GATEWAY TO TEACHING

GATEWAY

TO TEACHING

R. Lee Martin, Ed.D.
Department of Education

Alvin M. Westcott, M.S.
Department of Education

State University of New York
Oswego, New York

Illustrated by Alvin M. Westcott

WM. C. BROWN COMPANY PUBLISHERS
135 SOUTH LOCUST STREET • DUBUQUE, IOWA

BROWN

EDUCATION SERIES

Edited by LOWRY W. HARDING, *Ph. D.*,
The Ohio State University, Columbus, Ohio

Manufactured by WM. C. BROWN CO. INC., Dubuque, Iowa
Printed in U. S. A.

Acknowledgments

The authors wish to acknowledge their indebtedness to the many people who have helped them in this endeavor — students, colleagues and friends — some of whom must be left unlisted because of space limitations. They are indebted also to Miss Helen Hagger, librarian, and members of the library staff, State University College, Oswego, New York, who helped with bibliography and other items. Appreciation is expressed for the aid given by Mrs. Beatrice Lee of the Research Division, NEA, in reading parts of the manuscript and in offering pertinent suggestions. Special thanks are due Dr. Lowry W. Harding of The Ohio State University, advisory editor for William C. Brown Co., who read the manuscript and offered many helpful suggestions during the preparation of the book.

Mrs. Helen Gilbert, Mrs. Ginger Westcott, and Mrs. Mary Phillips, each of whom typed parts of the manuscript, are thanked for their very valuable help.

The authors express deep appreciation to Dr. James A. Smith of Syracuse University for his constant help and encouragement.

Dr. Martin acknowledges the inspiration of a lifelong friend, former teacher, and colleague, Dr. John Rufi, University of Missouri.

Gratitude is expressed to publishers, editors and authors for the use of excerpts and materials from their works. Specific acknowledgment of their permissions is made at appropriate places throughout the book.

July, 1963

R. Lee Martin
Alvin M. Westcott

v

To:

Virginia Martin and Ginger Westcott whose patience and understanding have made this book a reality.

Introduction

College students, right now you are probably standing on the threshold of the greatest experience in your entire professional training — your student teaching! You are, perhaps, reading this book as part of the preparation for your first teaching assignment!

As a beginning student teacher you suddenly feel butterflies in your stomach. You wonder if you will remember all the facts you were taught in your methods courses. You hope you will like the classroom to which you have been assigned, you pray the children will like you and you tremble at the thought that you may have a problem child whom you cannot handle.

For you, student teaching is both an end and a beginning. It is the end of long hours of "book" study, of classes in theory, of heated debates over vital issues, of observing and participating in classrooms, of being a full time college student. It is the beginning of long hours of child study, of practical application of theory, of on-the-job dealing with vital issues, of actual teaching experience, of being a part time teacher. And, although student teaching is still a part of your total college career, it is also the beginning of your life career.

Suddenly, many of the things you talked about in your education classes begin to take on meaning. Suddenly, too, you are faced with a multitude of problems you never before sensed.

Your college coordinator understands the tenseness of your situation and the ambivalence of your feelings. The chances are he was once on the same spot, probably not too long ago. He sees all your faces turned to him in expectation. He sees the unfamiliar look in the eyes of familiar students. He sees the hope, the anxiety, the misgivings, the uncertainties and the doubts in your heart. He can even hear those butterflies (rather wildly fluttering by now) in your stomach. He, too, senses the importance of this moment. He remembers his own misgivings of a few years past and he has planned a program to orient you to this new phase of your total experience. His main function at this point is to help you; to ease you into teaching, to give you enough security, assurance and reinforcement for trembling butterflies so you will feel competent and independent and you will go forth to meet your new challenge head on!

That is why he has chosen this book; it will help him to do the job. The authors were, themselves, once student teachers (and not so long ago). They were once teachers of children and now are campus co-ordinators helping to prepare young adults for the teaching profession.

Their wealth of personal experience has given them the background and understandings necessary to write a book which orients teacher aspirants into student teaching and the teaching profession. They have conducted countless orientation programs and student teaching seminars and know the problems and questions which students encounter as they go into their teaching careers by way of the student teaching experience. They have written this book with those problems in mind hoping their meditations will help students in finding answers.

Unlike many other books on student teaching, this one is not a rehash of material covered in former methods courses and other education courses. In the first part of the book, the authors deal directly wtih problems you are facing NOW. They explore all aspects of these problems, hoping to give you that coveted reassurance and security you are seeking. Once this is accomplished they ease you into the classroom situation and remind you of your obligations and duties there. The last part of the book helps you think through the many problems which will come to your mind as you assume the total role of the teacher, many of which you cannot, at this moment, anticipate.

The authors do not attempt to solve the *specific* problems you may encounter in student teaching; they make general suggestions about dealing with these problems realizing that each classroom is different, each child is different and each student teacher is different. They guide you through many of your problems by keeping before you general principles of good education which apply to all teaching situations, and by providing many valuable references and resources where you may go for help.

They realize that your campus coordinator and your cooperating teacher will help you translate the theory and the learnings of your education courses into actual practice and have devoted the major portion of their text to those problems which are closely allied to teaching but are not part of the actual teaching act.

Gateway To Teaching is a book you can use *NOW* to help you cross the threshold into student teaching, and one you can use later to help you cross another threshold — that which leads into the teaching profession.

1963
James A Smith,
Syracuse University

Table of Contents

for learning experiences. Discipline. What are the goals of pupil discipline? There's a place for routine. Functional planning for children. Custom tailor your plans. Teachers manuals can help. Flexibility is the keynote. Pupil-teacher planning. Creative teaching.

PART II

THE TEACHER AND THE PROFESSION

status of teachers' salaries. Legal state minimum salaries. NEA salary goals. Salary schedules. Merit rating and salaries. Teacher supply and demand.

Certification — what it is. Legal basis of certification. Brief historical background. Current status of teacher certification. Some problems and issues. Trends in teacher certification. Teacher tenure. Teacher retirement. Social security for teachers. Insurance for teachers. Credit unions for teachers. Leaves of absence.

College placement office. Commercial employment agencies. Have you considered these? Bon voyage! A job in another state. Should I teach in a private school? Letter of inquiry. The application form. Smile at the birdie. The personal résumé! Personal references — the stamp of approval. The tried and true trio. The team interview. Pyramid interviewing. Preparing yourself for the interview. What to expect from your interviewer. Topics discussed during job interviews with teachers. A preparation check list for the job candidate. Special requirements often requested by employers. The teaching contract. You've got it — what now?

PART III

EDUCATIONAL FRONTIERS

Seminar around the flag, boys! It can merely be a gab session. Educational frontiers. Wanted — fearless frontiersmen. Automation in education. Resourceful school plant planning. More effective and efficient use of our teacher resources. Well constructed, controlled and expanded programs of educational research and dissemination of information. Research into practice. Funds for educational research scarce. Exploring the limits and horizons of educational TV. What's your best camera angle? Greater individualization of instruction. More effective and functional grouping in the classroom and total school. Creative and functional curriculum development and implementation. Professional maturity and recognition of teaching as a profession. Visionary public school finance. High quality, consistent, democratic, inspirational school administration, supervision and leadership.

Part I

Student Teaching

introducing
Mr. "Stew" Dent
Teacher

Chapter 1

Student Teaching
What Is It?

> *They who educate children well are more*
> *to be honored than they who produce them;*
> *for these only gave them life, those the art*
> *of living well!*
>
> *Aristotle*

Student Teaching — What Is It?

Student teaching is an apprenticeship or internship which constitutes the gateway to one of the world's greatest professions — teaching.
It has been said with some appropriateness that while the medical
profession may lengthen and preserve life, good teaching is the only
vehicle leading to a full rich life. Just to be kept physically alive is
hardly enough for most people.

Man is naturally a curious creature. He desires to understand and
esthetically appreciate various elements of his environment. He is also
desirous of having children and youth informed of their cultural
heritage. Because of this inquisitiveness and ambition for the young,
the teacher and teaching take on tremendous importance. In conse-
quence, the experiences and procedures by which prospective teachers
are inducted into the profession have special significance.

What Actually Constitutes Student Teaching?

The program or course labeled "student teaching" includes all of
the experiences which a teacher preparing for active work with pupils

encounters during assignment to a school. It includes a great variety of activities such as mixing finger paint, mimeographing, applying first aid, locating materials, outlining lesson plans, filing, correcting papers, instructing, and yes, sometimes even cooking!

IT'S NOT A TRIAL

Student teaching is not a trial period; it is a preparatory period. It is an opportunity for you to put into actual practice many of the things you have learned in your teacher education classes. It is designed to ease you successfully into practice from a predominantly informational and theoretical background.

Professional Internship.

The internship or apprentice method of training is embraced by the professions of medicine, law, nursing, and others. It is traditionally the responsibility of the practitioners in a profession to participate directly in the preparation of its future members. What is more, professional preparatory schools for teachers in this country seem to be demonstrating increased support to the value of practical, on-the-job experience. This is exemplified most graphically in teaching, medicine, law and nursing.

A Brief History of Student Teaching

Historically, the professions and the trades have subscribed to the concept of internship, apprenticeship, or "on-the-job training" as a method of preparing the neophyte. While some of you might not care to associate the term "apprenticeship" with a profession, basically it embodies the same principle as student teaching, internship, or whatever other similar term you prefer. The evolution of the apprenticeship idea in the manual trades is quite readily traceable through the guild system of the Renaissance period and later through trade unionism.

The very early development of the apprenticeship or internship idea in the teaching profession is somewhat of an enigma. There is only fragmentary information about teacher preparation programs that included student teaching prior to the development of normal schools in the United States. The following summary presents some of this information.

An early example of teacher education (containing student teaching) in Europe can be found in the teacher preparatory school established at Rheims, France, about 1685. That program was aimed at preparing the Christian brothers to teach the children of the poor. The brothers learned, under close supervision, how to teach in charity schools.

During the rebirth of learning that occurred during the Renaissance, there developed a growing concern with methods of teaching. It began first among religious orders and then spread to nonparochial schools. This movement blossomed into a host of teacher preparation programs in *many* countries of Europe.

A milestone in that development was the normal school established at Yverdon by Johann Pestalozzi, a Swiss. It existed between 1800 and 1825. Pestalozzi suggested that all education begins with the nature of man and from this base teaching methods must be derived. His influence led to mass establishment of normal schools. Noteworthy among these was the first state supported normal school in the United States which was established in 1839 in Lexington, Massachusetts, under the guiding hand of Cyrus Peirce.

JOHANN HEINRICH PESTALOZZI
(1746-1827)

The Pestalozzian idea was firmly implanted in the United States by Edward Austin Sheldon at Oswego, New York, in 1861. The so-called "Oswego Movement" (containing provision for student teaching) had considerable influence upon early teacher education.[1]

Regardless of its location, the student teaching program the reader may be entering has its roots deeply embedded in these early teacher preparatory programs. You will be participating in a program which began in Europe and later flourished in the normal schools of this country.

---

[1]Dorothy Rogers, *Oswego-Fountainhead of Teacher Education,* Appleton-Century-Crofts, Inc., New York, 1961.

What Value — Student Teaching?

"Learn by doing" is the keynote of student teaching. The following famous statement by John Dewey clearly describes a buttress for the learn-by-doing premise that is the heart of student teaching:

> The most direct blow at the traditional separation of doing and know-ing and at the traditional prestige of purely "intellectual" studies, however, has been given by the progress of experimental science. If this progress has demonstrated anything, it is that there is no such thing as genuine knowledge and fruitful understanding except as the offspring of doing. The analysis and rearrangement of facts which is indispensable to the growth of knowledge and power of explanation and right classification cannot be attained purely mentally — just inside the head. Men have to do something to the things when they wish to find out something; they have to alter conditions. This is the lesson of the laboratory method, and the lesson which all education has to learn.[2]

The specific values of student teaching are somewhat elusive and are difficult to prove by research. As a matter of fact one of the strong-est justifications for continuing student teaching programs has little to do with research; it is the high value assigned to it by student teachers themselves. One of the interesting aspects of student teaching is that there has been little controlled research to evaluate its merits as a preparatory experience for teachers. Most teacher education institu-tions allot relatively large amounts of time and credit hours for student teaching with little evidence to justify this expenditure except for the reactions to it from students.[3]

In the absence of clear-cut research evidence then, both professional tradition and favorable student reaction were the basis for including student teaching as a part of teacher preparation in the past.

In fairness to researchers, student teaching contains so many vari-ables that it is extremely difficult to structure clear-cut studies. Some research is currently being undertaken, yet much more is needed. To the prospective teacher the authors are saying that they do not know conclusively that student teaching will help to make him a better teacher in comparison with other experiences his college might provide. Nevertheless, he can be assured by the knowledge that in the past participants have rated student teaching as a very valuable personal and professional experience.

---

[2]John Dewey, *Democracy and Education,* The Macmillan Company, New York, 1961.

[3]Kate L. Boyce, "What Is the Most Important Part of Teacher Training?" *Ohio Sch.,* 30: 162-63, 1952.

In addition to its being your general introduction to the role of the teacher, student teaching will offer you opportunities to:

1. Develop general teaching competence
2. Test educational theory
3. Evaluate yourself
4. Observe and study children

In the final analysis, the value of student teaching is a highly personal matter. As a result of student teaching you may be able to sense an increased feeling of security in your own poise and facility with language when speaking in front of your class. You may not trip over your tongue as often when trying to give a concise clear explanation. You may better understand why at certain ages the boys tend to line up on one side of the gym and the girls on the other at a school dance and try to avoid the opposite sex at all costs (understanding human growth patterns). More assuredly student teaching will foster growth toward professional maturity (in varying degrees) depending upon what *you* bring to it in the way of strengths and weaknesses. It definitely will develop in you a more realistic self-awareness since good teaching incorporates a projection of one's self as well as other variables. While this may sound silly, student teaching will help *you* to get to know *yourself* better.

You'll Get to Know YOU Better

A Coat of Many Colors.

Student teaching, in addition to having a great value to you as an individual also has value to (1) the college or university in which you are being educated; (2) the teaching profession; (3) the school in which you do your student teaching and (4) the children in your classroom. It probably is obvious to you that the foregoing is true; however, just to "tickle" your thinking permit us to support the last item (4) a bit:

Has it occurred to you how valuable you can be to children as a student? You can bring special personal skills to the classroom which will enhance its program beyond what your cooperating teacher could do alone; provide extra individual help for pupils who need it; bring another source of help and stimulation in the form of your college supervisor and furnish other benefits which we will not stress here.

Student Teaching Takes Many Forms

Perhaps you have already raised an eyebrow. You may have found in reading this material devoted to student teaching that some of the descriptive material is not congruent with the student teaching program in which you are enrolled. The authors are perfectly aware that this might occur.

The Variability of Programs Across the Country.

Student teaching programs are, to use a writer's phrase, "many splendored." They vary tremendously across our country. For example, some programs require that the individual spend the full day student teaching for a specified number of weeks (or clock hours). Still other programs schedule student teaching for an hour or so daily, spread over many weeks than in the previously mentioned scheme. There is disagreement even as to what constitutes a "clock hour" of student teaching. Is student teaching merely total time spent in a classroom? Is observation rather than actual teaching to be counted as student teaching? At present there is much confusion. Regardless of how student teaching is interpreted in terms of academic credit, the fact remains that all teacher preparation programs are committed to some form of practice teaching. This means that you can expect to undergo some form of professional on-the-job experience irrespective of its academic credit assignment.

As the teaching profession and the fifty states strive to develop reciprocity of teaching certificates, we can expect the establishment of definite minimum specifications regarding the amount of student teaching required for a nationally reciprocal teaching certificate (along with other specifications, of course). If the term "reciprocity" as related to teacher certification is not familiar to you, turn to the certification section of this text in Chapter 8. Other significant differences in student teaching programs in the several states include such considerations as:

1. The point in the student's college career at which student teaching is placed.
2. The character of the student teaching center — i.e., a college sponsored practice school or a public school.
3. Is it a "living way" from campus teaching center or is the student teacher permitted to remain on campus during student teaching and to participate in college activities?
4. The college personnel assigned to supervise the student teachers —does the professor who taught the theory to the student also oversee the practical training or is it someone else? (Very often

the professor who instructed the student in teaching methods has no contact with him during student teaching.)

5. The process and specifications for selecting cooperating teachers — would you rather do half as much student teaching with a topnotch cooperating teacher or have an opportunity to teach twice as long with an average cooperating teacher?

   How much control does the college exercise in screening cooperating teachers? Does the college have a wide choice of cooperating teachers? Does it pay them in some way for their services?

As is true in medicine and other professions, many beginners today are better prepared than those who supervise them. This is not to say, however, that you cannot learn a great deal from someone (your cooperating teacher) who has *experience* in the profession. As an example, Van Cliburn's piano instructor probably does not have nearly the proficiency Cliburn has at the piano, but this does not mean that the instructor cannot effectively guide, inspire and teach his gifted pupil.

There Are Bugs In It!

You might wonder why in presenting some of the differences in student teaching programs we have also pointed to some of the unsolved problems in relation to student teaching. We want you to understand that student teaching is in a constant state of flux. It is constantly evolving and there are no "perfect" student teaching programs. Even if someone were to come up with what everyone agreed was a perfect organizational pattern for student teaching, there still would remain so many human elements in its implementation that it would soon become sprinkled with flaws. Just accept the fact that there are "bugs" in all programs, yet every program can offer you a rich professional experience if you will take full advantage of the opportunities presented. Try to explore the limits of the experience.

If you should find what you consider to be serious deficiencies in your student teaching setting, feel free to discuss them (in professional confidence) with your college supervisor. All colleges and universities are anxious to improve their programs and recognize that reactions of students represent one vital evaluative channel.

THERE ARE "BUGS" IN IT

The Stage Varies But The Cast Is The Same.

Regardless of the uniquenesses of your particular program the same *general* characteristics are present in all programs. Because this is true, your personal objectives for student teaching and those of your college would be generally consistent with other student teachers and student teaching programs nationwide.

"I'M LOOKING FOR SOME OBJECTIVES FOR STUDENT TEACHING"

As is emphasized in Chapter 2, you will want to identify carefully your own personal objectives for student teaching as they will enable you to evaluate your progress. In setting these objectives the authors want to emphasize once again that student teaching is *not* a test to determine how effective a teacher you are at the outset but rather a learning situation in which you are guided toward professional competency. It is to be hoped you will have an opportunity to experiment with theoretical principles in a practical, realistic classroom setting.

The Paramount Values of Student Teaching To You

Undoubtedly you have been introduced to a host of lofty objectives for student teaching as part of your orientation. They often are invented solely by educators and may or may not have meaning for you. Let us get down to cases. What value can student teaching have for you?

Surgeon, Cut!

Student teaching is your opportunity to put your professional preparation into action, much as the surgeon performs his first operation. In contrast to the surgeon, however, in most instances you will have the opportunity to go back and correct mistakes that you make.

Student teaching is a chance for you to "get the feel" of a very important responsibility — that of a teacher. You will be orientated toward this goal gradually as your maturity and intellect permit. At some point in this professional progression you will be permitted to have total responsibility of the classroom for a full day or several full days. In many ways this is the pièce de résistance of student teaching. It is not until you have responsibility for the children from the moment they enter the classroom in the morning until they leave at the close of the day that you will "feel" the complete physical, mental, and emotional demands that accompany full time teaching.

What Is A Teacher?

Between the innocence of infancy and the dignity of maturity, our children fall under the influence of a group of people called teachers.

Teachers come in assorted sizes, weights, and colors. They have various interests, hobbies, religions, and beliefs, but they share one creed: To help each child to reach the highest possible degree of personal development.

The teacher is a composite. A teacher must have the energy of a harnessed volcano, the efficiency of an adding machine, the memory of an elephant, the understanding of a psychiatrist, the wisdom of Solomon, the tenacity of a spider, the patience of a turtle trying to cross the freeway in rush-hour traffic, the decisiveness of a general, the diplomacy of an ambassador, and the financial acumen of a Wall Street wizard.

She must remember always that she teaches by word, but mostly by precept and example.

A teacher may possess beauty, or grace, or skill; but most certainly she must possess love, a deep, abiding love, and respect for children.

She must love your little girl who has the song of a bird, the squeal of a pig, the stubbornness of a mule, the antics of a monkey, the spryness of a grasshopper, the curiosity of a cat, the slyness of a fox, and the mysterious mind of a woman.

She must also cherish your little boy, that inconsiderate, bothersome, intruding bundle of noise with the appetite of a horse, the digestion of a sword swallower, the energy of an atom bomb, the lungs of a dictator, the imagination of Paul Bunyan, the shyness of a violet, the audacity of a steel trap, and the enthusiasm of a firecracker.

A teacher must teach many things: reading, writing, arithmetic, spelling, geography, history, music, art, health. She must also manage during her 6 1/2 hours to teach manners and morals to children whose parents have despaired of the task during their 17 1/2 hours.

A teacher is Truth with chalk dust in its hair, Beauty with a backache, Wisdom searching for bubblegum, the Hope of the Future with papers to grade.

A teacher must possess many abilities. She must not mind explaining for the tenth time the intricacies of two-place multiplication to the whole class, then explaining it again to the one who didn't listen.

She must know when to talk and when to listen. She must learn to judge between encouraging and pushing a child. She must sense what decisions to make and which must be made by the child. She must be steadfast without being inflexible; sympathetic without being maudlin; loving without possessing.

She must live in childhood without becoming childish, to enjoy its great joys, satisfactions, its genuine delights; while understanding its griefs, irritations, embarrassments, and harassments.

She must do all this while worrying about how to pay the utility bills, what to have for supper, whether her baby has the chicken pox, if her lesson plans will meet the supervisor's requirements, how Mrs. Smith will take the lower grades on John's report card, where to get the extra money for summer school, and who took the dime from Susie's purse. . .[4]

JANE C. BUTLER
Castleberry, Texas

It is important that you experience the entire role of the teacher if you are to appraise *your* fitness to do the job. This opportunity to appraise the work load of teaching is one vital contribution which student teaching can make to your preparation for teaching.

As mentioned before, student teaching also will help you to get to know yourself better. You may find that you have to pace your output of energy very carefully in order to work within the boundaries of your physical stamina. You might decide, as some few students do, that the teaching profession is not for you on the basis of your student teaching experiences. You may find that you need to project your voice and personality a great deal more in order to be an interesting, effective teacher. For certain you will learn important things about teaching and about yourself.

> To find success or satisfaction in his work, a teacher must begin and end with faith — in the worth of all men and especially in his students; in all learning and particularly in what he teaches. But most of all, the teacher must believe in himself and in the value of what he is attempting to accomplish.
>
> In the days in which we live and teach, it should not be difficult to sustain that faith. Wherever men have believed that the human mind and spirit should be illuminated, the good teacher has been held in esteem and respect. It is so here and now, as it always will be where freedom, opportunity, and excellence are valued. In twenty centuries, no one has been able to answer Cicero's question: 'What greater or better gift can we offer the republic than to teach and instruct our youth'[5]

TOPICS AND QUESTIONS FOR STUDY AND DISCUSSION

1. Having read Chapter 1, what meaning does this statement have for you: "Student teaching takes many forms"
2. Attempt to list, in concise form, your feelings about student teaching. Now try to analyze why you have these feelings.
3 You undoubtedly have heard the term "readiness" applied to many skill areas in education (such as reading). What do you think are the major components of readiness for student teaching? After completing this task read Chapter 2 to compare your personal assessment of readiness with the points it stresses.

---

[4]*Congressional Record,* 1957.
[5]John H. Fischer, "Why Teach?" *NEA Journal,* April, 1962.

Whatever the outcome may be you can be certain that student teaching will be an exciting challenge and an experience that you will never forget. We wish you success as you enter student teaching, a gateway to a great profession.

SELECTED REFERENCES

1. Brown, G. W., "Day in the Life of a Student Teacher," *California Teacher's Association Journal*, Vol. 56, May, 1960, pp. 6-8.
2. Carroll, Margaret L., Dorothy McGeoch, and Carl Proehl, "Four Went To Teach," *Thirty-Fifth Yearbook, The Association for Student Teaching*, 1956.
3. Clothier, G., "Off-Campus Student Teaching Programs," *School and Community*, Vol. 42, November, 1960, p. 21.
4. Cox, D., "Why Should Public Schools Accept Student Teachers?", *Ed. Administration and Supervision*, Vol. 45, September, 1959, pp. 275-9.
5. Cummins, R. E., "Role Study In Teacher Training," *Journal of Educational Sociology*, Vol. 35, November, 1961, pp. 119-120.
6. Dickhart, A., "Student Teachers Are People," *Journal of Teacher Ed.*, Vol. 12, September, 1961, pp. 302-9.
7. Hamilton, Charles E., "Student Teaching," *California Teachers' Association Journal*, Vol. 50, December, 1954, pp. 16-17.
8. Hatfield, A. B., "Experimental Study of the Self-Concept of Student Teachers." *Journal of Educational Research*, Vol. 55, October, 1961, pp. 87-89.
9. Hazelton, P., "Student Teaching: A Hard Look." *Journal Of Teacher Ed.*, Vol. 11, December, 1960, pp. 470-3.
10. Horton, B. H., "Student Teaching Can Be a Worthwhile Experience." *National Association of Secondary School Principals*, Vol. 45, October, 1961, pp. 162-5.
11. Inlow, G. M., "Comparative Study of Student-Teaching Practices in Thirty-Eight Midwest Institutions." *Journal of Experimental Education*, Vol. 28, June, 1960, pp. 337-349.
12. Jones, R. M., "Off-Campus Student Teaching Programs." *Journal of Teacher Education*, Vol. 11, December, 1960, pp. 512-19, Vol. 12, March, 1961, pp. 97-100.
13. Kuhl, R. E., "Guide For Student Teachers." *Education Administration and Supervision*, Vol. 44, September, 1958, pp. 278-81.
14. Kuhl. R. E., "Time For Student Teaching." *Journal of Teacher Education*, Vol. 12, March, 1961, pp. 43-7.
15. Lewis, J., "Me As A Student Teacher." *Illinois Education*, Vol. 49, April, 1961, pp. 335-6.
16. Lingren, Vernon C., "Three Proposals for Improving Student Teaching." *Educational Administration and Supervision*, Vol. 43, November, 1957, pp. 385-389.
17. Ramsey, B., "Student Teacher Speaks." *Virginia Journal of Education*, Vol. 52, September, 1958, pp. 22-4.
18. Shaplin, J. T., "Practice in Teaching." *Harvard Educational Review*, Vol. 31, winter, 1961, pp. 33-59.

19. Steeves, Frank L., *Issues In Student Teachings A Casebook*. New York: Odyssey Press, Inc., 1963.
20. Steeves, Frank L., "Student Teaching is Essential." *Clearing House*, Vol. 32, March, 1958, pp. 430-2.
21. Steeves, Frank L., *You'll Have Fun in Student Teaching*. Minneapolis: Burgess Publishing Company, 1955.
22. Warren, R. L., "In Behalf of Student Teaching." *Clearing House*, Vol. 34, February, 1960, p. 344.

Chapter 2

Getting Yourself Ready For Student Teaching

There's a special providence in the fall of a sparrow. If it be now, 'tis not to come; if it be not to come, it will be now; if it be not now, yet it will come; the readiness is all.

Hamlet. Act V
Shakespeare

Readiness for Student Teaching

Readiness for student teaching really means the extent or quality of one's total personal resources necessary to complete the task successfully. Readiness for student teaching encompasses a variety of variables because of the complexity of the task. It involves the individual student teacher's social and emotional maturity, physical health, general intelligence, and professional background. As with all challenges in life, different individuals bring varying degrees of readiness to this task.

Much of your own readiness for student teaching is based upon your past life experiences and formal education. Your emotional maturity, for example, is the product of all of your experiences from birth to the present. In the existing product of that long series of developmental experiences, there can be very little modification or remediation during the brief time between registering for student teaching and reporting for duty.

The question of what actually constitutes satisfactory readiness for student teaching is one about which we know very little at present. Appraisal of readiness is based largely upon intuition and personal judgments of college personnel responsible for the program. Much research is needed relative to the identification and definition of the vital human qualities involved.

In the interim between now and the development of research, you should assume that if your college has approved you for a student teaching assignment it believes you have at least the minimum abilities necessary to succeed. We therefore direct this chapter toward helping you to understand more fully the roles of various individuals involved in the total student teaching experience. Also discussed are some of the mechanics of preparation and important details which should be attended to prior to beginning student teaching.

Your Role as a Student Teacher

There are many plans, systems, or patterns of student teaching across the country but in general all contain the same elements and dynamics. Regardless of the program in which you are enrolled, you can think about your student teacher role as analogous to the hub of a wheel around which revolves an interplay of many individuals and obligations. The diagram following may help clarify this point.

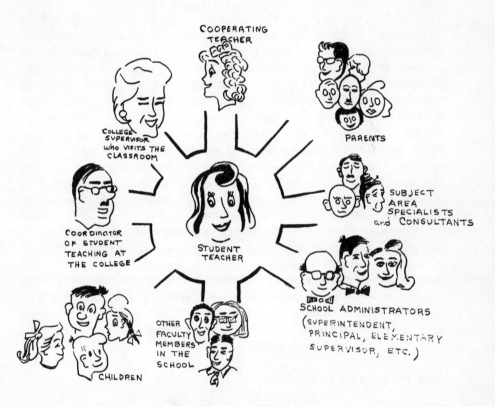

In order for you to operate with any degree of self-assurance in your student teaching setting, it is necessary that you understand your role as a student teacher. Student teaching is, among other things, a trial experience in human relations. There are of course many other related professional skills and objectives, but in essence your student teaching success will hinge in large measure upon your sensitivity to the elements of good human relations. It is a cliché carrying some grains of truth that "we teach *children* fundamentally, not subject matter."

Anyone who has actually done student teaching will attest to the fact that it is at best quite complex in nature. Do not let this disturb you, for in truth any given set of human relationships is very complex regardless of occupational factors, if one is able to understand *all* of the dynamics such as environment and personality which interplay.

First of all be comforted in the knowledge that you will be located in a school because school officials, teaching staff, children and parents *want you to be there*. They want you there for many reasons. They realize, for example, that your services can greatly enhance the instructional program of a classroom, that it is their professional responsibility to assist in training new teachers, that your presence can provide professional stimulation for their regular staff people, etc. Be comforted therefore in the knowledge that, in general, the total school community views you as an important asset. Do not take their hospitality and help for granted, however. While you are in the school as a student teacher, you should at all times realize that you are a guest of the school which has volunteered to help train you for teaching. At the same time, you often are looked upon by those in the school as an ambassador from the college you attend and your actions can reflect favorably or unfavorably directly upon your college and you.

Remember that although you are a guest and an ambassador in the school, your basic role remains that of a trainee for a vital profession. You are, as a student teacher, a learner. It is expected that not only throughout student teaching but throughout your teaching career you will never cease to be a learner or self-improver. This emphasis upon learning the multiphasic role of the classroom teacher as a firsthand experience is the basic contribution of student teaching to your professional preparation.

Your Professional Partner

"He rises by lifting others"[1]

The foregoing quote might well be the motto of the teacher who has offered his classroom and professional guidance to you. He or she can be given various names such as master teacher, cooperating teacher or critic teacher in different student teaching programs; however, his or her function is generally the same in all programs. We will refer to this person as the cooperating teacher throughout the rest of this text. This does not imply that other teachers in the school are uncooperative, but only that this particular teacher is cooperating with your college in preparing you for teaching.

---

[1]Robert Green Ingersoll (1833-1899).

In getting yourself ready for student teaching it is vital that you understand the role of the individual we choose to call the cooperating teacher. The quality of the relationship which you establish with your cooperating teacher may very well determine the degree of success you have in his or her classroom.

In helping you to understand the motives of your cooperating teacher better, let us discuss this question briefly: Why has this person chosen to work with a student teacher? As you might guess there are a great many reasons, oftentimes precipitated by the particular school setting or the uniquenesses of the individual teacher.

Some colleges and universities offer some kind of remuneration to the qualified teacher who will work with a student teacher. Often this remuneration takes the form of free tuition which the cooperating teacher can use to take advanced courses at that particular college or university. Perhaps the cooperating teacher is working on a graduate degree; this tuition thus is very important in terms of helping him reach this goal. Perhaps, on the other hand, the cooperating teacher wants to take a refresher course in some area in which he feels he either needs additional work or has a special interest. The monetary rewards offered him for taking you as his student are advantageous in many ways; however, it is hoped that this is not the sole stimulus which prompted his taking you.

Many cooperating teachers have little or no concern about any monetary rewards related to working with a student teacher. They volunteer because they sincerely enjoy sharing the joys and sorrows of the classroom with another person preparing for the profession. There are also those who want student teachers because they are burdened with a large class or classes and realize that the children will profit from having another teacher in the room. In addition there are those teachers who look forward to having a student teacher because he has recently been exposed to the latest in teaching methodology and research and they view him as a source of new classroom methods and ideas. With few exceptions, however, cooperating teachers assume responsibility for the preparation of future teachers because they receive a great deal of personal satisfaction in helping a neophyte ascend the ladder toward professional competence. In helping they are helped. As has previously been pointed out, student teaching is a complex of human relationships. While you as the student teacher are the pivotal point, your cooperating teacher plays a vital role in determining your success. There are a few tips which you might find useful in establishing a comfortable working relationship with your professional partner.

1. Be forthright and completely honest in all your dealings with your cooperating teacher.

2. If criticism (both negative and positive) is not given to you in relation to your work, ask for it. The student teacher who is mature and interested in improving his classroom techniques wants criticism. *Some* cooperating teachers are reluctant to offer it unless you request it. Do so.

3. Have your lesson plans and all other responsibilities ready on time. Your cooperating teacher should not have to badger you for them. It is a good idea to have your plans for the day on your cooperating teacher's desk first thing in the morning so he can check them if he desires to without having to ask you for them. Be punctual in all of your professional obligations.

4. If you decide you would like to try some innovation or departure from the regular classroom routine, check it first with your cooperating teacher. Always keep him posted as to what you have planned for the children.

5. Listen carefully to any suggestions given to you by your cooperating teacher. Take notes during your conferences if need be. It is very disconcerting to a cooperating teacher to feel that a student teacher does not listen to or take seriously what is said to him. You will want to take some things with a "grain of salt" as you might in any professional discussion, but at least listen carefully to what is said.

BE ALL EARS!

6. While the need for these may be obvious to you, be courteous and appreciative. These "twins" will carry you a long way in human relations.

7. Endeavor to be open minded in your dealings with your cooperating teacher. If a suggestion is offered to you, at least try it. You can reject it after a fair trial but student teaching should be a time of much experimentation on your part. Don't assume that you have pat answers to any teaching situations. Absolutes do not exist in a dynamic profession such as teaching.

8. Try to be as friendly and pleasant as possible. A smile often will hide grave misgivings on your part. Your cooperating teacher and the children will be gladdened by a cheery personality. You will be working very close to one another for quite a long time so try to make your presence a spark of enthusiasm and zest. Don't be afraid to let your sense of humor show. It can be a professional buttress for you.

9. Emphasize mentally the positive and/or strong points which your cooperating teacher has to offer you. Do not expect him to be

perfect or even highly competent in *all* areas of the curriculum. Some student teachers tend to pick apart tiny inconsequential flaws in the cooperating teacher's program, overlooking its many fine elements from which they can strengthen themselves. It is possible to learn *some* positive and helpful techniques, skills, etc. from any teacher, so look for the strong points in the classroom program and digest these. All classroom programs have some weaknesses. It is expected that you will recognize them but not use them as a reason for a poor job of student teaching.

10. Do not carry tales out of the classroom. Occasionally your cooperating teacher may confide some personal information about students or even himself which he does not want to go any farther. Be discreet about discussing your classroom setting.

Cooperating teachers come in assorted sizes, shapes, ages and personalities. As previously mentioned, you will be working very closely with your cooperating teacher. It is therefore your job to adjust as best you can to him to the point where you two can work well and effectively together in the classroom. Mimicry is probably one of the highest forms of flattery, but you are not expected to mimic him. It is more than likely you will want to adapt some of the techniques and procedures of teaching displayed by your cooperating teacher. However, you must develop methods to suit your own philosophy of education and personality which are harmonious with what you know to be sound principles of learning and child development.

Student teaching is also a two-way street in that, while you actually are the learner in the situation, your cooperating teacher and other teachers can learn many positive things about teaching from you. For this reason most cooperating teachers will encourage you to try out your ideas in methods of teaching, classroom activities, organizational techniques, and the like.

A point which a student teacher may forget in working with his cooperating teacher is that it is not simple for him to share his classroom with another individual. Any teacher who loves to teach and who receives great personal rewards from working with children is making a considerable sacrifice in sharing this experience with a student teacher. He is placing his responsibility to the profession above his own personal satisfactions. Hence in some situations you may have to press the cooperating teacher a bit in order to get him to give you more and more responsibility for control of the class. It is your job to let your cooperating teacher know your desire and readiness to take on various responsibilities and lessons. Act anxious and ready to assume any reasonable work assignment offered you. You are more likely to receive additional opportunities to participate in the program if you appear anxious to do so. Further, the more actual teaching time you have the more confidence, poise and technique you will acquire, assuming the teaching is reasonably successful.

It's Not Easy!

Your cooperating teacher, as you may have concluded by now, has a delicate role to play in the student teaching experience. While he is trying to provide opportunities for you to grow and mature in teaching he also has a responsibility to parents, children and the school administration to maintain a balanced, well organized and high quality program in his classroom. For this reason we re-emphasize the necessity for consulting with your cooperating teacher before attempting innovations in the established program. You probably will *not* be able to try out *all* of the ideas you have in teaching methodology in any one student teaching setting, but most cooperating teachers are very generous in providing room for your experimentation in their classroom programs. Student teaching is a time when you should experiment in many phases of the teaching process.

Co-Op Teacher

Quality Control

In some student teaching programs the cooperating teacher is referred to as the critic teacher. There is nothing wrong with this term providing the students do not immediately associate the word critic with only negative criticism. One function of the cooperating teacher is to give you *both* negative and positive criticism of your classroom work. He will accentuate the positive side but as a mature learner you should desire to know your weaknesses as well as your strengths. The cooperating teacher (and the college supervisor to some extent) therefore serve as quality control instruments for your classroom work. The old concept of "snoopervision" has faded and you will find your professional partners constructive and fair in their criticisms. Their job is to build upon your strengths, not to tear you down and discourage

"MR. MORSE, I'D LIKE YOU TO MEET YOUR NEW STUDENT TEACHER"

you from trying. Learn to accept criticism as being part of the teaching job.

Other Professional Helpers

We have previously mentioned the very important role the co-operating teacher plays in student teaching. There will be, however, other individuals involved either directly or indirectly with your work, and this group we choose to call the professional training team. The size of this team will vary somewhat, since student teaching programs vary. The number is not important; the vital factor is your attitude toward the team. You will notice that in the diagram on page 17 the professional team consists of your cooperating teacher, the administrators of the school in which you are located, the college supervisor and sometimes some consultant/specialists. This team is set up to assist you in achieving maximum success in student teaching.

Who's the Boss?

It is natural and proper for you to want to understand the power structure assigned to the professional team. Both your college and the school to which you are assigned share the responsibility for your performance as a student teacher, but initially and basically the college has the assignment for your professional preparation. There isn't any boss in the situation but rather a team-type effort with the college taking final responsibility.

Each member of your professional training team is sincerely interested in making you the very best teacher possible within your individual limits. The team consists of your *cooperating teacher* who is directly charged with your day-to-day classroom work. His (or hers) is probably the most vital role in your student teaching experience. Your cooperating teacher will be the person most familiar with your work and in the best position to evaluate it on the spot.

The *college supervisor* has many functions. He represents the college and acts as a catalyst for the team. He may act as a resource person for you, your cooperating teacher and the school administrators. He is charged with assisting all concerned with your student teaching in making it the highest quality experience possible.

The *school principal* often takes charges of orientating you to the school and setting up the administrative structure necessary to facilitate a high quality student teaching experience for you. If his time permits he may aid in evaluating your work and in serving you as a general resource person.

Specialists/Consultants

Specialists/consultants such as subject area specialists — art, music, science, and reading, as well as the school nurse, psychologist, and guidance person — may be called in to help you plan a classroom lesson or to confer about a specific child. They may also observe your work and offer suggestions which will help you grow as an effective teacher in their specialized areas.

Other Team Members

In some student teaching settings there are other team members such as an elementary grade supervisor and helping teachers. In some instances the school superintendent and/or school board members help to orientate student teachers to the school.

What's Your Attitude (not altitude) Toward the Team?

The professional team has a supervisory as well as instructional role. In some students the mere mention of the word supervisor conjures up a negative reaction; they have somewhere formed the stereotype of the supervisor as being the "snoopervisor" who looks for skeletons in closets or the harsh critic who looks to pick apart their every motion in the classroom. This could not be farther from the truth. As previously stated the team will help you to recognize your strengths and weaknesses, but they are builders not wreckers. The team is organized to help you to succeed and your success is paramount to them. Try then, if you will, to view your cooperating teacher, college supervisor, public school administrator, etc., as professional friends. They are there to help you realize the best potential you have for teaching children. Work *with* them and they will be a constructive, objective source of help to you as a student teacher.

Assembling Your Materials

As part of your "readiness activities" for student teaching you will want to assemble and organize the teaching materials you have collected during your college training. These would include things such as a picture file, college textbooks related to teaching, general reference books, perhaps a pocket chart, an abacus, and miscellaneous other devices and materials. Together with your professional equipment you will of course need all of the personal belongings essential for your own maintenance during student teaching. This is assuming that you will be living in different quarters from those of your regular college accommodations. Here is where a high degree of organization will stand you in good shape. Your file of pictures and teaching materials will be much more effective if you have it systematically organized so you are able to locate any material in a matter of seconds. This is also true of personal belongings such as your clothes, toiletries and the like. Time will be of the essence throughout your student teaching experience and the well organized student teacher is ahead of the game. Cardboard boxes can serve you very well as portable filing cabinets. Organize all of your notes and other college material under various headings to make them easier to find when needed. You may want to do the same with a picture file. Use cardboard as index dividers. In dealing with materials from your picture file for a field trip, look for short cuts and organizational ideas which will help you to conserve your precious time.

In the event you have advance notification of the grade level in which you will be student teaching, you will find that it is of great help to do some background reading pertaining to your assignment. If, for instance, you are assigned to student teach in a third grade you may want to read the following material:

1. Child development and/or child psychology texts dealing with the 8-year-old.
2. The state guide for the suggested curriculum content for third grade.
3. Curriculum textbooks.
4. Several of the textbooks that are being used in the class.
5. A handbook for teachers or even one for student teachers which you could read in advance.

Background reading related to the characteristics of the age group and the general curriculum traditional for that grade level will help you adjust to the classroom setting.

Understand the game before you attempt to play it. This axiom of physical education is true also of student teaching. Be certain that you understand the college requirements, rules, and regulations before you go out on the assignment. Listen carefully to all instructions and explanations given during your orientation period at college and at the practice school (if there is one). Always feel free to ask questions pertaining to any of the policies and requirements governing student teaching.

Note the specific projects such as units of work, child studies, community surveys, etc., which may be a part of the student teaching experience. When you know them you can plan and pace yourself early so as not to have all of the work load come due simultaneously.

To obtain a reasonable understanding of the ground rules for student teaching, we reiterate, you must listen very carefully. Embarrassing incidences sometimes occur because the student teacher just didn't listen carefully. Listening well is a rare attribute and one which future teachers should cultivate. Much less tension and anxiety are involved in any endeavor in which you understand the rules governing the situation.

A certain amount of confusion at the outset of student teaching may be very normal as you are bombarded with many details. But take heart in the knowledge that if you plan your work well you will have ample time to complete assignments and that your professional partners will re-explain or clarify any parts you still have doubts about as student teaching progresses. The important elements are to understand what is expected of you in special assignments, lesson planning, and general performance considerations and then plan your work to meet these requirements comfortably. It is always wise, however, to begin assignments as soon as possible; if other matters crop up, as they have a habit of doing in student teaching, you still will be able to meet any deadlines set. As illustrated in the folk tale, be an ant and not a grasshopper! Plan ahead!

> *"A house is infinitely communicative and tells many things"* . . .[2]

Living Quarters for Student Teaching

A room, an apartment, a tent, a park bench . . . suitable living quarters for student teaching should be of paramount importance to you. If your student teaching assignment necessitates your securing housing off campus then you will have some firsthand experience in exercising professional judgment in relation to this need. Some colleges and universities have prepared lists of acceptable student teacher housing. Other institutions rely completely upon the maturity and judgment of the student teacher in selecting and securing his or her own housing. In any event you will want to find out what, if any, college housing policies are applied to  student teachers before taking any steps. Once you know the ground rules you are ready to seek a student teaching abode. In securing housing for student teaching you may want to consider the following elements:

1. What type of housing would best suit your personal needs? — a furnished apartment, a furnished room, etc.
2. Are the mode and setting of the housing congruent with the social status of a teacher in that particular community? How about living in a room or apartment over a dance hall, bowling alley, or local pub? While it might do wonders for your social life it might be unbecoming to a teacher.
3. Financial considerations.
4. What contacts are available in securing housing?
5. Facilities for meals — apartment eat-in — room eat-out.
6. Good atmosphere conducive to study and relaxation.

---

[2]Robert William Chapman, *The Portrait of A Scholar.*

How about rooming with the family of some school faculty member or the principal? The authors personally believe living away from campus during student teaching is an integral part of learning the role of the teacher in a realistic manner. It also helps the student teacher to cast off campus ties that might distract him from concentrating all of his attention, abilities and energies on the job.

The Physical, Mental and Emotional Challenge of Student Teaching

On guard! Student teaching is not only an intellectual challenge but also a physical and emotional one. It is important for you to be in good physical condition prior to entering student teaching. A physical examination is highly desirable whether or not it is required by your college. In comparison with attending college, which is too often largely a sit down type of existence, student teaching can be quite an abrupt and strenuous demand on your strength, energy and general physical health. While this is not meant to be alarming but rather, realistic, there also are other physical hazards in teaching and student teaching. One very notable one is a teacher's probable exposure to many contagious diseases. At times an assortment of communicable diseases such as mumps, measles, chicken pox, the common cold, etc., is present in the public schools. Despite all reasonable precautions you will find that children will accidentally cough and sneeze and breathe in your face. A teacher friend of ours jokingly says there ought to be cheaper Blue Cross rates for teachers since she felt she was exposed to everything short of leprosy. This of course is an exaggeration, but it is true that you might be exposed to numerous childhood diseases; however, no more so than while working in any job which requires proximity to the general public. The important thing is that you endeavor to keep yourself in as good a physical condition as possible, thereby increasing your resistance to diseases and practice the rules of good health as well as insisting that children practice them. For example, insist that children cover their mouths with tissue when they cough or sneeze. To stress the importance of this precaution view the charming Walt Disney film "How to Catch A Cold." An intelligent person always attempts at least to ascertain the hazards involved in any undertaking. If you do everything possible to maintain personal good health you have one fortification against disease, and in some instances immunization is available if you desire it.

Generally speaking, however, whether you are doing regular teaching or student teaching, maintaining good personal health is a specific responsibility of any teacher. Robust good health facilitates more energy and enthusiasm for the job. The physically worn out teacher is bound to be less effective than the healthy, rested one, assuming other things arc cqual. It is recognized that an individual teaches a great deal by his own personal example, so a student teacher who practices good health routinely may very well be the most effective means of developing these habits in children.

In addition to watching his own personàl health, the student teacher can minimize the spread of communicable diseases by being alert to the symptoms of illness in the class. In addition he can make certain that children who return to school after an illness are checked by the school nurse before being permitted to remain in the classroom. Obviously then, if you are not familiar with the rules of good health and physical hygiene, review them in a health education textbook.

To the added physical demands of student teaching there are the concomitant emotional stresses and strains. This is true particularly in the first few weeks of student teaching while you are making your initial adjustments to the delicate role.

Remember, however, that for many it is perfectly normal to have large "butterflies" in their gastric systems or rapid pulse rates as they walk into their new roles as student teachers. Because of many variables involved, adjusting to some student teaching situations may take longer than to others. Be patient with yourself and don't expect to feel at home right away. Observe your new work setting carefully and soon you will forget your self-consciousness and be caught up in the classroom work. If you are still upset about your adjustment to your student teaching situation after a reasonable length of time, by all means discuss your anxieties with either your cooperating teacher or college supervisor. It is part of their job to aid you in this situation.

It is very normal to feel considerable emotional and physical fatigue at the close of your day as a student teacher. You will find that you gradually become adjusted to the work load. Some of the goals of student teaching concern your determining your physical and emotional limits and learning to work realistically within them. There is always additional work to be done in teaching and you will have to learn to recognize your personal limits. These physical, emotional and intellectual limitations are different for each individual and you must know your own. Knowing them is part of a mature self concept. To repeat, you must expect that being a student teacher will be quite a contrast to being a full-time college student. This is part of the importance of student teaching — to help you, a unique individual, fit into the complex role of the modern school teacher. It is, as you will discover, a very difficult, important, physically-taxing job, yet its rewards are enormous and well worth the giving of your energies and human effort.

A Final Pre-Student Teaching Check-Out

*"The tide tarrieth for no man"**

As a Final Check List Have You:

1. Had a physcial examination?
2. Made the necessary contacts with the school and college authorities (letter of introduction, etc.)?
3. Checked your financial status? Student teaching is enough of a demand upon your resources without the added worry of money problems. You should not attempt it without at least enough financial resources to meet your basic needs. If necessary borrow the money needed previous to student teaching rather than having to scrape and worry about money all through the experience.
4. Secured suitable housing? See page 27.
5. Obtained adequate transportation? If possible try to arrange for this in advance of your first day of student teaching. If you must commute to the school, try to locate a ride which will get you there in plenty of time in the morning. Oftentimes transportation can be obtained by consulting the school principal or your cooperating teacher. They will know of the transportation resources available.
6. Assembled your professional and personal materials for student teaching?
7. Done some background reading to help better familiarize you with your assignment? For examples, do you know the characteristics of the age group you will be teaching; subject matter areas that are usually taught at that grade level; the introductory chapters of your student teaching textbook or manual, etc?
8. Taken stock of yourself in terms of what you hope to accomplish in student teaching as well as what you believe your special abilities and talents are which will aid you in reaching your goals?

_____

*John Heywood (1497-1580).

Your college and the school you are entering are confident that you have what it takes to be a good teacher. Resolve that you will prove their faith in you is not misplaced.

Good luck!

TOPICS AND QUESTIONS FOR STUDY AND DISCUSSION

1. How might the following motto affect your student teaching if you adopted it personally? "Next week I've got to get organized."
2. How do you think student teaching best can be explained to parents of a school and to other community members?
3. Discuss what you believe is meant by the statement: A student teaching situation is never the same for any two student teachers.
4. Discuss your expectations relative to a cooperating (supervising) teacher.

SELECTED REFERENCES

1. Adams, Harold and Frank Dickey, *Basic Principles of Student Teaching,* New York: American Book Company, 1956.
2. Applegate, Ivamae, "Many People Affect the Student Teaching Program," *Educational Administration and Supervision,* Vol. 44, pp. 205-12, July, 1958.
3. Brown, Thomas J., *Student Teaching in a Secondary School,* New York: Harper and Bros., 1960.
4. Burr, James, Lowry Harding & Leland Jacobs, *Student Teaching in the Elementary School,* New York: Appleton-Century-Crofts, Inc., 1958.
5. Duker, Sam, "Elementary School Principal and the Student Teacher," *Educational Administration and Supervision,* pp. 467-71, December, 1955.
6. Edmund, N. and L. H. Hemink, "Do Student Teachers and Supervising Teachers Communicate With Each Other?" *Journal of Ed. Research,* Vol. 53, pp. 355-7, May, 1960.
7. Elliot, J. G., "Role Perception: the College Coordinator," *Assn. Student Teach. Yrbk.,* pp. 46-53, 1961.
8. Etten, J. F., "Pre-Teaching Experiences," *Illinois Education,* Vol. 49, p. 337, April, 1961.
9. Grayson, W. H., "Student Teaching: Increasing Responsibility," *H. Points,* Vol. 44, pp. 28-32, June, 1962.
10. Haines, A. C., "Role Perception: The Student Teacher," *Assn. Student Teach. Yrbk.,* pp. 59-64, 1961.
11. Kramer, L. I., "Final Charge to Student Teachers," *Clearing House,* Vol. 37 p. 27, September, 1962.
12. Lingren, Vernon C., "Help Needed and Received by Student Teachers," *Journal of Teacher Education,* Vol. 10, pp. 22-27, March, 1959.
13. Lottrick, Kenneth V., "Student Teaching; Pain or Pleasure?" *School Activities,* Vol. 29, pp. 251-52, April, 1958.
14. McAulay, J. D., "How Much Influence Has a Co-operating Teacher?" *Journal of Teacher Education,* Vol. 11, pp. 79-83, March, 1960.

15. Miller, H., "Professional Use of the Self Through Group Work in Teacher Education," *Journal of Ed. Sociology,* Vol. 36, pp. 170-80, December, 1962.

16. North Central Association Quarterly, "Some Guiding Principles for Student Teaching," *North Central Association Quarterly,* Vol. 32, pp. 193-96, October, 1957.

17. Oesterle, R. A., "Content of Handbooks for Student Teachers," *Journal of Teacher Education,* Vol. 8, pp. 380-386, December, 1957.

18. Perrodin, Axel F., "Principal and the Student Teacher," *Educational Administration and Supervision,* Vol. 42, pp. 149-52, March, 1956.

19. Wilson, J. A. and E. J. Swineford, "Co-operating to Improve Student Teaching," *Journal of Teacher Education,* Vol. 10, pp. 478-82, December, 1959.

Chapter 3

Becoming An Effective Student Teacher In the Classroom Setting

Since each learner is unique and learns in relation to his uniqueness, we will need to change our schools in the next decade so that they will be human-centered instead of lesson-centered.

Earl C. Kelley[1]

Your Impact As a "Professional"

Did you ever, in your own school days, have a teacher who wore the same suit of clothes day in and day out?

Have you ever had to sit in a classroom all day long listening to a teacher speak in a raspy, unpleasant tone?

The first of these situations involves the visual impact of a teacher; the second, the auditory impact of a teacher.

If you have sat as a student in a classroom where the teacher wore the same suit or dress for days, or was generally careless about his or her dress, then you know how depressing this can be to your eyes — to say nothing of your spirits. To make the point clearer, let us refer to a teacher's mode of dress as his or her "packaging."

The industrial and commercial world knows full well the importance of packaging in relation to selling a product. Millions of boxes of a

---

[1]Earl C. Kelley. "The Road We Must Take." *Educational Leadership* 14: 286; February, 1957.

particular soap powder or other commodity of good quality but no better than a competing product are sold on the basis of packaging.

Several scientifically oriented and highly efficient corporations have been established to study the psychological effects of packaging upon consumer buying habits. Many corporations allocate large sums of money to finance motivational research projects aimed at determining what factors prompt consumers to make certain choices among commercial products. Obviously some packing elements involved in such studies would be color, texture and shape (basic design). Classroom teachers can employ the psychology of attractive packaging to sell themselves and their product (education) to their pupils. A visually attractive teacher not only has an esthetic appeal for children but sets up an example for tasteful personal attire which children may decide to imitate. A teacher's mode of dress is particularly important in the elementary school. Remember that the children in these grades often have the same teacher all day long. They are a captive audience and do not have the opportunity of moving from teacher to teacher as in a departmentalized program. This fact makes it all the more imperative for the elementary teacher to be as visually attractive as possible. This does not, however, in any way excuse upper grade teachers from this responsibility.

It seems incongruent that some communities expect their teachers to dress in an exemplary fashion yet, despite such expectations, pay them very poor salaries. With ingenuity, however, it is possible to assemble a very functional wardrobe at a minimum price. If you purchase suits and skirts and sweaters (girls) or coats and trousers (men) that can be worn interchangeably, you can come to school in many combinations from a limited wardrobe. Clothing can be greatly enhanced by adding a flash of some bright harmonious color. For the ladies this means perhaps an assortment of costume jewelry, colored neck scarfs, necklaces, etc., while for men bright, colorful neckties will provide a focal point for a visual impact. Much can be done with a small budget if you keep such points as the foregoing in mind. The mode of dress for teachers varies considerably, running the gamut from quite formal to very informal. As a student teacher, it is wise for you to dress conservatively for the first few days at school. During that period, observe the mode of dress of the regular teachers and take your cue from them as to what is conventional. While you may not desire to dress conventionally when you become a full-fledged teacher, it is wise not to deviate very much from convention while you are a student teacher. You will have enough matters to consume your energies without coming under fire of colleagues and school administration for an unorthodox mode of dress. "When in Rome do as the Romans do" regarding mode of dress is a serviceable motto for student teaching.

Your clothing must be not only clean, neat and attractive but also functional for the type of lessons you will be teaching. A student teacher wearing spike heels will have difficulty teaching the kindergarten children a jumping-skipping type game, for example.

The following are two anecdotes which actually happened during student teaching:

A young lady engaged in student teaching in an intermediate grade habitually wore unusually tight skirts to school. One day while leading a game of "Simon Says" she did some deep knee bends. In the course of the game there was a very noticeable ripping sound. The bends were too much for her skirt, so she had to back gracefully out of the classroom for hasty repairs!

Another student teacher who was placed in a primary grade was in the habit of coming to school dressed as though she were going to a high society ball. One particular day she arrived at school in an overly frilly dress with a wide flowing skirt. The first activity of the day was finger painting. Following the lesson, she retreated to the washroom more than slightly soiled.

"Simon Says I'll Be
Back in a Few Minutes"

Select clothing which will permit you to engage freely in all phases of the classroom program.

Other aspects of your personal grooming include such items as care of finger nails, your breath, (is it offensive?), and for girls, the use of cosmetics. Cosmetics such as lipstick, eye shadow and rouge can add much to a woman's attractiveness if they are used tastefully — which usually means, among other things, *sparingly*. A truly "professional" teacher is always concerned about his or her visual impact on others and therefore is meticulous in matters of grooming. Professional attire is not to be taken as an inconsequential matter since it can greatly enhance or detract from your general impact as a teacher. It can communicate a very positive esthetic quality as well as being the hallmark of a cultured person.

Developing a Wholesome Classroom Climate for Learning.

There is much we need to know in relation to what actually constitutes the most wholesome classroom climate for learning. It is more than likely that research data will be collected clearly supporting the idea that there is not any single type of learning environment which is ideal for all children. Perhaps as more evidence becomes available we will be able to identify positively the indispensable elements of a wholesome classroom climate. In the meantime, however, we must employ all that we know of the principles of mental hygiene, child development and principles of learning in order to establish the best working environment possible for children. There is no magic formula which we who are writing this advice can suggest you employ as a student teacher. Undoubtedly a clarification of the task will help you to develop further insight into the subtle, complex and vital element of teaching known as classroom climate.

As components of a wholesome classroom environment, you will want to provide for the children a certain amount of freedom, creativity and spontaneity. At the same time children should realize a sense of purpose and order. Establishing a balance of these elements is indeed a classroom dynamic. How does the teacher encourage and nurture the development of individualism in children and at the same time not neglect teaching the cooperation skills involved in the group process? Further, how does the teacher promote dynamic and child-interest centered learning while working within the structure of a prescribed curriculum of content areas?

Many of these questions are very perplexing and unresolved in the minds of experienced teachers. This whole area of a wholesome working environment for children is going to be one with which you may wrestle for many years beyond student teaching. Do not, therefore, be impatient if you do not recognize any clear-cut answers to the problem during student teaching. In any event it probably is impossible to establish a classroom working environment which is best suited to *all* children. What you are trying to do is to establish an atmosphere in which you and the children can work best and with enjoyment, within the limits of the specific variables involved in your classroom setting. This is a very tall order at best. When we speak of establishing this wholesome working environment we do not mean to imply that a teacher or student teacher can come in and put the wheels in motion which will instantly, as with a magic word, establish the atmosphere. In most cases this working atmosphere is jelled over a considerable length of time. The time it takes will depend upon the group of children with whom you are working. We do feel, however, as though there were certain guidelines which can help you to tackle this delicate aspect of teaching.

In establishing a healthy classroom learning environment it is fundamental that you *know yourself* well — that you have a realistic self-concept. It would be disastrous for a teacher to permit a large measure of permissiveness in her classroom if she cannot live comfortably within this type of atmosphere without jeopardizing her own mental and emotional health. Some individuals by the nature of their personalities need to maintain tighter controls than others upon a classroom setting in order to be secure and effective as teachers. There will always be room in teaching for many types of personalities but there is a great need today to screen out those particular types who are not suited to teaching. This screening process is very complex and controversial and since it does not directly pertain to you as a student teacher we mention it only to make you aware of the fact that some thought and research are occurring concerning it.

If you will take a few minutes to jot down on paper what you consider to be the characteristics of the *best* working relationship *you* feel can be established with children, you will have graphic evidence of your present feelings in the matter. Then plan steps to initiate some of your goals into your student teaching setting with help and guidance from your cooperating teacher.

It would be very desirable to compare and discuss your description of a wholesome classroom climate in relation to what is known about principles of mental hygiene, sound principles of learning and child development. Is your idea of a learning atmosphere in harmony with them? Where does it conflict or contradict them?

While we recognize that much is yet to be learned about what constitutes a truly wholesome classroom climate, we advance the following suggestions to help you tackle the problem:

What Children Expect From a Wholesome Classroom Learning Environment

1. A teacher-leader whom they sincerely believe has their best interests at heart and who wants them to succeed in as many classroom tasks as possible.
2. A teacher who recognizes that making errors is a natural part of learning process and provides room in the program for them and their correction.
3. To feel that they play an important part in planning classroom work and that their opinions and suggestions are considered valable in terms of receiving serious consideration.
4. To know where the limits or boundaries are in relation to acceptable and unacceptable behavior. They should have a part in establishing the rules. They will have much more respect for rules which they have helped make and for which they see need and reason.
5. A teacher who thoroughly understands the general characteristics of the age group with which he is working and thus is patient and understanding when weaknesses and mistakes occur.
6. A teacher who freely recognizes the fact that he makes errors as well as the children and that he too is a learner in the classroom.
7. A teacher who lets his sense of humor show. He does not make children the butt of jokes but mixes a goodly portion of wholesome humor in his teaching.
8. A teacher who believes in the importance of teaching the concepts of democracy by *practicing* them as much as possible and by helping children to understand democratic principles and responsibilities. Democracy is not a subject but a process.

We have previously stressed the point that the development of a wholesome classroom environment rests fundamentally with the teacher. It is the teacher's personality and general sensitivity to human relations that have the greatest single effect upon any classroom learning environment. There are other elements such as the children themselves, the physical features of the classroom, and the school curriculum program and administration. We reiterate, however, that *you* as the teacher in large measure will determine the learning environment of your classroom.

What are some methods of establishing a wholesome environment for learning? As previously mentioned, children will work most comfortably in a classroom where they know the boundaries or limits of a situation. Here is where group discussion can play an important part. You may want to guide the children in setting up rules of good conduct. Through class discussion for example, your class might talk over why it is necessary to raise their hands to answer or ask questions. Why couldn't they just talk whenever they want to providing they do not interrupt anyone else? This question can lead the children to thinking about the reasoning or lack of it behind imposed social rules and regulations. The class may decide, with the teacher's guidance, to try to eliminate hand raising as a procedure. Other issues such as gum chewing, homework, etc., may also be raised. It is vital throughout these discussions that the children feel they have a voice in deciding rules for governing the class and that rules have been arrived at as a result of thoughtful teacher and pupil consideration. Children will have much more respect for rules they have formulated as a class than those imposed upon them by a teacher.

Encourage the children to write out their expectations for a teacher. What do they consider to be the characteristics of a good teacher? As discussion over these papers takes place, both children and teacher will come to understand better the other's point of view.

Use Reaction Reports at Least Once a Month

Reaction reports should be a *must* for you as a student teacher and throughout your teaching career. They are one technique for appraising and modifying the classroom learning climate. Pass out identical paper to all children. Encourage them to disguise their handwriting if it makes them feel more secure. Impress upon them emphatically that you will not make any attempt to associate a person's name with any paper submitted, since this is not your purpose. Then ask the children to write down the reactions they have to *any phase* of your teaching and of the classroom setting in general. The comments may be negative or positive or both. Impress upon the children the fact that you want to know how they feel about the classwork in order to help you make improvements and modifications. Unless you can convince the children that all reactions are kept anonymous they will not be candid and the papers will be useless. If some teachers would employ the reaction report technique with their classes, they would get a much-needed shock of their lives. Of course if children never have done a reaction report before you may have to structure their reports a bit by requesting they answer specific questions about your classroom teaching. If you do not do this you will get back reports which say things like "I think everything is O.K." This really does not tell you a great deal as you want children to develop much more mature analytical techniques than are reflected by a single ambiguous statement.

You may ask the children to include in their reports the answers to questions such as these: What activities have you liked most in our classroom work so far? Which ones haven't you liked? Why? Do you feel you have enough freedom in our classroom? Give a reason for your answer. Do I give too much homework? Is there anything about our classroom work which particularly bothers you? Why? These and similar questions will help the children to be more explicit, thus making the reports more useful. Encourage children to make a positive suggestion for improvement if they make a negative statement. In other words if there is something about our classroom workings you don't like, tell me about it, but also tell me how we might improve the situation.

While we have to read the reaction reports from children as a general barometer rather than an absolute judgment, they serve at least

two important purposes: (1) They let the children know that you are concerned about their reaction to your classroom teaching and are interested in improving it and (2) they provide an emotional outlet for children to say anything to you they desire in an an anonymous way.

A teacher is not worth his salt who is unconcerned about the reactions of the learners. Too many teachers are not concerned. We hope throughout your teaching career you will always use student reaction reports as *one* important piece of evidence for measuring your impact upon learners.

When children know you are concerned about making your lessons and general classroom work as exciting and interesting as possible, the general atmosphere of your classroom will be greatly enhanced.

Just keeping the children quiet is not what is meant by a wholesome learning environment, nor will the classroom climate for learning be similar at *all* times. Many factors can affect it. Establishing a wholesome learning environment for children in your classroom is a delicate, intricate job of human relations. Upon this phase of teaching can rest the foundations of your success or failure as an effective teacher or student teacher.

What's Packed in Your Voice-Box?

In addition to the intellectual and visual impacts you will have upon children there remains, your auditory impact. A great deal of your success as a student teacher will be determined by the sound impression you make. Your voice can portray zesty enthusiasm for what you are teaching or suggest abject boredom.

Your voice is a teaching tool. It can be employed to enhance or detract from the things you are endeavoring to teach. The children can hardly be expected to be enthusiastic and interested in what you are teaching if you yourself don't sound interested. Inflections, variations in tone and volume together with animated facial expressions and hand gestures will help you to "sell" whatever you are trying to teach. Teaching is partly a selling job. You must sell yourself and your program to children before optimum learning can occur.

Contrasts in all facets of your voice will add interest to it. At times during your teaching you should be almost shouting and at other times speaking in a whisper. These contrasts will help you to hold the attention of the students and will add interest to your speech.

Your auditory impact upon children can also affect your classroom control (discipline). A voice that portrays uncertainty, lack of self-confidence, or acquiescence can precipitate lack of respect for you from children and adults.

It is also important to remember that the teacher represents a very important language and speech example for her students. Many times children will adopt certain speech mannerisms from teachers, especially those whom they admire greatly. For children who come from culturally deprived homes the teacher very often is the best linguistic model to which they are exposed in their early years.

One wonderful device for self-help in relation to your speech impact is a tape recorder. Most schools today have one and if you will bring it into your classroom and push the record button before you begin your lesson you will have a tape which you can play back later for evaluation. If you keep the recorder for an extended period in the classroom the children will become adjusted to its presence and after awhile forget that the lesson is being taped. When you play back your tape, ask yourself if your voice sounds interesting. Does it provoke attention? — Portray enthusiasm and liveliness? — Exemplify good grammar? The taped lessons can also help you and your cooperating teacher to evaluate other aspects of your teaching, i.e., the manner in which you handle children's responses and questions, the suitability of your vocabulary, and the pace or speed of your lesson.

If you purchase a tape recorder before starting student teaching you can keep certain recorded lessons for later reference. You might want to send a lesson to your parents so that Mom and Dad can have the thrill of hearing you teach. This tape may also be amusing to listen to years later when you have had a good deal of teaching experience.

The Classroom as a Setting For Learning Experiences

Children learn through their life experience. Some of these learnings are of a positive nature, some negative. For example a child may *learn* to discriminate against a particular racial or religious group. The classroom is one segment of a child's life experiences. It is a learning laboratory in which the learning is to some extent planned and controlled by various agents such as the teacher, the school administration, and the board of education. It is the job of the teacher to set up situations in which the children can efficiently and interestingly learn certain knowledges, attitudes (appreciations) and skills. How can you as a student teacher make efficient use of the classroom setting to foster the prescribed learnings for the children? With the increasing amounts of subject matter being pressed upon the public schools and no change in the length of the school hours, it becomes imperative that the teacher budget his time very carefully each day.

Discipline

The maintenance of wholesome pupil discipline has been shown to be one area in which student teachers tend to be weakest.[2] Since classrooms are composed of individual children, total group control depends upon the behavior of each child.

An unbridled class of children who constantly go beyond the boundaries of propriety is as desructive to the learning climate as a class of children who are rigidly held to unrealistic behavioral rules. We must be careful to prevent the classroom as well as the total school establishment from becoming an awesome giant which stifles creativity and wholesome learning. Some teacher's actions seem to say "I am the sole judge of what is right and good. Why can't you children be more like me?" Good teaching does not suggest that pupils mimic the teacher — it promotes thoughtful behavior and increases healthy differences in children.

---

[2]Jesse A. Bond, "Strengths and Weaknesses of Student Teachers," *Journal of Educational Research* 45:507-16; 1952.

An exciting, stimulating classroom program tends to eliminate disciplinary problems. Children who are vitally involved in classroom work are not apt to misbehave, so if you are having disciplinary problems examine your classroom program first. As previously mentioned, the character of your voice can affect your classroom control a great deal. Check yourself with a tape recorder and discuss the results with your cooperating teacher.

What Are the Goals of Pupil Discipline?

Children should be constantly in training to develop inner self-discipline. The weakest type of classroom control is that which is *imposed* by the teacher. Children should behave within the boundaries of propriety and social conscience because they see the logic in doing so, not because some teacher is standing over them as a threat. You should be aiming to help children to:

1. Act in a socially desirable manner and eliminate undesirable behavior.
2. Associate pleasure and satisfaction with desirable behavior and displeasure and dissatisfaction with undesirable behavior.
3. Habituate desirable behavior so that it becomes automatic.

As a student teacher you must *be consistent* in implementing group control measures. What is unacceptable behavior at 10 A.M. should be unacceptable at 11 A.M. In order to be *consistent* it is important that you have thought out your philosophy of classroom discipline. Unfortunately the term discipline to some teachers means getting the children to do *exactly* what they want them to do. Is sound group control based upon manipulating children?

Here are some suggestions which may be helpful to you in pupil discipline:

1. Incorporate the children in planning activities, making rules and evaluation.
2. Get to know each child — his mannerisms and moods.
3. Guide your standards for child behavior according to the background of the children.
4. Seek to discover the cause of misbehavior when it occurs. The cause might be, for example, physiological, social, or perhaps inherent in the situation.

Wholesome pupil discipline involves helping children to develop intelligent self-direction, yet what constitutes intelligent self-direction

can be interpreted widely, depending upon things such as social strata and religious and nationality background.

As a student teacher you will have to be sensitive to unique local behavioral mores held for children in your particular teaching setting.

Sociometric techniques and devices can assist you in group control. For example you may want to do a sociogram of your class. This can chart various cliques in your classroom group as well as the relative social position of all class members. The information gleaned from a sociogram can be extremely useful in setting up committees, work groups, and classroom seating and in better understanding the behavior of individual children.

Remember, however, that this device has limitations. If you are not familiar with constructing a sociogram check a reference source.

There is no panacea for classroom control. Healthy classroom control has as its foundation good self-discipline of each *individual* pupil. When you find children who are discipline problems you may have to try many disciplinary techniques to determine an approach which works. Some respond favorably to certain techniques, others do not; there is no *one* solution.

Foremost in your mind should be the understanding that you have a responsibility to the *total* class in terms of maintaining a healthy learning situation. You cannot permit one or two youngsters to disrupt this continually, therefore at times the disruptive element must be removed.

Recognize that there are short-term and long-term disciplinary measures. A short-term measure seeks to end the disturbance as quickly as possible but usually is not remedial or corrective in character. Some examples of this would be requiring a child to leave the room or calling attention to his infraction of the rules in the presence of his classmates. These measures may quell the disturbance but they do not locate the cause of the misbehavior nor help the child to understand why he is being punished. Long-term measures involve such techniques as a series of conferences with the parents and the child, referral to the school psychologist, and private talks with the child.

Discuss often with the children the need for rules in our society and what would happen if we didn't have them.

Try to be creative in working out disciplinary problems. For example, when two boys who were fighting on the playground return to the classroom, have them used hand puppets (they are easy to make) and re-enact what transpired on the playground except that you ask each child to take the part of the other fellow. Then discuss the whole incident with the class.

Discipline is a complex classroom element. Some disciplinary problems are too serious to handle there and other agencies must be called upon. Your school principal can be helpful in this regard.

Try these:

1. List, with the help of your cooperating teacher, as many disciplinary techniques as you can think of and then discuss their relative merits.
2. The following are quotations from classroom teachers regarding discipline. React to each of these; it will help to crystallize your thinking.

    a. "I won't tolerate any foolishness in my room"
    b. "I like to have as few rules as possible in my room"
    c. "I like to be known as a strict teacher"
    d. "I let my children know who's boss in no uncertain terms"
    e. "Children really want to be told what to do, anyway"
    f. "Children never can be given too much love"

There's a Place for Routine

Another important element in general classroom management is the establishment of some type of routine to take care of such items as housekeeping chores, morning exercises, attendance, laboratory time, and lunchtime procedures. Young children in particular need some routine in their school schedule to promote security and orderliness. This stress upon a certain amount of classroom routine is not meant to imply that innovations are never introduced. Routine can, however, save precious teaching time when it is applied to the incidental elements of classroom management. You therefore may want to decide with the children what housekeeping chores must be done in the classroom and make a list of them. Then perhaps each week a team can be chosen to assume these tasks. An eye-catching bulletin board can assign these duties as well as serve as a remainder to the children.

Other elements of classroom management include the regulation of

light and ventilation, seating of children, the provision of suitable places for the children to keep personal belongings in a neat fashion and the storage and management of the many audio-visual teaching aids of the modern classroom.

Classroom management also encompasses keeping many kinds of records and reports and other miscellaneous paper work. You will need to develop a personal system for fulfilling these requirements.

Functional Planning For Children

Why plan? Superficial needs for teacher-made plans are often bandied about with remarks such as: You need written plans so that a substitute teacher can use them if you are out of class for some reason, or I (an administrator) must see your written plans each week as they are one indicator of your teaching pace and quality.

In reality all planning done by teachers and administrators serves two fundamental purposes, namely to foster continuity of the learning and to facilitate good teaching. In the final analysis of planning, what really counts is *not* the quality of the planning as written down but what is happening to children in the classroom as a result of the planning — the quality of teaching that evolves from it. There is no one format for teacher-made plans that is sacred or best for *all* teachers to employ. In general, however, all plans ought to contain certain basic elements. These are simply common sense elements.

The first element is your *objectives* for the lesson — (what you hope to accomplish). You wouldn't want a surgeon to operate on you without an objective firmly in mind or a lawyer to defend you if he weren't sure of his objective. It is equally important that a teacher recognize his objectives before commencing a lesson.

Another element is the *method or methods* to be employed in teaching the lesson (how it is to be taught). Incorporated within the method would be the introduction to the lesson. The introduction oftentimes is in our judgment the most crucial point of the lesson. It is at this point you try to capture the children's interest — you attempt to motivate children highly. You should give a great deal of consideration to dreaming up excitement, thought and interest-provoking introductions to your lessons.

The teaching methods you use in your classroom we believe are *as* important if not more important than the subject matter itself. A teacher must be well informed on subject matter but how he presents this material to children can stimulate or kill their desire to

"Dreaming Up an Idea"

learn it. Those who have led the wholesale condemnation of teaching methods courses are grossly misinformed as to the role teaching methodology plays in the learning process.

Sometimes you will find that the nature of the material you are going to teach to some extent dictates or limits the methods you can employ, but these instances are rare.

There is nothing as tragic as a teacher who has a wealth of information and knowledge to offer to children (she knows her subject matter) but fails to employ teaching methods which motivate them to want to explore the subject matter with her. Teaching methodology is a crucial issue in your success as a student teacher.

Other elements of a lesson plan are the *content* (what you plan to teach), *materials* (the resources you plan to draw upon), and *evalua-*

tion (the success you had or degree to which you accomplished your objectives).

Planning should be viewed as being short or long term in character. As a student teacher you are expected to engage in some of both. Short-term planning generally involves your daily lesson planning and/or weekly planning, whereas long-term planning may involve several weeks, as with a unit-type plan, or yearly planning (such as the minimum year's work required in arithmetic or social studies).

You may not have an opportunity as a student teacher to be involved in grade level total curriculum planning. Your daily plans are really small parts of your long-term plans. Your professional helpers will aid you if you still are confused about teacher-made plans.

Custom-tailor Your Plans

Student teaching can help you to work out the type of planning which best facilitates your personal teaching. Planning is highly individualistic, especially in regard to detail. Some of you will find through experimenting with your own teaching that you need only a few simple notes on a 3 x 5 card to teach effectively. Others will need to write out their plans in more detail in order to feel confident and to do a good job. As an analogy some individuals can give an hour long speech using one 3 x 5 card with a few sentences on it while others would need copious notes to give the same talk. This principle is also true for teacher planning. The important factor is the quality of the teaching which results from the plans, not the plans themselves. Some teachers are capable of writing out beautifully engineered plans but cannot translate them into action.

There are some commercial teacher plan books which have blank spaces under the days of the week for you to fill in your weekly teaching plans. You might find one of these useful.

You will be expected to plan in detail at the outset of student teaching. Detailed plans are necessary to prove your competency to your cooperating teacher and others concerned with your development and to insure a better chance of your first lessons' going smoothly. Once you have proved competency in detailed planning, strive to streamline your plans so that a minimum of writing is involved without affecting your teaching effectiveness adversely.

There is so much paper work embodied in the teaching profession that it is vital you learn how to develop top quality written plans in a minimum amount of time. Here again, your cooperating teacher and college supervisor may give you some aid.

Team teaching, which is being given considerable attention in some areas of the country, presents many new challenges to teacher planning. Space does not permit a discussion of them here. You and your cooperating teacher may want to do some reference reading about team teaching and experiment with it in the classroom.

Teachers' Manuals Can Help

One buttress for your planning can be the teachers' manuals which some textbook companies publish to accompany their particular books. You will find them of great help as a beginner in teaching. The only caution here is to use them as *one* source of ideas for teaching a particular lesson and couple this source to *your* professional judgment. Teachers' manuals are written for the express purpose of helping you plan and teach specific lessons in a particular textbook series; however, you should modify the manual in relation to what you feel you can handle and in relation to your particular group of children. Some ideas for presenting lessons may fit your program and children very well, others may not. You may, for example, want to change the method of motivating the lesson suggested in the manual to suit some special interest of your class. You might also feel that some of the manual's suggestions for teaching a particular lesson are too juvenile or too sophisticated for your particular class. Even better, you may be able to think of a more unique and interesting method for teaching the textbook material. Teachers' manuals were not intended to be followed literally in all classroom situations but rather to be used as aids for the free thinking teacher. You can and should be a source of individual ideas and techniques for presenting lessons. Try out some of your ideas. Do not let rigid adherence to a teacher's manual stifle your own creativity.

Flexibility Is the Keynote

Since it is impossible to determine the response of children in advance of a lesson, it is necessary that teacher-made plans be flexible.

There are so many unexpected occurrences in the modern day classroom which dictate a change in plans that every teacher learns to be flexible to some extent.

In teaching a lesson, for example, you may find that the children would like to approach a topic from another avenue than you had originally planned. Their special interests may point to a slightly different focus on a topic than you had intended. Flexibility must, then, be a basic characteristic of a teacher-made plan oriented to the needs and interests of children.

Pupil-Teacher Planning

Much has been written about the positive and negative tenets of pupil-teacher planning. Unfortunately an aura of negativism surrounds pupil-teacher planning in some areas because it is associated with that supposed demon, progressive education. We cannot hope to present adequately in limited space all of the facets of this most important teaching skill and therefore suggest that if you are not familiar with the area you do so some related reference reading. There are, however, certain fundamental points which we feel should be emphasized to student teachers.

Pupil-teacher planning permits the learner to take a shared responsibility in outlining his own learning as well as that of his peers. It also may develop a deeper personal involvement on the part of the child in relation to such elements as human relations and group dynamics. In addition pupil-teacher planning can, if well implemented, offer children an opportunity to develop the important skills connected with planning.

How Important Is It for Children to Learn to Plan Effectively?

Planning is a part of almost all endeavors of adult life and yet how often in school do we give children an opportunity actually to make plans and to carry them out? Successful adult living may very well be hinged to one's ability to plan his or her life well, yet where are real planning experiences in our school program? They are scarce.

As a student teacher it will be a thrilling experience to try some pupil-teacher planning.

How Can It Be Done?

Pupil-teacher planning cannot be suddenly thrust upon children who have had no preparation in handling it. There is a readiness element related to pupil-teacher planning in both pupils and the teacher. It will take different groups of children differing amounts of time to *learn* to plan together, depending upon the general maturity of the groups. You must expect some setbacks as well as progress during the readiness period. You should begin by permitting the children to plan simple things before moving to the complex. Perhaps you will want the children to plan the *order* of the subjects they will have each day with the exception of those already scheduled such as music, physical education and art.

Small-size committee work in social studies, language arts, etc., is a good lead-up step for children in pupil-teaching planning. In doing any type of committee work with children you will find it is valuable to discuss these things with them *before* the committees or groups begin to function:

1. What are the values of committee work? What are the advantages of working with other people in a group as opposed to trying to do a job alone? What are the disadvantages?
2. What are the responsibilities of a good committee or group member?
3. What specific problem or task are we attacking today? (Be certain the children understand the purpose of the groups.)

At the close of a period of group work it may be well to ask the children how they felt the group work was done. Did they accomplish their goals? Did they find any pitfalls to beware of when next they work in groups?

Do not give up on committee or group work with children just because your first experiments do not go as well as you expected. Discuss with the children the failures and successes and make provision to avoid repeating the same mistakes. Later you may want to have them choose among various activities or methods of approach to the subject matter in language arts, science, or social studies activities.

In many instances it is not possible for the children to help you determine *what* is to be taught but certainly they can share in choosing *how* it is to be done. For example they may discuss various methods of approaching the next unit in social studies. Group discussion, individual reports, and projects can all be explored as possibilities, with the children arriving at a decision. In your early experiments with cooperative planning you probably should be a very active member of the planning session, but as time goes on you may find it possible to fade gradually into the background and eventually permit the children to do it alone.

Your class might evolve from limited planning of a single activity to that of a full day's work. One thing to keep in mind is that in learning to plan, as in all types of learning, children will make errors. They will learn from these errors if they are guided to find the reasons why their plans were unsuccessful. Sometimes they are too ambitious in biting off a work load or they may not foresee that certain obstacles might arise. If you analyze the success of your planning together at the end of each day, children will soon become astute in their planning.

We deem it realistic to recognize that many teachers will probably never be able to incorporate real pupil-teacher planning in their classrooms because of the nature of their personalities. Their personal security in the classroom hinges upon rigid control of the children and the program. They are unable to permit children the degree of freedom of action which undergirds the cooperative process. Most teachers, however, can *learn* to employ pupil-teacher planning successfully.

Some Suggested Readiness Activities:

1. Group or committee experiences where children are required to operate with self-discipline.
2. Experience as a class in planning some single activity such as taking a trip or organizing room duties.
3. Experience as a class in planning single subject areas like social studies before you try to plan a whole day with the children.
4. Having the teacher explain at various times in the morning what his plans for the class are for the day and how he arrived at these decisions.
5. Having the children hold class meetings run by the class officers (elected).

What Are the Pitfalls?

1. It does take extra time, but democratic decisions are always more time consuming than dictatorial ones.
2. Children must be slowly eased into the full job by a system of well planned readiness or lead-up experiences, or chaos might result.
3. It may be that some children will have a long way to come in terms of gaining enough self-discipline to handle this job so there may be some added disciplinary problems.
4. It takes a very skillful teacher to guide the children so that they will develop a worthwhile program; therefore it may challenge your skill and security more.
5. You certainly never know what children are going to suggest so you must be ready for anything.
6. Some children may try to monopolize the group.

Some Common Criticisms of Pupil-Teacher Planning

Here are some of the criticisms you will frequently hear from teachers and administrators. Are they accurate criticisms of well implemented pupil-teacher planning?

1. The children tell the teachers what to teach.
2. It wastes too much time.
3. The children always get disorderly.
4. Children don't know what's good for them anway, so how can they make intelligent decisions about their progress?
5. It destroys the role of the teacher.
6. I can't use it and still use a textbook sequence or prescribed curriculum.

Creative Teaching

Creative teaching stems from creative personalities. There is a dire need in our nation to utilize the creative talents of our people if we are to survive. Creativity begets creativity. Creative teachers foster creativity

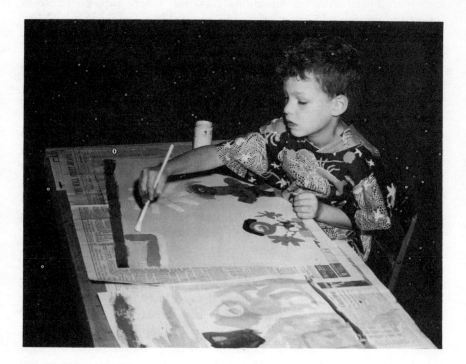

in their students. The professions and business and industry are clamoring for creative people since they recognize the tremendous contribution original thinkers can make, yet most agree that these people do not fit in readily as organization-type persons. Creativeness implies an element of or nonconformity. We could labor the semantic aspects of the word creative, but let us assume creativity is not so much an aptitude as it is an attitude. It implies, however, that the individual possesses in large measure certain characteristics which enable him or her to excel in the ability to be flexible and adjust rapidly to new situations, be original and fluent in dealing with ideas, and handle problems in a broader framework of possible solutions.

You have a certain degree of creativity in you though you may find it difficult to exercise. The exact process involving creativity remains shrouded in many mysteries, yet all of us are capable of developing new ideas — perhaps not big ideas but useful and contributory nevertheless. Creativity in your teaching implies injecting a part of yourself into it.

Creative elements can be incorporated in practically every teaching endeavor. There are some situations, however, where rather strict conformity is desirable. For example, serious problems might result if you decided to be creative about interpreting fire drill procedures or encouraging the children to interpret them.

Some types of record keeping in which uniformity is valuable might also be handicapped by a teacher who decided to be creative. We do, however, need to incorporate more creative ideas in what seem to be routine, obligatory areas like record keeping.

Creativity in your teaching can mean dreaming up new activities to enrich learning and experimenting with new methods and materials that *you* have thought of. Creativity is contagious. The children will feel a creative classroom atmosphere. You can deliberately plan activities and situations which will encourage creative thinking in the children. You might, for example, try brainstorming solutions to realistic problems. Try beginning a lesson by telling the children that you are the president of a hoola hoop company and that you have three big warehouses full of hoola hoops. The problem is that the fad for hoola hoops has lessened greatly. What uses can we find for these hoola hoops in order to sell them?

CONTAGIOUS CREATIVITY

All types of writing activities in which the children are encouraged to react to their environment in prose and poetic form will enhance creative thinking. You might say to the class, "What do these things make you think of, boys and girls? Chocolate, walking barefoot in the mud, a spring breeze, a caterpillar, fresh paint."

To some, any structuring of the classroom program presupposes placing limits on the creative spontaneity of children. This point of view is debatable.

Dare to be creative and thoughtfully different in any phase of your teaching. Transpose your ideas into action; creativity implies action and resolution. There is a story regarding a woman who said to Fritz Kreisler following one of his inspirational concerts: "I'd give my life to play as you do." Mr. Kreisler replied soberly, "I did."

No one can *tell* you how to be creative. You must learn to give to your teaching a part of your unique being.

> No other job in the world could possibly dispossess one so completely as this job of teaching. You could stand all day in a laundry, for instance, still in possession of your mind. But this teaching utterly obliterates you. It cuts right into your being: essentially it takes over your spirit. It drags it out from where it would hide.[3]

TOPICS AND QUESTIONS FOR STUDY AND DISCUSSION

1. List some of the elements which are a part of good mental health. Now discuss what conditions in a classroom can help to establish and/or nurture (in children) these elements.
2. The title of this chapter contains the phrase "effective student teacher." Using the sample evaluation forms shown on pages 103-113 in Chapter 5, identify some of the factors which contribute to a "student teacher's effectiveness."
3. Classroom control (discipline) historically has been a problem for student teachers. How can a teacher effectively involve his class in establishing disciplinary limits?
4. What is the role of criticism in the student teaching program? How can it be helpful? When does it become a disintegrating factor?

SELECTED REFERENCES

1. Anderson, Harold H., ed., *Creativity and Its Cultivation*, New York: Harper & Brothers, 1959.
2. Getzels and Jackson, *Creativity and Intelligence*, New York: John Wiley and Sons, 1962.
3. Ghiselin, Brewster, ed., *The Creative Process*, New York: Mentor Books, 1952.

---

[3]Sylva Ashton-Warner, *Spinster*, Simon and Schuster, Inc., p. 9, 1959.

4. Lowenfeld, Viktor, *Creative and Mental Growth*, New York: The Macmillan Company, 1957.
5. Mearns, Hughes, *Creative Power: The Education of Youth in the Creative Arts*, New York: Dover Publications, Inc., 1958.
6. Miel, Alice, ed., *Creativity In Teaching*, San Francisco: Wadsworth Publishing Company, Inc., 1961.
7. Zirbes, Laura, *Spurs to Creative Teaching*, New York: G. P. Putnam's Sons, 1959.

GATEWAY TO TEACHING

Chapter 4

Teaching In the Total School-Community Setting

*There's many a life of sweet content
Whose virtue is environment.*

Walter Learned (1847-1915)
*On the flyleaf of
Manon Lescaut*

The immediate environment of the teacher is the classroom, but no classroom exists in a vacuum. It is definitely not an island, but one in a series of interdependent organizational units. It is part of a total school program. The school in turn has a specific setting as an integral part of a community or rural school district. Still further, the community or district exists within a particular state as part of our nation, the world, and in the space age — our galaxy. All of these interdependencies affect every classroom setting directly or indirectly. This means that the role of the classroom teacher extends far beyond the classroom itself. Many dynamic forces — political, social, economic and geographic — outside of the classroom act upon it and the teacher. In order to evaluate adequately your impact as a teacher in any classroom setting it will be necessary that you become aware of the character of these forces and variables. Achieving this will help you to: (1) be a more effective student teacher, (2) better evaluate your teaching effectiveness, (3) develop a more realistic concept of the expanded role of the teacher and (4) select your first teaching position more wisely.

57

It is the purpose of this chapter to identify some of the facets of the school and community which you may want to observe and evaluate during and after student teaching.

The Educational Philosophy of the School

If you will turn to page 219, you will notice that the advanced education students who were sampled in the two teacher preparing institutions considered a school's philosophy of education to be a major factor in selecting a first teaching position. Why have these students placed prime importance on philosophy? Perhaps you think it is for philosophers to haggle over in their cozy ivory towers, devoid of contact with reality, and not a functional part of everyday living. This could not be farther from the truth. Actually everything you do in life is in some way influenced by your philosophy even though you may not be conscious of it. Similarly in your classroom the way you teach as well as what you teach will be the result of your philosophy of life and/or education and the forces that act upon them. One of these forces will be the philosophy of the school in which you are employed.

"I'LL NEVER GET OFF THE GROUND"

Its philosophy of education will affect the type of teaching methods that are deemed acceptable as well as the school curriculum. The school's philosophy also will determine the type of discipline that is enforced, the allocation of funds for school needs and even such a fine point as the style of furniture that is bought for the school. Literally everything that goes on in the school is, in some way, acted upon by its philosophy.

The authors have used the phrase "the philosophy of the school" in the preceding paragraph. In reality, however, a school rarely adheres to one basic philosophy although its staff is composed of some individuals who do. You will find that the philosophy of education varies considerably from teacher to teacher, and so it should be. However, there is some kind of general philosophical climate which can be detected in all schools, and it is to this that we refer. This climate is determined to some extent by the school administrators. While inserting many of his own beliefs regarding education, the principal is also reflecting the feelings of the superintendent and the board of education. This is to be expected, since the schools belong initially to the people and these are the people's representatives. What does all of this mean to you as a student teacher or a first-year teacher in a school? It means that you can expect to find a wide range of philosophies of education among teachers and administrators. Teachers, however, are expected to operate within certain limits which the school administration may set down in clear-cut terms or imply indirectly through its policies. Sometimes these limits are wide and liberal and sometimes they form a very narrow avenue within which the classroom teacher must work.

There's More In the Act!

In addition to the philosophy of the school there usually is a general philosophical climate in the community which affects the public schools. If the philosophy of the school and that of the community are not relatively harmonious, there may be open conflict. Educational conflicts are not difficult to precipitate as there usually are some laymen in every community who feel they are experts in the field of education.

As previously stated, you can expect to find a general philosophical climate in every community. What should be kept in mind is that this climate to some degree is constantly changing. Conditions change in a community and often result in abrupt changes in the community's attitude toward education and the public schools. One task of the professional educator is to be sensitive to the signposts indicating a general change in attitude. It is also part of the professional educator's role to help mold a sound, healthy community attitude toward education. It will be your responsibility as a teacher to help educate the community as to the needs of the school and to interpret the school program. All teachers have this public relations aspect in their role.

A Kingdom For the Cause!

The foundations of community educational philosophy are hidden in a complex sociological maze. Such things as the nature of the social stratification, economic conditions, religious and ethnic elements, local prejudices, the quality of the community leadership, political variables and the like all play active parts.

If the school board represents the people of the community in the true sense of the word, then you can in some measure detect community feelings by examining the policies of the board. Many of its decisions are made in the light of the will of the general public. Its will is governed by its philosophy of education. This community philosophy of education, while not always immediately apparent to the student teacher or the first-year teacher, can affect all aspects of education from the role of the teacher in the community to what is to be taught in the classroom. Even more vital it affects the purse strings (financing) of the school program.

You have undoubtedly taken professional courses during your college career. In them, you probably developed some personal convictions regarding such things as the general purpose of education, curriculum content and the role of the teacher. Many students, however, fail to crystallize their thinking enough to develop an organized philosophy of education. As a result, their teaching may lack well-defined purposes and direction. This can be embarrassing as well as confusing to them and to the parents of children they are teaching, to say nothing of the school administration. In addition, when they are unsure of their beliefs they become very vunerable to those who would impose their own ideologies upon them. It is also a reflection upon their professional training if they appear illiterate in the philosophical issues of the profession. This is not meant to imply that they should have definite, absolute answers to the philosophical issues, as there are no right answers. They should be able, however, to state clearly and sensibly their stand regarding them and why they have taken their particular stands.

Student teaching will help you make your philosophy of education operational to some extent. The teaching methods you employ and the disciplinary climate of your classroom will be the manifestations of your philosophy of education and/or philosophy of life. These two cannot be divorced. For example, if you use pupil-teacher planning as the framework for your classroom program, you are manifesting a belief in certain specific values related to pupil involvement in learning, the rights of individuals to self-determination (within certain limits) and the advantages to be gained from group effort.

You will want to examine and discuss various classroom teaching methods in the light of your philosophy of education. Why have you selected one method rather than another to teach a specific lesson? It will not be at all unusual to find that at times you are inconsistent. As an example, you may firmly believe that personal independence is an important characteristic to teach developmentally to children. You may find, however, that your methods of teaching promote strong pupil dependence upon the teacher rather than pupil self-reliance. Your classroom may be too tightly structured in terms of prescribed pupil behavior to permit children to make behavioral choices which lead to self-direction and independence.

While evaluating various teaching procedures such as the lecture method, be certain to include not only its philosophical underpinnings but the principles of learning and findings of educational research which apply to the particular method under scrutiny. Using methodology as a starting point, probing the philosophical and research foundations of the teaching process can be an emotionally exciting and intellectually stimulating experience for you and your cooperating teacher. The process may help you to develop more internal consistency in your philosophy of education and philosophy of life. You may find, as many students have in the past, that in crystallizing your beliefs and values you have an eclectic philosophy — one built upon fragments of many different philosophical schools. In any event, the process of philosophizing in education will enable you to better understand other teachers, students whom you are charged to teach, and yourself. To enable teacher candidates to do just this, teachers' colleges and universities offer courses in general philosophy as well as in the philosophies of education. If such a course is available in your institution you should by all means elect it if it is not a required course. It is lamentable but true that some colleges still do not offer courses in educational philosophy. It is assumed that the students pick up threads of the various philosophical schools as they progress through other professional courses. Some of this does occur, perhaps by "osmosis"; however it does not supplant an organized course in comparative philosophies of education. If you have not been fortunate enough to have had such a course and will not have the opportunity to take one before you begin teaching, you should do some reading and thinking in this area on your own time. The authors provide at the end of this section some selected questions and readings you may find useful in investigating educational philosophy.

It's Not Just By Chance.

The authors have deliberately placed philosophy of education as a lead-in topic to this chapter because they sincerely believe that it is of primary importance. Before seeking your first teaching position, take time out to think out and write out what you believe to be the kind of classroom you want to establish. Describe also the kind of educational system and/or program of which you want to be a part.

When you do this, you will find it impossible to avoid reflecting a good deal of your educational philosophy. In addition we suggest you investigate the questions which follow:

1. What does the term philosophy mean and how does it relate to education?
2. In what way does your philosophy of life affect your philosophy of education?
3. How do the four fundamental areas of philosophy relate to the roots of a philosophy of education — Ontology, Human Nature, Epistemology and Axiology?
4. What are the basic beliefs of the main philosophies of education, where are their origins, who were their founders, and who are their current proponents (Perennialism, Progressivism, Essentialism, etc.)?
5. What and who should determine the aims of public education in America?
6. What are the effects of John Dewey's work upon modern day education?
7. What role should religion play in education?

SELECTED REFERENCES

The following reference books will help you to tackle some of the foregoing study questions. They will also help you to better understand what constitutes philosophizing in education.

1. Brameld, Theodore, *Philosophies of Education*. New York: The Dryden Press, 1958.
2. Brubacher, John S., *Modern Philosophies of Education*. New York: Mc-Graw Hill Book Co., 1950.
3. Burns, H. W. and C. J. Brauner, *Philosophy of Education*. New York: The Ronald Press Company, 1962.
4. Butler, Donald, *Four Philosophies and Their Practice in Education and Religion*. New York: Harper & Bros., 1957.
5. Dewey, John, *Democracy and Education*. New York: The Macmillan Company, 1916.
6. Hansen, Kenneth H., *Philosophy of Modern Education*. Englewood, Cliffs, N. J.: Prentice-Hall Inc., 1960.
7. Hughes, James Monroe, *Education in America*, Elmsford, New York: Row Peterson and Company, 1960.
8. Mayer, Frederick, *Philosophy of Education for Our Time*. New York: Odyssey Press Inc., 1960.
9. Morris, Van Cleve, *Philosophy and the American School*, New York: Houghton Mifflin Co., 1961.
10. Phenix, Philip H., *Philosophy of Education*, New York: Henry Holt & Company, 1958.
11. Wahlquist, J. T., *The Philosophy of American Education*. New York: The Ronald Press, 1942, Chapters 1-6.

12. Weber, Christian O., *Basic Philosophies of Education*. New York: Rinehart and Company, 1960.

The School and Its Community Setting

The community constitutes the immediate environment (setting) of the school. It therefore is in a strategic position to exert considerable pressure upon the school; in fact schools usually mirror the community in which they are located. While the community directly affects the school the converse is also true. Some sociologists believe the public school to be the most potent organ for social change, so to some extent the school serves to mold the community. Certainly there is constant interaction between them and often a cause-and-effect relationship. As a result, modifications occur in both. Whether or not social change *should be initiated* by the public school is a philosophical issue. As challenging as this issue is, it does not suit the authors' purposes in this chapter to discuss it here.

Many student teaching programs require a community study or survey. Its major purpose is to make student teachers aware of the strong interdependence and cause-and-effect relationship which exist between the school and community. Among some of the more *specific* purposes for surveying the community are:

1. To become more aware of the influence of the community upon the lives of children.
2. To become familiar not only with the services of the community but also with its needs.
3. To become acquainted with the resources of the community upon which the school can draw.
4. To recognize some of the forces which act upon the community.

Most student teaching programs which contain a community study requirement also suggest that the student teacher use a particular format. As a result the authors are attempting to present only some helpful orientation and procedures which may augment any prescribed format.

Even though you do not conduct a formal community study, you cannot avoid its effects. It is impossible to teach a group of children without being exposed to the community forces which act upon them. As a teacher of children you automatically become a student of society since one is the product of the other.

In all communities there is material — human, natural and man-made — which can be used by the teacher to enrich his classroom program. Surveying a community will help you to identify it. In making a survey the student teacher will discover suitable places for class field trips as well as educational resource material.

There are several limiting factors to face before attempting a community study. First there is the element of time. Thorough study of a community with all of its complexities would require more than a lifetime. It is therefore only realistic that the student teacher select a few elements of the community to study in depth.

Second, you may be restricted by certain school policies. There may be some areas of community life which are considered too delicate for a neophyte teacher's involvement.

Third, there may be a lack of records, data, and information to which you can gain access. Fourth, there are the limitations which each of us possesses as an individual.

The quality of your study will in large measure be determined by the sensitivity and maturity with which you compile, handle and interpret the data. You definitely will need to budget your time meticulously to fit a community study into your total student teaching work load.

Due to the complexities of large communities and the time required to collect data, many studies are undertaken only from the vantage point of a teacher. In other words, they are written as a study of community effects upon education. Even this task is monumental, but it narrows the scope of the study considerably. If more than one student teacher is located in a particular locale, a group community study can be organized. It would be ridiculous for one individual to attempt a full-fledged community study of a large city while student teaching.

The Melon Needs to Be Sliced Down to Size.

You will learn a great deal more by systematically studying *one phase* of a community *in depth* than by tackling an entire city. At best a city could be studied only superficially in the time available to you.

"SLICING THE COMMUNITY MELON"

The mere copying of material from a chamber of commerce brochure does *not* constitute a community study. It is one informational source, but many others should be sought. Some information can be secured through personal interviews with key people in the community. Other types of information can best be obtained by a questionnaire or through personal observation. A city directory and/or telephone book can be of great assistance. In simply riding around a community you can observe such things as the conditions of the streets, recreational facilities, the physical appearance of neighborhoods, etc.

Your study of a community will of necessity entail two facets. One will be quantative data. In collecting the data you may want to keep some numerical tally or record. For example, you will want to know the number of physicians, dentists, and other professional people available to the community. A count of the stores selling similar products also may be significant. The number of industries located in a community and the total of their employees can also be a vital community statistic.

The second facet is a qualitative one. After collecting the quantitative data you will need to interpret and evaluate them. For example, does the community have enough physicians and hospitals as compared with other communities or the American Medical Association recommendation? To record your *general* qualitative judgments about eleven aspects of the community you may want to use the "Community Grading Sheet." If properly employed, this can serve as a summary of the study. The authors suggest that you grade each of the eleven elements listed and then write out a brief defense of the grade you have assigned for each area. What evidence or data do you have to justify the grade you have assigned? The grading scale is calibrated 1-5 as follows:

5 — excellent
4 — good
3 — average
2 — inadequate
1 — poor or nonexistent

After totaling the numbers on your grading sheet it is possible to derive a general grade for the community. Since there are eleven categories and the number three is equivalent to average, then a total of 33 would be the lowest limit of an average rating. Likewise a grade of 44 would be good and 55 excellent, with various gradations in between.

Of course this grading sheet is not a scientific instrument and is designed only to enable the student teacher to record his value judgments. A great deal of subjectivity is involved in such a grading sheet; however, it will raise many valuable questions. As a result it can form the basis for the development of more mature insight into community analysis.

Name _____ Date _____

Community grading sheet

		Grade 5 4 3 2 1
I	Cultural Resources — theaters, museums, libraries, concerts, lectures, etc.	
II	Over-all Community Spirit — optimism toward its future; willingness to support its improvement and growth	
III	Religious Dedication and Activities — implementation of religious principles in daily living; support of organized churches.	
IV	Public Health and Safety — adequacy of fire, police and health services, etc.	
V	General Economic Conditions — business climate, distribution of wealth, employment opportunities, available sources of capital	
VI	Recreational Facilities — playgrounds, clubs, equipment, personnel, maintenance, etc.	
VII	Political "Health" — citizen participation, free from "boss-ism." Capable, honest leadership, etc.	
VIII	Support & Effectiveness of Community Organizations & Charities — service clubs, united fund, private charities, etc.	
IX	Physical Appearance of Community — free from litter & refuse, homes well-kept, general neatness, etc.	
X	Education — schools, colleges, support of, etc.	
XI	Communication & Transportation	
	Total grade points	

KEY TO CITY

SCHOOL ZONE

VINE STREET

The use of study consultants is very desirable. A psychologist, a sociologist, an anthropologist, and an economist scheduled to discuss community study with groups of student teachers can develop additional understanding of the task.

Suggestion Box For Community Study

1. Very small communities are often more difficult to study than large ones, as printed material is not readily available.
2. Support your conclusions about a community in your written study with footnotes. These should refer to sources of information in support of your judgments.
3. Employ a research format in writing your community study.
4. When controversial issues are discussed include *all* sides of the argument.

5. Permit only those persons who are recommended by your college to read the community study. A good deal of bad feeling can be created by passing around a community study indiscriminately — especially one in which the community does not fare too well.
6. Check the appropriateness of any questionnaire you may want to distribute with school authorities before sending it out.

SELECTED REFERENCES

1. Bartky, John A., *Social Issues In Public Education*. New York: Houghton Mifflin Company, 1962.
2. Cook, Lloyd A. and Elaine Cook, *A Sociological Approach To Education*. New York: McGraw-Hill Book Company, 1960.
3. Dahlke, Otto H., *Values In Culture and Classroom*. New York: Harper & Bros., 1958.
4. Gross, Wronski and Hanson, *School and Society*. Boston: D. C. Heath & Company.
5. Gwynn, J. Minor, *Curriculum Principles and Social Trends*. New York: The Macmillan Company, 1960.
6. Hodgkinson, Harold, *Education in Social and Cultural Perspectives*. Englewood Cliffs, New Jersey: Prentice-Hall Inc., 1962.
7. Mercer, Blaine, and Carr, Edwin, *Education and The Social Order*, New York: Holt, Rinehart & Winston, Inc., 1957.
8. Steeves, Frank L., "Student Teaching in the Community." *The Phi Delta Kappan,* 36:193-196, February, 1955.

Educational Resources of the School

A plumber would have great difficulty in repairing even a leaky faucet without tools. Tools make work lighter, extend a man's power, and save time.

A Horn O' Plenty.

FAUCET FIRST AID

Educational resources such as textbooks, maps, films, charts, and other audio-visual aids are the tools of teaching. They do not supplant the teacher but enhance his teaching effectiveness. Literally all things which contribute to the education of children in a school are educational resources. This then includes the faculty and the physical plant itself (school building).

The foregoing elements are discussed under separate headings in the text, therefore we are devoting this space largely to what are generally termed audio-visual instructional materials.

Audio-Visual

There is voluminous research evidence to support the use of audio-visual materials in the classroom. In most instances research indicates that correct use of them can greatly increase the quality and quantity of learning. A simple two-dimensional picture or diagram can be a springboard to building an accurate concept in a child's mind. Perhaps you will want to use a bullietin board as a kickoff for a lesson and as an attention getter. A picture can be worth a thousand words.

A well chosen film about Japan can help textbook material come alive. In-

AUDIO-VISUAL

viting a Japanese-American resource person from the community to speak to your class can also increase the chances that your class will absorb some of the flavor of the Orient. The beauty of the Oriental mode of life cannot be conveyed by a textbook alone.

A teaching machine can reinforce certain learnings with slow children or teach bright children some advanced material that you would not ordinarily have time to present.

Observing the launching of a space vehicle on network TV or a demonstration lesson on closed circuit TV are other examples of exciting educational resources.

The student teacher or experienced veteran teacher who fails to use modern teaching aids is analogous to the physician who attempts to practice medicine without employing modern drugs. As a student teacher you must become familiar as quickly as possible with the educational resources of the school in which you are placed. Survey the library sources, the number and kinds of films and filmstrips and the type of projection equipment available, locate picture files, flannel and magnetic boards, models, mock-ups, maps, charts, and the like. Find out the correct procedure for reserving and operating the equipment. Be certain to return it on time to the correct storage location after use.

It's a Case of Supply and Demand.

What kind and how many educational resources are necessary to teach a particular subject matter most effectively is highly debatable. Good teaching is certainly attainable without any educational resources excepting a good teacher. This is not to say that the proper implementation of educational resources coupled with a good teacher cannot further improve his effectiveness. They also can make day to day teaching more interesting for students by providing a variety of materials. This is particularly true when repetition such as drill work is necessary in the classroom program. Presenting the work to children on a flannel board one day, magnectic board the next and perhaps with the help of a hand puppet the following day can add spice to routine drill work. There is no doubt that proper use of such materials can add at least interest value for learners.

A HAND PUPPET TEACHING AIDE

The availability of educational resources in the school should be of vital concern to you as a student teacher and in selecting your first teaching position. Many schools have a grave shortage of these materials because of inadequate budgets or the failure of teachers and administrators to recognize their value and to pressure the budget sources for them.

You can, as a student teacher, construct some of these aids such as a flannel or felt board, an abacus, magnetic board, etc. If you make some of your own teaching aids then you can use the money you ordinarily would spend to buy these materials for other educational aids.

Bombardment!

In this era of dynamic mass communication media we as educators are challenged to keep the voice of the school and the teacher from being smothered. The youth of today are being bombarded by commercial TV, movies, radio and periodicals which attempt to usurp their attention, interest and time. These pressures also tend to divert youth from school responsibilities and to dictate values and tastes. An example of the exertion of pressure lies in the attempt to manipulate consumer buying habits. There are several books devoted to this topic. A notable one is *The Hidden Persuaders*.[1]

MASS COMMUNICATION
BOMBARDMENT

Since the school must compete with modern commercial mass communication media, it must employ resources which are as stimulating and efficient as possible. The ever increasing volume and complexity of subject matter commitments in the public schools make mandatory the implementation of the most efficient and interesting educational resources available. This is one of the great challenges to education in this space age. How will you meet it?

Perhaps the following questions will be of help:

1. What do you consider to be the *basic* educational resources *every* school should contain?
2. Select one topic, such as magnetism, which might be taught in your classroom and list as many educational resources as you can which could be used as teaching aids.
3. How does a teacher decide which educational resources to employ in teaching a particular topic? Is there a hierarchy of resources as regards one's being better than another?

---

[1]Vance Packard, *The Hidden Persuaders*, David McKay Company, Inc., 1957.

4. How might the child development characteristics of a particular grade level affect a teacher's choice of audio-visual aids?
5. How can a school administration best make audio-visual materials accessible to teachers?

SELECTED REFERENCES

1. Brown, J., Lewis, R., Harcleroad F., *A. V. Instruction.* New York: Mc-Graw Hill, 1959.
2. Dale, Edgar, *Audio-Visual Methods In Teaching.* New York: Holt, Rinehart & Winston, 1954.
3. Finn, James D., *The Audio-Visual Equipment Manual.* New York: Holt, Rinehart & Winston, Inc., 1957.
4. Kinder, James S., *Audio-Visual Materials & Techniques.* New York: American Book Company, 1950.
5. Sands, Lester B., *Audio-Visual Procedures in Teaching.* New York: The Ronald Press, 1956.
6. Wittich and Schuller, *Audio-Visual Materials.* New York: Harper & Bros., 1957.

Astronauts are probing what appears to be limitless space. This text, however, has space limitations which will not permit extensive coverage of the topics that follow. They are all integral parts of the total teaching environment. You will want at least to consider the relative importance of them during your student teaching experience. In actual job selection you may want to consider their relative merits more thoroughly. The authors are simply attempting to acquaint you briefly with them.

Physical Features of the School

The school plant (building) can be characterized as an educational resource in and of itself. It also can be simply a sterile container of educational resources. School buildings are sometimes designed on the architect's drawing board to house a specific type of educational program but more frequently school programs are bent to suit a physical plant already in existence.

What is the circumstance in your particular school? How much floor space is available per pupil and is the floor space used functionally? Are there adequate playground facilities? Is the school plant designed in such a manner so that air, sound and lighting can be well controlled? Perhaps there is an overuse of glass, as in some of our more modern buildings, so that a greenhouse effect is created.

Is the interior decoration of the building bright and cheerful? Is it restful to the eyes or confusing and disorientating? Does the school plant contain comfort facilities for the professional staff as well as personnel? A teachers' lounge and conference rooms not only help to cement the faculty team but provide a place for the free exchange of ideas.

These are but a few aspects of the school's physical plant to consider from the vantage point of a teacher. Among others are the safety features of the building and special facilities such as cafeteria, auditoruim, gymnasium, swimming pool and photography darkroom.

Are the school buildings today being constructed with enough foresight to serve tomorrow's needs?

"THAT GREENHOUSE EFFECT"

Perhaps all new schools should be built underground in this age of the atomic bomb! This is but one of a myriad of puzzlers which face school planners.

We have much to learn about constructing functional, economical school buildings. You can find this problem discussed further in Chapter 10, which deals with frontiers in education. The basic consideration related to the physical facilities of a school plant is whether the school augments or restricts the program.

While student teaching try to be aware of how the physical features of the school building affect your classroom program and the total school program. You may get some "glimmers" despite all of your other responsibilities.

Where In the World?

The geographic location of the school can have drastic effects upon the school program. This fact is mentioned here especially in relation to selecting your first teaching position. School programs in New Mexico may be markedly different in many aspects from those in Maine. A school in Alexandria, Egypt, will contrast sharply with one in Uganda, British East Africa. There are basic purposes which are similar in all schools but excluding cultural and economic differences, geographical elements alone can affect the school program. The climate and topography plus accessibiilty of basic goods and services are all determined to some extent by the geographical location of the school. In evaluating a school program or in job selection, geographical location of the school should not be minimized. What aspects of the total school program might differ between a school located in a temperate climate and one located in a semitropical climate? How might the topography of the land affect a school program? In what manner does climatic change affect teaching and the teacher? Bathhurst[2] points out geographical affects upon the curriculum.

Faculty of the School (including administrators)

In jest, it was once said that a faculty consists of a group of people who have lost their faculties. In reality the faculty of a school represents its primary educational resource. The nature of the school faculty can in large measure determine your success and happiness as a teacher or student teacher. Certain characteristics of a school's faculty are of particular significance. They are the (1) age range, (2) professional training, (3) rate of turn over, (4) ratio of men to women, and (5) general morale. How can each of these factors influence the instructional program of the school and your role as fellow teacher or student teacher?

Tow That Barge — Lift That Bale!

The teaching work load is comprised of all professional demands upon the teacher. It is another variable of teaching which should be seriously considered. A particular salary can often take on a different dimension when you know what is expected of the teacher who receives that salary. Some teaching positions, for example, make unusual physical demands while others have many busy-work or nuisance chores.

Many surveys have been taken regarding teachers' attitudes toward busy-work or noninstructional tasks and the results are very similar. The part of their work load for which teachers seem to have the most distaste are noon hour and playground duty, cafeteria supervision, collection of money, bus supervision and supervising school corridors.[3]

A characteristic of all professions is that the work load is not always clearly defined. This fact has both positive and negative aspects. In some school systems the classroom teacher is *required* to assume a large quantity of out-of-classroom chores such as chaperoning school social activities, advising school club activities, coaching and/or supervising athletic events, and leading charity collection drives in order to win administrative favor. While many consider it unprofessional, there have

---

[2]Effie G. Bathhurst, *Where Children Live Affects Curriculum*, U. S. Dept. of Health, Education and Welfare, Washington, D. C., 1950.

[3]Meta F. Williams, "A Step Toward Curriculum Improvement," *NEA Journal*, January, 1961, p. 15.

been some attempts by teacher organizations, especially teachers' unions, to persuade school authorities to spell out clearly what constitutes the job of the teacher. Work falling outside of the defined job or work load could thus be identified and school officials would then be required to pay additional remuneration for the extra work or teachers could legally refuse to assume it. There is a great vacuum in state legislation which defines in any terms what constitutes a maximum teacher work load.

Components of teacher-work load include such items as: (1) length of the school day; (2) class size and character; (3) quantity and complexity of subjects taught; (4) duration of teacher contracts — ten or twelve months; (5) quantity of teacher-aide services available — i.e., secretarial help, teacher aides, consultants; (6) out-of-classroom responsibilities, and (7) quantity, duration and placement of rest periods.

A good deal of superfluous weight could be subtracted from the teacher work load by modernizing and streamlining record keeping. In an age of automation it seems incongruent, for example, that a teacher's valuable time should be consumed in keeping attendance records in an archaic and frustrating manner.

Teachers and school administrators need to cooperate in reviewing and evaluating the types of chores required of teachers and to delete as much of the deadwood as possible. Teachers should devote the lion's share of their time and energy to planning, teaching and evaluating. We need to free teachers to teach. Employing teacher aides and the implementation of automation in school record keeping are but two small steps in the right direction. It is an awesome waste of professional talent when teachers have to take time to count milk money, perform janitorial tasks, and patrol school grounds. Much is yet to be accomplished. You can help achieve progress along these lines by participating actively in your local, state and national professional organizations.

Historically teachers have failed to stand together and defend against the demeaning of their professional role. We are still reaping the results of this failure today. It's time for a change! To check your own feelings in relation to these matters, the following questions are posed:

1. If a teacher has a very heavy teaching load what effect *might* this have upon the quality of his teaching?
2. What school tasks or chores do you feel should *not* be a part of the teacher's role?

3. How might faculty morale in a school be affected by the teaching work load?
4. Should all teachers in the school have an equal work load assuming they are on the same salary schedule?
5. How should a teacher's work load be computed or in other fashion determined?

The Effectiveness of the School Program

With a thunderous expulsion of dust and vapor a giant missile ascends into cloudless sky from its launching pad. From the moment it leaves the launching pad, tracking stations, like ultra-sensitive ears and eyes, trace its progress and performance. It would be wasteful and scientificially purposeless to send a missile aloft and not record and evaluate its performance. The awareness that one is part of a highly successful and effective team is as satisfying to a member of a faculty "team" as it is to a member of a missile team. In order to feel valid satisfaction, however, there must be some record or evidence of success. It is simply amazing how many schools continue the so called educative process without the vaguest idea of how effective the program is.

Can you imagine a soap manufacturer producing millions of boxes of soap without keeping a watchful eye upon sales volume? If the soap production were not carefully geared to its sales performance, the manufacturer might soon be up to his ears in unsold soap. Every manufacturer directly or indirectly attempts to evaluate the sales performance and quality of his product as compared to his competitors' products and consumer reaction to both. Any educational institution, regardless of whether it's an elementary school or a university, needs to check the performance of its products — (students). This means not only their immediate performance as students but their long-term performance as adult citizens. A follow-up program of the school's graduates therefore is necessary. The general public image and academic reputation of a school are often established upon the performance of its graduates.

The effectiveness of the school has to be measured in terms of some predetermined expectations, goals, or objectives. It is vital that the total school — students, faculty, administration and parents — know toward what objectives the school is striving. It is equally important that they have a part in determining them. Effectiveness of the school program can then be measured in terms of meeting these objectives. Without clearly stated realistic goals a school program is adrift to an uncertain destination. Worthwhile objectives will form the basis for curriculum decisions as well as general school organizational policies.

The worth of evaluating the effectiveness of the school program is stressed because the authors believe that one of the greatest satisfactions in teaching can come from an association with a school that maintains high standards. What is more important, the school has some tangible evidence that these high standards are being reflected in the performance of its graduates.

Chasing a Rainbow.

In fairness to the schools it must be emphasized that the task of evaluating the effectiveness of a school's educative program is extremely difficult and can add considerable expense to the school budget. As in many evaluation tasks, numerous variables complicate the process immensely. Nonetheless, we must make the best effort possible. The "fly in the ointment" lies in trying to prove a direct cause-and-effect relationship between the school program and the adult behavior of its products. Fortunately it isn't necessary to establish (if it were possible) which agent (school, home or church, etc.) is solely responsible for developing specific traits in the final product (adults). What is most important is whether or not the job is being accomplished. For example, supposing the school feels that in an age of increasing automation and shorter work weeks a vital educational objective is to teach children constructive use of leisure time. Previously the school must spell out what constitutes constructive use of leisure time, which involves putting the objective into behavioral terms. Through surveys and similar techniques it then can be roughly determined how the "graduates" of the school are utilizing their leisure time. If the results are not favorable, certain curriculum changes can be made in the school to correct the situation. Of course other agents such as the home, church, service clubs, community social agencies and the like have responsibility in this area, but since the school has no direct control over them it must supply the remedy. The school naturally would solicit the help of these other agents.

At one school familiar to the authors, it was discovered that over ten per cent of the graduates ran afoul of the law before they were twenty years of age. A concerted effort was made to improve this statistic by the school and several cooperating agencies of the community. The school made some curriculum modifications aimed at this objective (lowering the crime rate). The result was a substantial reduction in the percentage of teen-age crime in that particular community during the time the project was observed. Schools have long-term effects upon human beings and hence upon society. These effects must be constantly evaluated.

Some of the Fish Are Easy to Catch.

There are certain types of data which are not as elusive as others and can help a faculty evaluate at least the short-range objectives of its program.

SOME FISH ARE EASY TO CATCH

The danger here is that too often short-range data are used to generalize about long-range school objectives. The results of standardized tests, the percentage of high school dropouts in the community, the percentage of the high school graduates who enter college, the number who graduate from college and the type of colleges they attend can all help in determining the effectiveness of the school program.

Some schools naively point to a *single* statistic such as the record their institution has established on standardized tests (or regents' examinations) or the percentage of their high school graduates who enter college as an indicator of the effectiveness of their school program. Any *one* statistic, however, cannot begin to tell the story of a school's effectiveness. It even may be misleading.

As a student teacher or a first year teacher it is extremely valuable to be affiliated professionally with a school that has educational direction. School officials know in what direction it is attempting to move and how it is succeeding. Often the objectives (direction) have to be re-examined and the process can be as valuable as the product. In considering school objectives such questions are raised as: What is the primary educational purpose of our school? Is it to produce educated adults? If so, what is an educated adult? Can we arrive at an agreeable, workable definition? Perhaps we are more concerned about developing loyal, productive, good citienzs. If so, what is the definition of a loyal, productive citizen? This type of probing which goes on too infrequently in our schools can be of immense help to all concerned with their educational institutions. If you can serve on a committee whose task is to re-examine school objectives you will be intellectually and professionally blessed.

Curriculum Establishment and Policies.

Once total school objectives are defined, curriculum can be intelligently formulated. The curriculum should not be imposed upon a faculty by administrative edict. Teachers should play an important part in its establishment. A standing curriculum committee composed at least partly of classroom teachers should be in existence in all schools. Teachers are most apt to teach fervently what they themselves have established as being important. While student teaching you may have some opportunity to determine how curriculum decisions are made in the school. Equally important is the question of who makes the curriculum policies and how they are communicated to the total school faculty. If you are very fortunate you may be permitted to sit in on a curriculum committee meeting. Since space does not allow a detailed discussion of curriculum establishment, the authors suggest the following references:

"CHARTING A COURSE"
(CURRICULUM ESTABLISHMENT)

SELECTED REFERENCES

1. Association for Supervision and Curriculum Development, *Balance In The Curriculum* (1961 yearbook), National Education Association, Washington, D. C., 1961.
2. Beck, Robert, and Cook, Walter, *Curriculum in the Modern Elementary School*. Englewood Cliffs, N. J.: Prentice-Hall, Inc., 1960.
3. Haan, Aubrey, *Elementary School Curriculum*. Boston: Allyn and Bacon, Inc., 1961.
4. Parker, Edwards and Stegeman, *Curriculum In America*. New York: Thomas Crowell Company, 1962.
5. Rogers, William, *Modern Elementary Curriculum*. New York: Holt, Rinehart & Winston, 1960.
6. Rucker, W. Ray, *Curriculum Development in the Elementary School*. New York: Harper & Bros., 1960.

Opportunity for Professional Growth

Another aspect which should concern you is the opportunity the school provides for your professional growth. This does not mean that in the interview for your first teaching position you will be informed that in a few years you will be installed as a school principal in the system. Professional growth is usually not meteoric or analogous to Jack's beanstalk. In fact, the term should not immediately convey the exchanging of one's teaching position for a so-called "better" one. Its accepted connotation is that of acquiring more proficiency in one's profession; an increasing of one's competency; and maturing toward an ideal concept of the teacher. It may be true also that the term professional growth suggests moving from classroom teaching to positions carrying expanded responsibility and authority, such as supervision and administration.

In-service Courses and Training. In-service courses are one example of a school's providing opportunity for the professional growth of its staff. These courses are taken while a teacher is employed by the school and usually meet on Saturdays, a week night, or one day a week after classes are dismissed. They are aimed at increasing the professional competency of the school faculty and helping keep it informed about new educational trends and ideas. These courses are taught either by a member of the school system or by an outside resource person such as a college professor. A teacher may receive salary credit for the course, college credit toward an advanced degree, or both. Frequently school systems will have a specific in-service course for first year teachers or new teachers in the system. These are particularly helpful as the first year teacher has an opportunity to discuss his problems with other first year teachers under experienced professional guidance. This makes your first year of teaching a continuing part of your professional preparation. It becomes a type of internship. Consider yourself very fortunate if you locate in a school system having such a program. While some school systems do not sponsor in-service courses for teachers, they encourage them to take advanced courses in nearby colleges by paying a portion of or the entire tuition fee.

Supervision As a Helping Hand.

Professional growth and maturity can result also from the guidance and help that teachers receive from school administrative and supervisory personnel. Wholesome rapport between teacher and supervisor based upon mutual respect is the foundation of the supervisory process. Supervision becomes ineffective without mutual respect.

Is There Room at the Top?

If a candidate feels that he definitely would like to seek a position carrying expanded responsibilities such as that of a school administrator, then he should deliberately seek a teaching position in a system which is growing. Very often in an interview the hiring official will explain what opportunities for advancement are likely to occur in the future for that particular system.

Additional opportunities school systems frequently offer to teachers aimed at increasing professional standards are:

SCHOOL ADMINISTRATION
TOTEM POLE
IS THERE ROOM AT THE TOP?

1. One or two days (with pay) which they can spend visiting another school system of their choice.
2. Paid time off and expenses to attend professional meetings and conventions.
3. Internship programs in which a classroom teacher can train (while on full salary) to assume an advanced position (i.e., administrative or supervisory internships).
4. Special consultants, as in reading, psychology and speech therapy, to foster the professional growth of the classroom teacher.
5. Professional libraries, particularly for teachers, as part of the school library. This is a trend in elementary and secondary schools. In addition to housing current professional reference books "the library" subscribes to many professional journals.
6. Sabbatical leave or leave-of-absence for study and/or travel.
7. Participation in teacher exchange programs.

Does the School Really Encourage Professional Growth?

Is there sincere encouragement from the school administration for teachers to grow in the profession? This sometimes means the school may lose the teacher to another system. It takes a big administrator to put the professional growth of his staff uppermost in his thinking. There is great temptation for him to attempt to retain the teacher to solve staffing problems. It is a wonderful feeling to be a staff member of a school system which promotes the maximum professional growth of its teachers. It is a foregone conclusion in such a school that each teacher should be encouraged in every way possible to seek the greatest professional horizons that his ability will permit. You can find such a school.

Grouping Within the School

A school consists of a community of children and teachers. The manner in which they are grouped can affect the instructional program immensely. Elements of group dynamics and principles of child development enter in here.

To Group or Not to Group — That Is Not the Question.

All schools employ some form of grouping despite what they might say. Even random grouping is a type. Specific factors are frequently considered when establishing groups (or grades) of children within the school community. Some of these are chronological age; I. Q.; academic achievement; exceptionality (i.e., retardation, deafness, physical handicaps); socio-economic background; ratio of boys to girls; social maturity and special interests of students.

There has been much debate in past years concerning the relative merits of homogeneous and heterogeneous grouping. If you are not familiar with these terms, check the selected references which follow this section.

Currently, the non-graded classroom as a grouping pattern is enjoying much attention in educational circles. Reference book number 2 is recommended for this topic.

In many communities school grouping procedures have been a hot issue. The most ingenious grouping pattern imaginable is worthless, however, in the absence of good teaching.

As a nation we tend to be "groupy." It certainly is possible that we have overplayed the importance of grouping within our schools. Grouping has taken on the aura of motherhood and the American flag in the minds of some educators. The quality of any group is only as good as its individual members. Too often when *individual* thought is needed we retire to "buzz groups."

It is important for you as a teacher to help children identify those tasks within the classroom which can best be accomplished by groups and those which can best be accomplished by individuals. Could "Macbeth" have been written by a committee or Michelangelo's "David"

sculptured by a club? Could the Gettysburg Address have been composed as a conference report?

Once again space limitations do not permit adequate coverage of the topic. Perhaps the questions and references which follow will aid your further exploration. Your work as a student teacher and as a fully certified teacher can be greatly influenced by the grouping pattern employed in the school. There is no single solution or pattern which is universally desirable. At this juncture, grouping experimentation within your own classroom will be *your* best instruction.

TOPICS AND QUESTIONS FOR STUDY AND DISCUSSION

The following questions may assist you in exploring the many avenues of grouping:

1. Is there ever actually a "homogeneous" group? Give reasons to support your answer.
2. What possible effects can the grouping of boys and girls have upon them? — upon teachers in the school? — upon the instructional program?
3. Is homogeneous grouping in keeping with the principle of equal educational opportunity for all? Defend your answer.

4. What *facts* could a teacher employ in justifying ability grouping to parents?
5. What educational objectives can be accomplished through group work within the classroom as opposed to the children's doing *individual* projects.
6. What direction (if any) does educational research give us in terms of school grouping procedures?
7. Suppose that the children of one grade level are divided into three ability grades — the bright group, the average group and the slow group. What do you consider to be the advantages and disadvantages of teaching each of these groups?

SELECTED REFERENCES

1. Cartwright, Dorwin and Alvin Zander, *Group Dynamics: Research and Theory,* Elmsford, N. Y.: Row, Peterson and Co., 1960.
2. Goodlad, John and Robert Anderson, *The Non-graded Elementary School.* New York: Harcourt Brace, 1959.
3. Hock, L. E., "Classroom Grouping for Effective Learning," *Educational Leadership* 18:420-4, April, 1961.
4. Kelly, F. C., "Ungraded Primary School," *Educational Leadership,* 18:79-81, November, 1960.
5. Massoglia, E. T., "How Children Learn and Live Together," *N.E.A. Journal,* March, 1962.
6. Morrison, N. C., "Instead of Ability Grouping, What?" *Childhood Education,* 36: 371-3, April, 1960.
7. Smith, Lois, "*Group Processes in Elementary and Secondary Schools,* Department of Classroom Teachers, N.E.A., Washington, D. C., 1959.
8. Strang, Ruth, *Group Work in Education.* New York: Harper & Bros., 1958.
9. Wolfe, J. B., "Planning for Teaching Different Groups," Conference on Reading, Chicago University, 1959: 171-4.
10. Wrightstone, Wayne J., *Class Organization for Instruction,* Department of Classroom Teachers, N.E.A., Washington, D. C., 1957.

GATEWAY TO TEACHING

Chapter 5

Appraising Growth
In Your Pupils and Yourself

*I, who have so much and so universally
adored this "excellent mediocrity" of ancient
times, and who have concluded the most
moderate measure the most perfect, shall
I pretend to an unreasonable and prodigious
old age?*

*Of Experience
Essays Book III Chap. 13
Michel de Montaigne*

How would You like to Wrestle an Alligator? One of the most difficult and frustrating tasks which will confront you as a student teacher
is that of attempting to test, measure and evaluate human effort. To
accomplish this in the truest meaning of the phrase may well be
impossible in the light of human frailties. Yet it is mandated that
teachers make an intelligent attempt at it with reasonably acceptable
results as it is a vital part of the educative process.

Perhaps the knowledge that evaluating pupil progress accurately
has been one of the frustrating requirements of education since the
dawn of education itself will be some comfort to you.

In order to educate yourself or a pupil it is necessary to identify
two specific elements related to learning. One is the quantity of the
learning which is taking place; the second is the quality of that learning. In order to appraise these elements a classroom teacher must

engage in three basic processes namely (1) testing, (2) measuring and (3) evaluating. Each of these is defined later in this chapter.

"How Would You Like to Wrestle an Alligator?"

All learning can be classified roughly into three general categories: intellectual learning, affective learning, and mind-muscle learning. Intellectual or cognitive learning can be broken down into sub-parts such as concepts, understandings, facts (arbitrary associations). Affective learning applies to attitudes and appreciations which involve emotions and value judgments. Psychomotor learning deals generally with skills requiring the development of specific neuromuscular coordinations. Examples of this are learning to drive a car, roller skate, or throw a ball accurately.

Teachers do a pretty fair job of testing the intellectual type of learning, especially in testing children on "facts." The weakest part of the total testing picture is that teachers do a very poor job, if any job at all, in testing children's attitudes and appreciations related to what they are learning. Why is it important to know not only what a child is learning but how he is reacting to the learning — how he feels about the material being taught as well as the learning process itself? It is quite possible to teach a child to read very skillfully but at the same time teach him to loathe reading. We need desperately to test children's attitudes and appreciations related to school and learning as they can have an awesome effect upon later learning. These elements, however, are difficult to measure and as yet we have few reliable instruments (tests) with which to evaluate.

Space limitations do not permit a technical discussion of the pros and cons of all the various types of tests and test items. However, to familiarize yourself with some of the tests available to the classroom teacher you may find the *Mental Measurement Yearbook* of particular assistance. This volume includes not only comprehensive lists of tests but gives a brief synopsis of the character of each test and its major specifications. Here, in addition to the commonly used I. Q. and achievement tests, you will find tests designed to measure such things as personality characteristics, attitudes about sex, tolerance to ambiguity, occupational aptitudes, and the like. Unfortunately, many teachers are unaware of the availability of some of these important measuring devices.

Another method of familiarizing yourself with different kinds of tests is to incorporate as many of them as time and energy will permit in your student teaching experience. For example, it is actually constructing an "open book" test and then attempting to grade and evaluate it that you will come to grips with the many pitfalls of this type of test as contrasted with other types. Reference books number 1 and 3 on the selected readings list at the close of this chapter will help you identify some of the types of tests and test items available to you as a student teacher. The "hunt" for them and their trial implementation into your classroom can be very exciting.

Testing: One, Two, Three!

Testing is the means by which we derive a measurement of a learner's progress. As previously stated, you will need to employ testing to estimate the quantity and quality of the learning which is a direct or indirect result of your teaching. The actual *results* you obtain from tests will give you an approximate *measurement* of the growth of individual children, as well as their relative achievement as compared with the total class. Just as a ruler serves a carpenter as a device or tool for measurement, so a test serves a teacher. When the carpenter utilizes the ruler to determine that a board is six feet long he has arrived at a measurement. When a teacher uses a written test to determine that a child knew 90

"Testing: One, Two, Three"

per cent of the social studies information asked for, she also has a measurement. The test then, is the *implement* which gives the teacher an approximate, if not rough, measurement.

By definition a test is a collection of questions or tasks to which the student is asked to respond. In other words the questions on a test can be viewed as a stimulus to which a specific (correct) response is desired. With an appropriate and well planned stimulus (question) the teacher can test for almost any type of educational objective if he intelligently evaluates pupils' answers (responses).

"Shoot for the Target, Gridley!"

Unfortunately, many teachers set specific objectives as goals (targets) for teaching a particular unit yet fail to test (shoot) for these objectives. Their objectives constitute one set of factors and they test for other factors.

"My prime objective in this unit," said one student teacher, "is to teach children to think critically." Yet the written test she had constructed asked the children simply to recall information (facts). There were no test items (questions) which required that the children utilize facts in a thought provoking problem situation. She was not testing in relation to her prime objective. If you set clear-cut objectives at the outset of your teaching, any test you construct should be aimed at determining to what extent you are achieving your objectives. Otherwise you have little or no evidence of your teaching effectiveness in terms of your original objectives.

Popularity Plus.

Tests fall into three general classifications namely verbal, nonverbal and performance.

Verbal tests are those in which students are called upon to use *written or oral language.* This type of test enjoys widespread popularity and usage in our schools.

Nonverbal tests (while the directions may be given orally) require no language, written or oral. Usually, through drawings and three dimensional materials the student taking the test points to the correct response. These particular tests are useful in working with illiterates, children with poor mental endowment, and very young normal children who have limited language facility.

Performance tests require that the person being tested *perform* some simple task. For example, a teacher might test children in physical education on the number of "push-ups" they can do, in driver education on parallel parking a car, or in cursive handwriting class on demonstrating the formation of specific letters.

They're Tests But They're Not?

Many techniques or devices are available to the teacher for collecting growth data about children other than verbal and nonverbal tests.

Some of these are anecdotal records, questionnaires, reaction reports, sociometric devices, personal interviews, and check lists of skills.

In the *literal* sense of the word "test," the foregoing techniques for collecting evidence about students are not exactly congruent with the definition given earlier. Still there can be in all of them the element of measuring students against specific expectations or of determining whether or not a student has passed a particular hurdle. It may be a social adjustment type hurdle or an emotional hurdle but still present are expectations against which the student is being "tested." Space does not permit us to define all of these meticulously and to describe their implementation. Consult one of the texts at the close of this chapter for further delineation of these devices.

Three Delicious Flavors!

Written (verbal) tests take many forms (flavors) and originate from many sources. Three of the most popular written tests are: (1) standardized tests, (2) teacher-made tests and
(3) commercial progress tests.

Standardized tests are constructed by specialists in test making and usually are sold at commercial rates to schools. They are called standardized tests because they are administered to thousands of boys and girls of varying intellects and age and grade levels in different parts of the country. Then they are revised as need dictates before being distributed commercially by the publisher. After having administered the test to the

"THREE DELICIOUS FLAVORS"

sample of boys and girls in advance of sale, the experts determine what constitutes an average or standard score for the fourth grade child (4.0), a fifth grade child (5.0) and so on. By employing these *standards* a teacher, after administering the test to her class, can compare the achievement of her children with national "norms." If used properly this feature of standardized tests makes them a source for some quality control in education. Utilization of standardized tests as the *only* source of evidence upon which to promote or retain pupils, or as a merit rating device for teachers, constitutes an improper use. Even with standardization, these tests represent only one narrow measurement statistic for evaluating total human achievement of pupils or teachers at any grade level.

Standardized tests can be of immense aid to the classroom teacher along such lines as:

1. Charting pupil progress.
2. Comparing an individual's achievement in various subject matter areas.
3. Diagnosing difficulties and weaknesses in pupil achievement.

Teacher-made tests, as the name implies, are those constructed by the classroom teacher. Groups of teachers working at the same grade level in the same school often will cooperate in making tests for their own grade level to be used in only their school. One distinct advantage of teacher-made tests is that they can be geared closely to what has actually been taught. In a sense they are custom-tailored to the particular group of children involved. There are disadvantages of teacher-made tests. First, the scores derived from them compare children only with the limited number of other children in this one school setting who took the test. Because of this fact it's difficult if not impossible to know how the children's achievement as reflected on these tests would compare with national standards. Second, classroom teachers are usually less sophisticated about the mechanics of sound test construction than testing experts so therefore their tests are sometimes poor instruments for obtaining an accurate appraisal of a child's achievement. You can't secure an accurate measurement with an inaccurate measuring device; however, since teacher-made tests usually are closely related to what is actually being taught they are useful to some extent. Their use as evaluative evidence should always be combined with other data such as teacher observation of the child's work, samples of classwork, etc.

Commercial progress tests are developed and distributed by educational publishers, and in many cases are designed for use with a specific textbook. Let's say, for example, you have just finished a social studies unit. Rather than constructing a unit test yourself you can obtain a progress test from the publisher of the text you are using with your class. Some of the advantages of such tests are: (1) they save you the time it would take to construct a test of your own, (2) the tests are developed by experts thus would contain fewer pitfalls for children in terms of such things as the ambiguity of test items (questions) than teacher-made tests.

Some limitations of these tests are: (1) they cost money, and (2) they are aimed at testing the material presented in one particular textbook so if you were using several texts and other resource books the tests would be of limited value.

The strength of a test depends upon the quality of test items (questions) comprising the text. It is very difficult to write test items which do not contain a great deal of language ambiguity. Further study coupled with experience will add to your proficiency. Consult reference book 5 at the close of this chapter for specific aid in writing test items. This book explains the strengths and weaknesses of the various types of tests such as true-false, matching, completion, multiple choice, etc.

Written tests certainly should not be given unless the test papers are going to be corrected. Tests, as well as everyday classwork, should be corrected and handed back to students as soon as possible. If a child makes a mistake on a test or in his regular classwork and doesn't receive correction until two weeks later, the value of immediate correction is completely lost. This factor of immediate correction is one of the great strengths of teaching machines. The learner responds and immediately knows whether or not he is correct. If correct he receives immediate reenforcement for his response; if not correct he is led to modify his incorrect response.

The more tests you give the more correction time is required. Some student teachers spend a disproportionate amount of time correcting papers. One suggestion is to use more performance tests which require no written papers or use oral tests which can enable you to obtain *some* of the same data a written test can furnish.

We have not touched upon the "mechanics" and/or processing techniques in handling test scores. These include such things as plotting a curve, computing the class median, mode, mean, standard deviation from the mean, a difficulty index related to each test item, etc. If you are not familiar with these technical considerations you should consult one of the texts listed under Selected References at the close of this chapter.

Test data (the scores of measurement) should be used to diagnose the errors children are making, to chart progress and as a basis for planning future learning experiences for the children.

Unless test data are effectively used, time spent testing children is largely wasted. Many teachers test too much, others not enough. Tests should be given when a sample of students' achievement is required to lend direction to teaching, assess the learners' progress or plan the instructional program.

Standardized tests, for example, cost money as well as classroom time. Their use is not justifiable unless the test data derived from them are used effectively. Some teachers test frequently in an attempt to give children and parents the impression that a vigorous program is being implemented. The *number* of tests given is no barometer for indicating the instructional quality of a classroom program.

S-O-S!

Some Testing Life Preservers

1. When working with young children particularly, it is better to employ short tests frequently than to use lengthy tests less frequently.
2. Try to alleviate children's anxieties about testing in general and about the single value of any *one* test.
3. Use many types of testing media.
4. Include several types of test items within any one test — some true-false, multiple choice, matching, etc. (All types of items [questions] have weaknesses. Some students perform better on certain types of items than on others.)
5. Recognize that some children because of emotional elements do not perform well on *any* type of formal test thus other less formal measuring devices are necessary.
6. Use objective test data as only one facet of evaluating the growth of children. Your own professional judgment (reaction) based upon observation of the children will always be a vital part of evaluation.
7. When employing any test which utilizes printed material recognize that a child's achievement can be greatly affected by his ability to read the material. (He may know the answer but be unable to read the question — keep language simple!)
8. Make the testing environment as physically comfortable for the student as possible — good lighting; ventilation; freedom from distractions. Take occasional breaks during a long test.

9. Many variables can affect test results. Included are the day or time of day, physical condition of child, emotional state, etc.
10. When you secure test results you have only an estimate of how much students know about the information called for on the test.
11. There is no such thing as a completely objective test. All testing has *some* subjectivity involved in it — if not in scoring the test then in selecting the items.
12. The first few items (questions) on a test should be easy ones as they promote confidence in the student taking it and encourage him to go ahead with the test. A very difficult beginning question on a test can be a psychological barrier for some students.

You've Tested; What Then?

Testing is merely the means for measuring students. After testing you are confronted with converting the data into measurement terms.

Measurement

The *measurement* element is essentially a descriptive entity. For example, a child might be *tested* with a Stanford Binet I. Q. test and receive a measurement score of 120. Measurement then is the end product whereas a test is the vehicle, device or instrument which results in a *measurement*. Measurement data, sometimes referred to as scores, are a relative commodity.

The act of measuring anything implies that a comparison is made or a relationship is drawn. Any measurement data can have meaning to you as a teacher only if you know something about the variables connected with the test. Obviously the more variables you take into account the more meaning the measurement has for you.

Some of the variables related to the test and resulting measurement are:

1. The reliability of the test.
2. The validity of the test.
3. Past performances of other pupils on the test or similar tests.
4. The conditions under which the test was given.

Consult a text such as one of those suggested at the close of this chapter if you are not familiar with these terms, as space does not permit ample discussion of these facets of test analysis.

Evaluation

What Is It?

Evaluating anything, including human effort, involves making many value judgments. If you are familiar with the components of philosophy you recognize that fundamentally any evaluation implies that a system of values is being implemented. This can lead to a study or discussion of axiology. Axiology is the branch of philosophy which deals with values. You may want to do further reading related to axiology. Any commodity has value only in *relation* to other commodities. When you are attempting to evaluate a child's progress or growth it is important you be conscious of exactly what values you are employing. For example, you may need to evaluate a child's handwriting in order to make some comment on his report card. If neatness is an important value to you then this value will greatly flavor your evaluation. Your personal conception of neatness will be involved here.

In evaluating a child's schoolwork, regardless of the subject matter area, certain variables should interplay in determining the value judgment you make about the child. They include such things as:

1. Intellectual capacity
2. Physical health
3. Emotional-social adjustment
4. Degree of academic motivation (how much interest does he have in the work?)
5. His background of life experiences.

It's All Relative.

The relativity of values can be easily exemplified for each of the five points just mentioned. A child's intellectual capabilities, for example, if being judged largely as a result of a verbal I. Q. test are being compared (through his scores) with the performance of thousands of similar children who have helped establish the norms for the test.

Evaluation's two fundamental dimensions are the individual in relation to himself and the individual in relation to others. You will find that these dimensions are frequently considered dichotomous and their importance carries different weight in different school systems.

Why Evaluate?

Evaluation can result in a clearer more realistic self-concept for the learner and sometimes for the teacher. It can express a child's relative position in the class in any number of achievement areas; illustrate the personal growth a child (learner) has made since the last evaluation; help the learner set new goals based upon his present position and a host of other elements as well.

It is vital that the learner play a part in his own evaluation. Too often evaluation is done apart from the child by some higher authority.

As a student teacher you will need to hold conferences with the children to exchange evaluation information and value judgments with them.

Let's Recapitulate.

Measuring and evaluating pupils' over-all growth in all areas of the classroom is done to:

1. Enable the teacher to help the child to formulate a realistic self-concept.
2. Enable the teacher to appraise the effectiveness of teaching methods and materials being employed.
3. Enable the teacher to help the child set realistic future goals.
4. Aid the teacher in determining what type of remedial work is needed by the student as well as what progress steps are necessary.

Try to remember that evaluation of a child's progress implies much more than merely taking a bunch of grades from your grade book and computing their average. Evaluation takes into account as many as possible of the variables confronting the child and then asks the question: How well is the child achieving or progressing while working under these *particular circumstances* in your *particular classroom setting?* An answer is not easy to determine. Evaluation is more than taking a lot of statistical data and using them *alone* to evaluate a child's classwork. To the statistical data must be added large portions of professional judgment, understanding and at least a quart of the milk of human kindness. Most important is that the child be permitted to play an important role in determining his own evaluation.

How Will You Know That You Teach?

As just mentioned, evaluation can help you to answer this question. From the vantage point of the teacher it is vital for you to have at least a general idea of your teaching effectiveness. Evaluating of the individual growth or achievement progress of your class members can act as a barometer of this effectiveness. Evaluation also results in some type of grading (or marking) the work of your pupils. The grading is used to report the pupils' progress to parents, other teachers, and anyone rightly concerned with it. This section of the text, in such limited space, cannot hope to cover all the ramifications of measurement and evaluation nor is coverage our objective. The authors are attempting to call your attention to the basic skills, understandings and issues in this area that are most likely to confront you during student teaching.

As a student teacher you will need to know *approximately* how much individual children are learning and something about the quality of that learning. Are children retaining what you are teaching them over an extended period of time (longevity of the learning)? Can they use the learning (transfer of learning) from one situation to another?

You will need to keep some records of the first two elements just mentioned and to report pupil progress to parents, school administrations and others concerned.

Permanent Records.

Most schools have some type of record of pupil progress which too often follows the pupil like a shadowy monster throughout his school years. These record folders or cards will be of great importance to you as a student teacher. On them you will find background information related to the pupil's intellectual, physical, social and emotional progress as well as family background and other vital statistics. These records take many forms. Space is not taken here to discuss the mechanics of keeping permanent records. *All* record keeping should have as its main purpose the fostering of optimum growth in the child. Busy teachers sometimes lose sight of this.

You will find that schools vary tremendously in their policies on handling permanent record material. A goodly number of schools permit the teachers unqualified access to these records while others guard

them in a "Fort Knox" type security system. The "professionally mature" manner of dealing with all confidential material is to place full trust in the judgment of the teachers and permit their open access to the records. Anything short of this procedure is to obstruct the free exchange of vital data about children to those directly responsible for them.

Familiarize yourself with the records related to your class as soon as possible in your student teaching. The notion to which some teachers adhere — "to read the personal records early in the teaching experience will bias their judgment" — is also professionally immature. A physician would not want to diagnose and treat a patient without knowing as much medical history as possible. If teachers cannot read the case history of a child and still reserve personal judgment about him, they are naive in handling data. Many facts about the children, which are important for the teacher or student teacher to be cognizant of *before* beginning instruction, are stated in these records. In fact a thorough knowledge of background data should facilitate, not inhibit, better instruction.

Handling Professional Records.

You would not want to consult a medical doctor whom you felt might discuss your case all over town. Similarly teachers should never discuss personal information about students excepting with those persons with whom it is ethically and professionally proper. Occasionally teachers and student teachers disregard the ethics of the teaching profession and carry tales out of school. This practice can result in serious trouble and embarrassment. For example, there was the case of two student teachers' discussing on a city bus the poor home background and poor mental endowment of a student, only to find the youngster's mother seated behind them. There was also the case of a student teacher who gave out an I.Q. score to a parent which resulted in a difficult and threatening situation for the child of this parent. In addition it was contrary to policy to give a parent an actual I.Q. score in this particular school system. Be certain that you know what type of information is confidential in your school setting and treat it that way.

Reporting Pupil Progress

You will need, at some point in your classroom program, to report children's progress. It may be to parents, school administration and/or to the children themselves.

There are many methods or vehicles for reporting pupil progress. None are perfect. Some schools use the report card method entirely. Others employ report letters, check lists, and parent conferences and some use various combinations of these devices. Sometime during the final days of your student teaching the authors suggest that you select a pupil (or perhaps several) and make out a sample report card and a sample report letter for him. Use all data and evidence you have collected related to the pupil's over-all work in your classroom to support your judgments. Then show the report card letter to your cooperating teacher and obtain his opinion as to how accurate a job you have done. Perhaps you will want to compare your sample report card with the last one your cooperating teacher made out on this particular child. You will learn many things in doing this project. You may get some notion as to whether or not you hold realistic standards for students working at your particular grade level. You will also get to know how much time, thought, and energy are connected with using the report card as opposed to the report letter. Perhaps you will see some of the limitations of using one or the other or both as a reporting device.

PARENT-TEACHER CONFERENCE

If possible try to obtain permission to "sit-in" on a parent conference so that you have some experience with the techniques involved. Discuss with your cooperating teacher and other teachers in the school their feelings about parent conferences as a reporting vehicle. Remember that the most important aspect of reporting to parents is accurate communication.

Support Your Judgments With Data.

If a parent should question the reason for a particular grade or comment in his child's evaluation you should always be ready to support your evaluation with some evidence. Unless you have supporting evidence a parent may feel you are expressing only an opinion. He may also feel his own opinion is as valid as yours unless you can support yours with evidence.

Perhaps you will want to maintain a personal folder, which can serve as a source of evaluation evidence with your class grade book, for each child in your class. Combine this with your own professional observations of the child.

The Folder System.

The folder system should permit the child to have free access to his own work. He should know what is in his folder and contribute samples of his own work whenever he desires. You should also place in each child's folder samples of handwriting, tests, daily classwork and even some samples of the child's art work. The folder then becomes somewhat of a cross section of the youngster's work.

In addition to having a sample work folder for each child to support evaluation and reporting, you can also employ such things as anecdotal records, sociograms and data from the child's permanent record folder as additional evidence. We all expect a physician to make his diagnosis and other professional judgments on the basis of evidence he has collected. As professional people, teachers are expected to do likewise. If they do not then evaluation becomes largely a guessing game.

Who Have We Been Kidding?

For too long a time many educators have been deceiving themselves, and kidding the public as well, about their ability to grade students' school work. Due to ignorance and a general naiveness on the part of the public as to the limitations of academic grading, some schools have been able to foist off on them rather ridiculous systems for reflecting the achievement of students. What is even more ridiculous is the fact that all too many teachers actually believe they are very accurate in reporting students' true achievements through the numerical or letter grades they assign.

Much has been written about the marking (or grading) systems in many schools. Many teachers have made an honest effort to improve conditions but accurate evaluation and reporting of achievement are very elusive targets.

We probably never will develop a perfect system for grading and reporting pupil progress but the authors feel certain that there can be much improvement in many existing practices. To be more specific, what does a 93 really mean as a grade in English or history or any other subject for that matter? What is the difference between one student's receiving a 93 and another a 94? What justification is there for high schools which compute students' numerical grades to two decimal places in order to determine such "life or death issues" as who is to be class valedictorian or who should be awarded a particular scholarship? Is a student with a 94.05 average in high school better suited to be valedictorian than a student with 93.95? Unfortunately at all levels of education grades are used with a great deal of asininity.

Some teachers attempt to grade even the creative work of children. In English composition, for example, if a child hands in a piece of creative writing just how does a teacher justify assigning an 87 as an accurate grade or for that matter an A or a B? It is possible to evaluate objectively the theme on the basis of the correct "mechanics" of the English language such as spelling, grammar, sentence structure and the like, but how does one assign an objective and accurate letter grade to someone else's creative effort? Nevertheless many school systems demand that teachers attempt the impossible by calling for a sensible numerical grade on report cards for such things as art, music, homemaking, etc. Such problems and issues may confront you either directly or indirectly as a student teacher.

Include the Children.

One avenue of reporting pupil progress which is little travelled is that of reporting their development to the pupils themselves. We often carefully inform school administration and parents about a particular child's progress via a report card but we leave out the learner (the child) in the process. Periodic conferences with each child (regardless of grade level) in the classroom concerning his general progress in school is essential. How can the learner be expected to improve and modify himself and set realistic goals if he has only a casual awareness of his progress? All reports sent home should, in our judgment, be explained and intrepreted to the child himself. One helpful technique is to duplicate for each child a copy of all items on the school's report card or check list, then have each child mark himself in all areas. Follow this with a brief conference with each child in which you show him the report card you have made out for him and discuss the differences between his and yours.

Regardless of the technique you employ the child should be directly involved in his own evalaution. When a child sees a sincere need for improvement he is most likely to take responsibility for and interest in self-improvement.

You're Next!

Just as you will need to collect achievement data, evaluate and report it about the children in your classroom, so also will your cooperating teacher and college supervisor be doing the same about your work as a student teacher. In fact, as awesome as it may seem, all those who come in contact with you as a student teacher — pupils, parents, school administrators, other teachers, etc — will be sizing you up (evaluating you) either formally or informally. Some of them will convey their reactions directly to you, others will not. Your greatest concern, however, will be the evaluation by those professional persons closely associated with your classroom teaching. You can and should have a part in collecting and evaluating the data related to your work as a student teacher. Evaluating your work is vital in fostering increased competency. Perhaps if you adopt the habit of talking over with your cooperating teacher the relative merits of the lessons you have taught during the day, the habit of daily personal assessment will become part of your mode of working. Habituating daily assessment of your teaching is part of becoming a self-improver. Self-improvers grow in competence each day throughout their lives as teachers, while others find a comfortable rut and repeat year after year essentially what they did their first year of teaching.

No one is permanently educated and likewise no one is permanently competent to teach. It is necessary to be a lifetime student yourself in order to keep pace with the exploding frontiers of knowledge. Evaluating your teaching each day with your cooperating teacher, even for only fifteen or twenty minutes, will habituate professional self-assessment and re-enforce its value to you.

Perpetual Motion.

In following the foregoing pattern of constant, ongoing evaluation, you will notice that evaluation takes on the character of perpetual motion. So it should be. Daily evaluation will eliminate anxieties for you as you will always know at least where you stand. Uncertainty can be anxiety producing. Sometimes you will need to take the initiative in seeking evaluative conferences with your cooperating teacher. If you request suggestions and critical analysis of your teaching, your cooperating teacher will feel less hesitant to offer them.

Your college will provide a pattern and/or specific forms for evaluating your student teaching. Here again there is no proven ideal form or method, but perhaps some of the following guidelines will be of help.

When discussing various aspects of your teaching such as classroom management, character of your voice, use of gestures,. etc., try to think of specific incidents which substantiate your evaluation. In other words, try to distinguish what behaviorisms are related to classroom management and to what extent you engage in them.. Strive also to isolate the values and educational philosophy exemplified by the various methods you employ. As previously suggested, tape recordings which you have made of some of your lessons can serve as a basis and as supporting evidence for evaluation.

It's A Togetherness Job!

It is hoped that you and your cooperating teacher together will do much evaluating of your work. Perhaps if you make out an evaluation of your work in private and your cooperating teacher makes out one separately then you can compare them and use the differences as a basis for your evaluation conference.

Remember that, in entering any profession, there are certain minimal standards that you must meet. You should not be evaluated however in terms of how you measure up against an experienced teacher, but rather how you rate in terms of expectations for a student teacher considering all of the variables of your particular student teaching setting.

One very fundamental evaluation-type question you may want to toss around with your cooperating teacher is this: What effect has your being there (in the school as a student teacher) had upon children, parents, and the total school? In reality this cannot be accurately determined but it will help to bring to the surface some specific reactions to your work as a student teacher.

Grade A Is a Better Label for Milk Than For Student Teachers!

Due to the tremendous complexity of student teaching plus the

great disagreement as to what constitutes good teaching, we feel it should be evaluated in terms of the accomplishment of skills and formation of attitudes rather than condensed into a single letter grade such as an A or B.

Because of tradition, some colleges and universities feel it necessary to bestow a letter grade on the student teacher. This coincides with the grading procedures in subject matter courses in the college program. In cases other than the foregoing, we feel a letter grade for student teaching is nebulous and communicates little or nothing. Rating scales which define specific skills, general report letters, conferences, and similar devices, if well implemented are better suited to reporting the many subtleties of student teaching.

The important facets of evaluation are: (1) it is done in terms of clear-cut, pre-established objectives, (2) it includes suggestions and plans for further growth, (3) you have an active part in it and understand it, and (4) it is based as much as possible upon objective evidence.

Working primarily for a specific letter grade in student teaching represents a poor form of motivation in terms of developing wholesome professional attitudes. There are, as previously stated, minimum competency expectations for any profession, but beyond these evaluation should consist of appraising your progress toward optimum professional competency, taking into consideration your individual abilities, talents and intellectual endowment.

You must learn to set realistic professional goals for yourself and evaluate your progress toward them, and perhaps most important of all it is desirable that you have a feeling of accomplishment and satisfaction about your growth in teaching or you are apt to forsake it. Of course we all meet failures but successful experiences should predominate in your early preparation.

At best, honest, realistic evaluation is very difficult, and it will require a personal maturity. The job would be greatly simplified if the teaching profession could clearly define the specific components of good teaching.

All Is Not Lost.

There are fortunately some general elements which most professional educators agree are necessary to a good teacher or teaching. It would however be difficult if not impossible to obtain strong agreement as to how much value or weight should be assigned to these elements. It would be equally difficult to obtain much agreement on an accurate description of the behaviors which portray these various elements. For example, how does a student teacher behave who is showing initiative in his work?

While your college will have its own particular forms and system for rating student teacher performance, perhaps student teacher rating sheets will help you. Rating sheets, with accompanying descriptive charts, are shown on the following pages.

Checklist for Evaluation of Elementary School Cadet Teachers[1]

1962-63

EARLY CHILDHOOD AND ELEMENTARY EDUCATION

SYRACUSE UNIVERSITY SCHOOL OF EDUCATION, SYRACUSE, NEW YORK

CHECKLIST FOR EVALUATING WORK OF ELEMENTARY
STUDENT TEACHERS

Name of student... School..................................

Name of teacher..

Date .... Check: Marked by teacher ....

Marked by student and teacher ....

(An appraisal of the above named student in terms of the following points is very much desired. If possible, a better learning situation may be encour-

---

[1]*Cadet Teaching at Syracuse University,* Dept. of Teacher Preparation, Syracuse University, Syracuse, N. Y. 1962-63.

aged if student and teacher mark the sheet together. Each point may be marked by checking the continuum *anywhere* along the scale and by making subjective comments in the place provided. These sheets may be used as often as desired during the student teaching experience but we should appreciate it if you would return a copy of all the evaluation sheets within a few days after the student teaching experience is completed.)

CHARACTERISTIC AND COMMENTS

---

1. Sympathetic understanding of boys and girls.
   Comments:

2. Ability to plan and acquire subject matter and general background for teaching.
   Comments:

3. Growth in skill in handling teaching techniques.
   Comments:

4. Personal appearance.
   Comments:

5. Initiative.
   Comments:

6. Dependability
   Comments:

CONTINUUM SCALE RATING

1.
1   10

| Disregards n a t u r a l characteristics of children at this age level. | Recognizes needs and interests somewhat but does little about them. | Capitalizes on children's needs and interests, heeds problem. |

2.
1   10

| Shows no pre-planning for lesson. | Shows some planning. Material fairly organized. | Careful planning. Material well organized and presented. |

3.
1   10

| Handles material the same at the end of experience as at beginning. | Acts on suggestions but shows little initiative. | Takes suggestions — improves constantly on them and goes out ahead. |

4.
1   10

| Careless in dress, clothes unbecoming. Untidy. | | Well-groomed, attractive, tidy. |

5.
1   10

| Ignores or is not alert to classroom needs. | Shows some initiative but misses much. | Takes advantage of teaching experience. Sees things that need to be done. |

6.
1   10

| Is tardy for appointments, work unfinished or unprepared. | Shows some reliability. Is sometimes forgetful or irresponsible. | Accepts responsibility. Prompt. Does assigned work. Notifies teacher and school of absences. |

7. Growth in ability to discern and provide for individual differences.
   Comments:

8. Skill in social control.
   Comments:

9. Ability to speak within the child's level of understanding.
   Comments:

10. Control of voice.
    Comments:

11. General professional attitude.
    Comments:

12. Willingness to assume additional school responsibilities (P.T.A. meetings, Mother's Club)
    Comments:

13. Willingness to accept and act on supervisory suggestions.
    Comments:

14. Ability to handle regular school routine.
    Comments:

7.

1   10

| Teaches always to whole class. Disregards individual differences. | Shows consciousness of individual differences. Does not do much about them. | Is conscious of differences in children and provides for them. |

8.

1   10

| Is disrespectful and inconsiderate of other teachers. No rapport. | Is thoughtless or self-centered at times. | Has good rapport with co-workers, gains respect of students. |

9.

1   10

| Speaks in terms too easy or too hard for children to understand. Does not communicate ideas well. | Vocabulary fairly well selected but ideas not always communicated readily. | Vocabulary on children's level. Communicates ideas easily. |

10.

1   10

| Rasping, too loud or soft, indistinct, too slow or fast. | Steady, lacking in control. | Well modulated, clear pleasant, expressive. |

11.

1   10

| Poor | Improves | Superior |

12.

1   10

| Shows no interest in school matters outside of the class. | Assumes duties when suggested. | Accepts extra jobs around school well. Co-operative. |

13.

1   10

| Resents criticism in any form. | Accepts constructive criticism but does little about it. | Welcomes criticism and acts on it. |

14.

1   10

| Has no follow-through of school routine. | Follows school routine with little understanding. | Anticipates necessities in school program and carries them out regularly. |

15. Enthusiasm for job.
    Comments:

16. Ability to make individual decisions.
    Comments:

18. Contributing member of the classroom.
    Comments:

15.
1   10

| Mediocre. | Average interest. | Exceptional interest. |

16.
1   10

| Relies on teacher to make judgments. | Comes to teacher sometimes for help in making decisions. | Uses good judgment in handling individual or group problems. |

17.
1   10

| No control over children. All a c t i v i t y without a purpose. | Knows most of the time what is going on in room and guides children into purposeful activity. | Knows what is going on everywhere in room. Has ability to direct children so that all activity is purposeful. |

18.
1   10

| Is part of furniture. | Brings in some material. | B r i n g s in material. S h a r e s experiences. Makes the classroom a better place by presence. |

Ability to handle particular skills we feel important: (please comment)

> Storytelling
> Pupil-Teacher Planning
> Musical Situations
> Games (new and old)
> Dramatization
> Discussion
> Making classroom attractive

SUPPLEMENTARY OR ALTERNATIVE REPORT

If you wish to do so, you may write out an evaluation of the student *instead of* check the scale on the preceding pages. A written-out evaluation may also be used in preference to assigning a letter grade.

STRENGTHS:

WEAKNESSES:

TEACHING PROMISE:

_____
Teacher's Signature

_____
Date

	Superior—Strengths Clearly Overshadow Weaknesses	Acceptable—Balance of Strengths and Weaknesses Potential Good	Weak—Definite Need for Improvement	Weaknesses Predominant Improvement Essential to Success In Teaching
STUDENT TEACHING EVALUATION CHART *(Consult the Expanded Chart in the Handbook for Sample Descriptions of Qualities Evaluated)*				
Evaluative Items				
Appearance				
Speech				
Language Usage				
Initiative and Responsibility				
Emotional Stability				
School Relations				
Community Relations				
Physical Health				
Healthful Room Conditions (lighting, heating, ventilation, etc.)				
Desirable Environment for For Learning				
Classroom Organization and Management				
Teacher Planning				
Pupil-Teacher Planning				
Professional Background				
Academic Background				
Evaluation of Pupil Progress				

STUDENT TEACHING EVALUATION CHART [1.]

(Expanded to provide sample descriptions of Evaluative items)

EVALUATIVE ITEMS	SUPERIOR	ACCEPTABLE	WEAK	UNACCEPTABLE
1. Appearance	Dresses appropriately; well groomed; no obvious personal inadequacies	Acceptably dressed and groomed; no flagrant violations in personal appearance	Grooming somewhat careless; occasional inappropriate dress; some lack of value of personal appearance	Inappropriate or unkidy dress; consistently poor grooming; little attention to appearance
2. Speech	Well-modulated; excellent enunciation; distinct; firm	Acceptable tone and enunciation; conscious of defects and striving to overcome them	Obvious defects in speech; needs much improvement; sensitive to speech defects	Defective speech definite handicap in teaching; lack of sensitivity to defects or effort to improve
3. Language Usage	Accurate usage; variety in expression; stimulating; effective	Adequate; few errors-conscious of these and striving to improve	Limited vocabulary and inaccurate word usage; persistent errors	Frequently incorrect, not aware of errors; lack of concern
4. Initiative and Responsibility	Skill in handling problem situations; creative and original; adapts plans and ideas of group; accepts responsibility; thoroughly dependable	Does assigned work well; offers a few suggestions; can deal with usual problems; generally dependable	Needs s o m e pressure; carries out minimum of plans; rarely tries anything new; tends to dodge responsibility; erratic	completely dependent; lacks self-reliance; requires almost constant prodding; lacks ideas and curiosity; procrastinates; cannot deal with problems
5. Emotional Stability	Well-balanced and poised; profits by experience and suggestions	Normally controlled; gets excited under stress; seeks assistance	Somewhat excitable; nags OR Is withdrawn; timid	Too easily moved to anger; touchy; resentful of criticism OR Apathetic; fearful; passive; unresponsive
6. School Relations	Aims to be a worthy and contributing member of the group; respects the ideas a n d contributions of others; is friendly and just in d e a l i n g s with colleagues; is aware of school policies and procedures and honors them; is concerned with welfare of others	Usually honors school policies and procedures; tries to adjust to being a member of a teaching group; is usually friendly; accepts colleagues as individuals with some discernment; usually identifies needs of others in consideration for their welfare; accepts ideas and contributions of others	Lacks perception of needs of others; may offend; neglects to regularly observe school policies and procedures; slow adjustment in becoming a member of the teaching group; does not always respect ideas and contributions of others	Lack of tact in dealing with others; anti-social; self-centered; is careless in observing school policies and procedures; lacks respect for ideas and contribution of others
7. Community Relations	Realistic understanding of the role of the teacher in the community; seeks participation in community affairs; participates effectively; adjusts well to community	Cooperates; does as much as expected; usually recognizes community standards	Rarely participates in community affairs; indifferent to community and its needs; accepts community standards reluctantly	Does not contribute to community affairs; ignores community standards

*Handbook for Student Teaching, State University of New York, College at Oswego, 1960.

EVALUATIVE ITEMS	SUPERIOR	ACCEPTABLE	WEAK	UNACCEPTABLE
8. Physical Health	Healthy, vigorous; regular attendance; exercises good judgment in maintaining health	Good health and stamina; seldom absent; is not always alert to maintaining good health	Lacks energy; occasionally ill; ignores maintenance of health	Frequent absences; general indifference due to physical deficiencies
9. Healthful Room Conditions (lighting, seating, ventilation, attractiveness)	Consistently alert to provide best conditions; needs little direction	Generally alert; needs some supervision	Needs much direction; quite often unaware of conditions	Indifferent; needs constant direction
10. Desirable Environment for Learning	Provides stimulating environment; has ideas to contribute to healthy learning situations	Aware of need for stimulating environment; needs some help	Makes little effort to stimulate pupils through environment; needs much direction	Indifferent; follows suggestions inadequately
11. Classroom Organization and Management	Carries out routine activities effectively; needs little direction; has good rapport; seeks help when in doubt	Aware of need for organization; generally carries out routine well; needs some help occasionally, but follows suggestions well	Has difficulty in organizing and managing; rapport often lacking; accepts suggestions reluctantly	Unaware of need for organization; profits little from directions and resists suggestions; uncooperative
12. Teacher Planning	Plans effectively; is aware of need for planning; needs little assistance and profits from suggestions	Plans adequately but needs some assistance; profits from suggestions; is generally aware of need for planning	Plans inadequately; lacks insight as to need for planning; profits little from suggestions; careless about submitting plans	Unaware of need for planning; plans rarely and very inadequately; does not profit from suggestions
13. Pupil-Teacher Planning	Recognizes need for pupil participation; is generally effective; profits from suggestions; exercises positive leadership	Aware of need for pupil planning; is generally effective, but needs some direction; profits from suggestions	Rarely attempts to solicit pupil participation in planning; needs continual help; lacks confidence	No evidence of pupil participation in planning; is unaware of need; profits little from suggestions
14. Professional Background	Deals effectively with children; understands them; uses effective methods; has good knowledge of materials; eager to learn; profits from suggestions; keeps up-to-date	Deals effectively with children most of the time; has generally good understanding of children and materials; profits from suggestions; has potential for growth	Lacks understanding of children and materials; does not seek assistance	Extreme lack of understanding; does not follow suggestions, and even resents suggestions
15. Academic Background	Has superior background; is well-informed; has skill in locating information; keeps up-to-date	Generally well informed; may have some weaknesses, but is eager to overcome them; may need some help and welcomes it; profits by suggestions	Inadequately informed; little skill in locating information; rarely seeks help	Has definite lack of background; seems unaware of difficulties; resents suggestions
16. Evaluation of Pupil Progress	Is alert to need for continuous evaluation; evaluation is generally good; has breadth of view, and experiments in improving techniques	Is aware of need for good evaluation; needs assistance, but profits by it, has generally sound point of view	Inadequate understanding of evaluation; seems unconcerned; has narrow point of view	Has little concern for pupil progress and seems to lack understanding of purposes and means; may resent suggestions

Student's name ....

GUIDE FOR GRADING

A. Excellent student. Seems to fit naturally into teaching role. Shows potentialities for being an excellent teacher. Has done an outsanding job.
B. Very good student. Has shown considerable growth in most areas and willingness to learn. Seems to fit well into the teaching role.
C. An average student. Has shown growth in many areas and an ability to progress. Needs more preparation and help.
D. A weak student. Not outstanding and not a failure but probably inadequate for teaching.
E. Totally inadequate for teaching.

As an overall summary of this student's work in student teaching in my room, I feel the above grade best represents his work. (   )

_____

Teacher's signature

_____

Date

TOPICS AND QUESTIONS FOR STUDY AND DISCUSSION

1. This chapter suggests that accurate testing, measuring and evaluating of human effort is a most difficult task. What are some variables in human nature that validate this statement?
2. Browse through *Mental Measurements Yearbook*, Oscar Buros, ed., Gryphon Press, New Jersey, 1959, and/or *Tests In Print*, Oscar Buros, ed., Gryphon Press, New Jersey, 1961, in order to become more familiar with the variety of tests available to the classroom teacher.
3. The character and utilization of permanent records can be a source of controversy in any school. The authors have made the following statement in Chapter 5: "Most schools have some type of record of pupil progress which too often follows the pupil like a shadowy monster throughout his school years." How do you interpret this sentence?
4. Discuss the statement that "No one is permanently educated and likewise no one is permanently competent to teach."

SELECTED REFERENCES

1. Ahman, Stanley J., Glock, Marian D., Wardeberg, Helen L., *Evaluating Elementary School Pupils*. Boston: Allyn and Bason, Inc., 1960.
2. Cronbach, Lee J., *Essentials of Psychological Testing*. New York: Harper Bros., Second Edition, 1960.
3. Remmers, H. H., Gage, N. L., Rummel, Francis J., *A Practical Introduction to Measurement and Evaluation*. New York: Harper & Bros., 1960.
4. Strang, Ruth, *How to Report Pupil Progress*. Chicago: Science Research Associates, Inc., 1955.
5. Travers, Robert M., *How to Make Achievement Tests*. New York: The Odyssey Press, 1950.
6. Wrightstone, Wayne J., *What Tests Can Tell Us About Children*, Chicago: Science Research Associates, 1954.

JUST FOR FUN

"You Say You Have Just Finished Student Teaching."

"I Don't Suppose I Can Use the Fifth Amendment Again" . . . .

Student Teacher Finishes a Unit.

"Prof, I Think Hector Was Workin' on Rocket Fuel Again."

Part II

The Teacher and the Profession

Chapter 6

Teaching As A Profession

*All the high hopes which I do avowedly
entertain of a more glorious future for the
human race are built upon the elevation
of the teacher's profession and the enlarge-
ment of the teacher's usefulness.*

Horace Mann in
The Teacher's Motives

This chapter deals with questions like the following: (1) What is
a profession? (2) How have professions developed? (3) Is teaching a
profession? (4) How does teaching differ from other professions? (5)
What is the current status of the teaching profession? (6) What are
some significant movements affecting teaching as a profession? (7)
How are standards affecting teaching derived and applied? (8) What
professional organizations are of chief value and interest to teachers?

What Is A Profession?

When you are asked "What is a profession?" what do you answer?
It is likely that you are at least slightly confused. If you are asked to
name a profession, you have less difficulty. You probably mention
medicine or law or engineering. The term "profession" often is used
quite loosely for you hear reference, for example, to the gambling profession, and many occupational groups claim to be professions. It is
small wonder there is confusion!

117

As a result, there is need for careful definition. We need to know what constitutes a profession. In a sense, the public attitude determines whether an occupational group has professional status. For example, the general public accords high status to physicians. Is the public regard for common laborers the same? How does the public view teaching? In most of the polls of the past decade or so, in terms of the public's views on the status of occupational groups, teachers have not ranked very high. Usually they have ranked above average, but such groups as lawyers, physicians, bankers, ministers, and chemists, among others, outranked them. It may be of interest to you to note a Gallup Poll[1] published in August, 1962. It points up a gain in prestige for teaching as a career. The three professions topping the list were physicians, engineers and teachers. Admittedly, public sanction is not the only criterion of status, but most authorities as well as citizens in general agree that it is most significant. Obviously, it is not enough to have recognition only within an occupational group. A group's self-view is important, even vital, but the general public must give the ultimate sanction as to status.

What then, constitutes a profession? Despite the confusion over exact meaning of the term "profession," and despite the fact there seem to be no final and authoritative criteria by which we can clearly and finally distinguish professions from other occupations, there are some characteristics more or less typical of and apparently unique to professions. By these criteria we can, in general, distinguish a profession from occupations. There also is wide enough agreement on certain characteristics to provide us with a good working idea of what is meant by the term profession.

What are these characteristics? There are several lists of characteristics or criteria which have common elements and are generally accepted. Perhaps the basic statement of criteria of professions is that of Flexner.[2] It follows:

1. They involve essentially intellectual operations with large individual responsibility.
2. They derive their raw material from science and learning.
3. They work up this material to a practical and definite end.

---

[1]American Institute of Public Opinion, "Opinion Poll of Public on Professional Prestige." Released in August, 1962. Princeton, N. J.

See also (for summary of past polls on professional status) Reiss, Albert J., Jr. *Occupations and Social Status*, New York: Free Press of Glencoe (Division of Crowell-Collier Publishing Co.), 1961.

[2]T. M. Stinnett, "The Teacher and Professional Organizations" — 1956, Washington, D. C. The NEA, 1956, p. 5.

4. They possess an educationally communicable technique.
5. They tend to self organization.
6. They are becoming increasingly altruistic in motivation.

Another list which has wide currency in educational circles is that proposed by the NEA Division of Field Services.[3] A profession:

1. Involves activities essentially intellectual.
2. Commands a body of specialized knowledge.
3. Requires extended professional preparation.
4. Demands continuous in-service growth.
5. Affords a life career and permanent membership.
6. Sets up its own standards.
7. Exalts service above personal gain.
8. Has a strong, closely knit professional organization.

As you can see, the two lists are quite similar. The latter has more items, one of which has come to have much significance. That is the one in the NEA list which states that a profession "sets up its own standards." More will be said about this later as we deal more particularly with the status of teaching.

Some Essential Considerations In Defining a Profession

There are other lists of criteria, as you can see by reading some of the references at the end of this chapter. It would appear, however, that in the light of the several lists we can seek a definition of a profession in terms of these considerations:

1. The nature of the preparation for entrance into the profession.
2. The nature of the services provided by the profession.
3. The nature of the controls used within the profession.
4. The kind of organizational life engaged in by members of the profession.

A profession calls for broad and specialized education. In other words, a broad general education and mastery of certain specialized knowledge and skills are required. Professional training emphasizes intellectual rather than physical techniques. It calls for problem solving. This involves defining problems, searching for relevant data, and formulating possible solutions.

Physical techniques may or may not be involved but if they are, as in the case of the surgeon, for example, they are guided by intellec-

---

[3]National Education Association, Division of Field Services, "The Yardstick of a Profession," Institutes on Professional and Public Relations, 1938-47, Washington, D. C., The NEA, 1948, p. 8.

tual operations. Long before he uses physical techniques, the surgeon has pursued a complex intellectual program of preparation.

It would seem that teaching meets this criterion. It involves activities which are predominantly intellectual in nature and commands a body of specialized knowledge. There is disagreement over the exact nature of that specialized body of knowledge, and some claim that it has not been sufficiently developed. Some even claim that general or liberal education is all that is needed for teaching.

Such differences of viewpoints are common in the development of a science. Educators point to the vast research in education as summarized, for example, in *The Encyclopedia of Educational Research* and in similar or related volumes. Some critics question the quality of some of the content, but there seems little question now that preparation for teaching involves a body of specialized knowledge that is not common in occupations or other professions in general.

Most of us would contend that extended professional preparation is necessary to produce a competent teacher. The majority of school systems expect their teachers to be college graduates, and many emphasize an additional year of study after some initial teaching experience. Throughout the nation, however, this concept is not universally enforced. In 1961, for example, while 44 states and territories required the minimum of four years of preparation for teaching in elementary school, there remained eight with lower requirements.

The requirements for beginning secondary school teachers more nearly approach a professional concept. In 1961, all states required a minimum of four years, or college graduation, and six required a fifth year.

In general, teaching meets preparation requirements for professional status. Close examination reveals, however, that such variation in actual practice exists, as is pointed out in some detail in a later chapter (Certification), a categorical conclusion can hardly be reached! Until there are a universal four-year preparation requirement and strict enforcement of this standard, we can hardly say that teaching is fully professional at least in this one aspect.

That teaching is an occupation or profession of essential social value cannot be denied. Literally everyone gives at least lip-service to the concept that teaching and education are essential to the welfare — even the preservation — of our society.

One eminent educationist[4] takes the position that if education has made any progress toward becoming a profession in the last century,

---

[4]Myron Lieberman, *Education as a Profession,* New York: Prentice-Hall, Inc. 1956, p. 2.

it is due in part to development of the idea generally that education is so important to the welfare of children and society that it must be made available to all children.

How Do Professions Develop?

The medical profession through its national organization, the American Medical Association, presents an example of the virtually autonomous group. Through its Council on Medical Education and Hospitals, and particularly since the historic Flexner report in 1910,[5] medicine has evolved from a rather chaotic and even shocking condition in the early part of the twentieth century into a strong, competent, highly selective and closely knit profession. There is no question but that it has earned the respect of the public at large. It has also set a pattern which other professions have followed in varying degrees. In the words of a medical authority, Dr. W. W. Bauer, some of the steps involved in medicine's road to professional status are as follows:

"How did medicine become a profession? In precisely the same way that education achieved professionalism, by concern over the needs of others; by observation, by recording of accumulated knowledge, and by the transmission of the same; by research, by strong organization for the defense of professional integrity and by a firm devotion to public service. This is the hard but sure road to professional eminence. There is no other."[6]

What, then, are some of the main roads to professional status as followed by medicine and other major professions, and on which there is much agreement as being necessary for the teaching profession?

Following is a brief summary of some of the major steps:

1. The emergence, development and general acceptance of a unified code of ethics. The Principles of Medical Ethics[7] of the American Medical Association stems from the ancient Oath of Hippocrates. Popularly, the physician's oath is referred to as the Hippocratic Oath. This code appears to contain more about the conduct of individuals than about their competence as practitioners. It seems effective, nevertheless, in guiding practitioners toward professional behavior.

---

[5]Abraham Flexner, *Medical Education in the United States and Canada,* New York: Carnegie Foundation for the Advancement of Teaching, 1910, 346 pages.
[6]W. W. Bauer, "How Medicine Became a Profession." *The Journal of Teacher Education,* 6:211, September, 1955.
[7]Principles of Medical Ethics of the American Medical Association. Chicago: The Association, 1955 (See close of chapter for reproduction of this code).

2. The development of research and education in professional procedures and services.
3. The determination of professional standards by the profession relative to:
   a. selection of capable persons for the profession and retention of these persons.
   b. establishment of adequate requirements for certification or licensure.
   c. removal of incompetent and unqualified members.
   d. accreditation of professional schools on a nationwide basis.
4. The establishment of appropriate conditions for the maintenance of adequate salaries, working conditions, and security of competent professionals against unwarranted attacks.
5. The development and maintenance of a strong, closely knit profession organization to speak for all members.
6. The placing of high priority on the ideal of service as a main motivating force, as done in all true professions.

It would be improper to imply that the teaching profession can follow all of these steps in exactly the same manner as other professions which are largely private in nature. There is however considerable belief among educators that teaching, though largely public, is following and will continue to follow in the same broad steps to full professional status.

It must be recognized that public sanction will, of necessity, have to be gained and to a greater degree than would be necessary for a private profession.

The authors take the position that teaching is a profession. True, its status is hardly that accorded medicine and some other professions, and there are areas such as those mentioned before in which serious problems need to be solved.

Teaching is an ancient profession, however, and one commanding a high degree of respect in many cultures. In ancient Greece, for example, the names of Socrates, Plato, and Aristotle, even in their own times, ranked above military conquerors!

Professional status can be indicated in part in another way in the following quote — "The legislature hereby finds and declares that teaching is a profession requiring the acquisition of specialized educational qualifications."[8] This is legal recognition by the legislature and governor of the State of New York that teaching is a profession.

We should not conclude from this exhibit that legal action alone will afford professional status. Indeed, while it has significance, there

---

[8]Chapter 417 (Educational Law) Laws of New York State which became a law of the state as of April 11, 1961 (excerpted).

are other more important areas of concern as teaching moves to full maturity as a major profession.

Such problem areas as selection and retention of qualified practioners; the development and improvement of adequate programs; the preparation and establishment of adequate standards of licensure and control; the acceptance of standards for accrediting professional schools; adequate salaries and working conditions; and the development of a stronger and more unified professional organization are of concern to both educators and the public. While the profession has made considerable progess in virtually all of these areas, there is still room for improvement!

TEACHING IS VERY OLD

How Teaching Differs From Other Professions

Teaching differs from other professions primarily in the following respects:

It is largely a public enterprise while most other professions are private in nature. This difference necessitates greater dependence on public sanction of teachers than of other professionals, as has been pointed out.

Related to this aspect is the matter of control. The legal control of education actually lies outside the profession in the hands of the public, through their duly constituted authorities. Controls are largely of two kinds — state and local. Hence, what the public wants education to be, at least in large part it will be. Likewise, the profession of teaching depends to a certain extent on what the public permits it to be. This, of course, brings teachers closer to the public, and demands greater and more intelligent interaction with it than is the case with other groups.

Teaching also differs from other groups in function. The term teaching denotes the primary function of the teaching profession. Physicians perform medical services of various kinds, lawyers perform legal and business services, and so on. In a sense, the teaching profession can be called the mother of other professions since all professional practitioners were taught in their preparatory studies.

The teaching profession has far greater numbers than any other profession. With a membership of over 1,500,000, it greatly outnumbers physicians, lawyers, engineers, and clergymen among the leading professions. In fact, there are more teachers in the United States than members of the four other groups combined!

The large size of the teaching profession affects selection of candidates in that it is difficult to limit membership to a highly qualified number, as in the case of physicians for example. This problem demands that much emphasis be placed on preparatory programs and on in-service training to obtain the most competent teachers.

Finally, a majority of the membership in the teaching profession are women. In this category, only the nursing profession and social work are comparable. Over the years, this characteristic of the teaching profession has affected salary primarily. Traditionally women have been paid less than men not only in teaching but in other fields. It seems that a kind of unwritten law has prevailed. Naturally there are exceptions; the single-salary schedule in public schools has done much to equate salaries on factors other than sex.

All of these factors of difference must be kept in mind in programs of improvement carried on by the teaching profession. They will affect selection of candidates and the program involved in the preparation and professional growth of teachers and may have a bearing on other aspects.

The foregoing is a résumé of current conditions stemming from the past, in which matters like local control and public sanction have long been traditional. This is not to say that such conditions will continue. There is some question, for example, as to the usefulness or the educational value of local control. One eminent writer on education[9] takes the position that the concept of local control involves much mythology. The same writer strongly supports the idea of professional autonomy. While such ideas are now minority views, who is sure in this century of radical changes that they may not become majority positions?

In time, the differences between teaching and other professions may be greatly reduced. Even the sex ratio is leveling; more men in recent years have entered the field of elementary education.

---

[9]Myron Lieberman, *The Future of Education,* Chicago: The University of Chicago Press, 1960, Chapter III.

MORE MEN ARE ENTERING ELEMENTARY EDUCATION

Current Status of the Teaching Profession

Later chapters will present detailed information and developments concerning salary and other welfare areas and certification. This section will, therefore, deal with these matters briefly and primarily as they affect other problems.

Public Respect.

As already stated, how the public views teachers and teaching is of some significance. There is considerable evidence of gains in the matter of public respect in recent years, though teachers have not as yet reached the status of some other professionals.

In some degree, the income received by members of a profession is a mark of public respect. No one in the profession is likely to claim that teachers receive munificent incomes! However, gains have been made in recent years in teachers' salaries.

As Figure 1 indicates, the average salaries of teachers have risen in the 22 years pictured from $1,441 in 1939 to $5,716 in 1961-62. As you will note, gains in teachers' salaries have been gradual but steady. With recent gains[10] in salaries and with current prospects favorable

---

[10]The legislature in New York in its 1962 session provided for a new state minimum salary schedule of $4,500 to $6,800. California and Alaska had already established minimums of $4,500 or higher.

for continued progress toward the NEA goal of a $6,000 minimum salary with appropriate increments, a goal considered as reasonable by many, we may expect perhaps a rise in public respect.

The chief point here is that there probably will be an increase in public respect for teaching and teachers as their economic status improves.

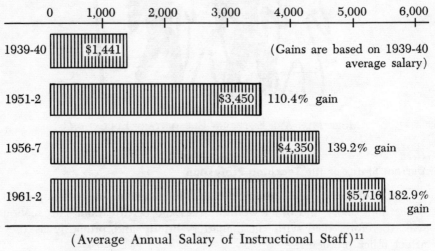

(Average Annual Salary of Instructional Staff)[11]

FIGURE 1.   Gains In Earnings of Teachers 1939 — 1961-2

Code of Ethics.

A basic characteristic of all professions is the adoption, general acceptance, and enforcement when and where necessary, of a professional code of ethics. The term ethics as used in this context refers to principles of conduct based on what is good or right, or what ought to be, as accepted by the individual professional.

In some early attempts to maintain what was then considered the ethical or moral behavior of teachers it was rather common for school authorities to spell out what they considered to be "do's" and "don'ts" for teachers as part of the components of their contracts. This left no doubt as to what was expected of teachers who were employed in a particular school system. The following provisions were actual sections of some teacher contracts at about the turn of the century.

[11]Adapted from "Estimates of School Statistics, 1961-62" Research Report, 1961 R22, Research Division, NEA, p. 12.

The "Do Nots":

(1) get married;
(2) keep company with men;
(3) leave home between 8 P.M. and 6 A.M.;
(4) loiter in ice cream parlors;
(5) smoke cigarettes;
(6) drink beer, wine, or whiskey;
(7) leave town without permission;
(8) ride in a carriage or auto with any men except their fathers or brother;
(9) dress in bright colors;
(10) dye her hair, use face powder, mascara or lipstick.

The "Do's":

(1) bring a bucket of water and scuttle of coal for the day's session;
(2) sweep the classroom floor daily and scrub it weekly;
(3) start the fire at 7:00 A.M. on school days;
(4) each day fill lamps, clean chimneys and trim wicks;
(5) wear at least two petticoats.

Fortunately, such demands are a thing of the past!

A code of ethics cannot or should not be imposed but it should be the responsibility of the total group — even the total profession.

The medical profession has perhaps the oldest code — the Oath of Hippocrates — some 2,500 years old. Its current code, the Principles of Medical Ethics, was written in 1848. The revision is reproduced at the close of this chapter for your examination and study.

Other professions have developed codes to guide the behavior of their members. Perhaps the latest is the NEA Code of Ethics, officially adopted in 1929, and revised several times until, in 1952, the current NEA Code of Ethics was adopted. This version also is reproduced at the close of this chapter. You are encouraged to study it together with the medical code. It should be noted here that the NEA Committee on Professional Ethics presented a proposed draft of a basic code of ethics for the education profession to the July, 1962 Representative Assembly of the NEA. It is now being studied by state education associations and other groups in the profession. This proposed revision may eventually replace the 1952 Code.

In addition, all state associations of teachers have either adopted the NEA code or have developed their own. Doubtless some local associations have codes. Yet the fact remains that today there is no single code that is recognized as generally applicable to all teachers. A careful check of materials supplied by the American Federation of Teachers fails to reveal a code of ethics for that organization.

We reasonably may question whether a single code might become applicable to all teachers. If this is a valid characteristic of a mature profession as most authorities seem to agree, however, the teaching profession has some unfinished work!

Possibly one answer may lie in the universal adoption of the NEA code with improvements[12] as felt necessary initiated, developed and approved by the profession. Local, state and national associations would appropriately be involved. Students preparing to teach may well enter into study and consideration of suitable codes of ethics. There seems to be a trend toward more widespread acceptance of the NEA code.

It would seem that if universal acceptance with the necessary improvements as determined by professionals could be secured, the profession would be greatly strengthened.

Professional Standards

Traditionally, the teaching profession has played only a small role in determining standards of certification or licensure of its members, in accreditation of professional schools for the preparation of teachers, and in selection of its members. Neither has it had much to say about removal of incompetent members. Standards that have evolved relating to these areas have been set up and managed by persons other than those in the teaching profession. Such standards are largely a function of the state through a state agency, the legislature, or state board of

---

12See Myron Lieberman. *Education As A Profession.* Englewood Cliffs, N. J.: Prentice-Hall, Inc., 1956. Chapter 13 and especially pp. 445-451. (This account offers a judgment as to possible improvements.)

education. True, in recent times, many enactments have been the reflection of standards held by teachers through their state association. Unfortunately for the profession as a whole, there has been little unity. The result has been a wide range of standards through the nation. This becomes apparent when we study certification standards, in which there is much variation among the states. This is presented in detail in a later chapter in the section on certification.

State departments of education along with regional accrediting associations have set the standards for accreditation of professional schools. Teachers have had very little to say or do about this matter!

Here it may be recalled that the medical profession through its professional organization, the American Medical Association, has long determined for itself what schools may operate and what programs may be instituted for preparing doctors in the schools approved.

There have been wide variations among institutions and states in standards of selection. Indeed, a rather common criticism has been that teaching attracts students of somewhat less than superior ability. Several studies[13] offer some basis for the criticism. They show, in general, that students in teachers' colleges, as judged by tests, ranked lower than students in some other colleges, primarily liberal arts and engineering.

At best, however, the information supplied by these studies is only a partial answer. In the first place tests are not necessarily appropriate measures of teaching ability. Secondly, we do not as yet know very much about the qualities needed for teaching. Mental ability is important, of course, but it seems apparent that willingness to work, personality, social adjustment, character, and liking for children are also important. With teachers' colleges and education departments lately giving more attention to more careful selection of candidates, there is reason to hope for improvement. Perhaps the most significant development of recent years is the work of the National Commission on Teacher Education and Professional Standards, NEA, particularly the 1960-61 New Horizons project, which offers much promise as a challenge to the profession. The following quote indicates the nature of the challenge: "The profession itself must take up the challenge. The profession must assume responsibility for identifying qualities that can be measured accurately enough to provide bases for evaluation. Instruments and procedures must be set up to insure evaluation of each

---

[13]See W. S. Learned, and B. D. Wood, *The Student and His Knowledge*. New York: The Carnegie Foundation for the Advancement of Teaching, Bulletin No. 29, 1938.

prospective teacher by competent personnel, self-evaluation by each student, and continuous analyses of the evaluation processes themselves."[14]

Accreditation of Teacher Education Programs

In addition to certification, the state exercises control over teacher qualifications by accreditation. Accreditation is a process by which the state or other accrediting agencies establish standards for a teacher education program or a program for medical education or law, for example. The particular program must be of such quality that it can be approved.

Historically, the state set the standards for approval of teacher education programs and for local school systems. Such is still the case with the result that there is much variation among the states as far as their standards are concerned.

"Blessings on Thee"

In addition to the state, regional accrediting associations have developed. There are six of these agencies. All are voluntary and largely multi-state in extent. They apply standards for the approval of colleges and universities and for secondary schools. They publish annual lists of approved schools and colleges within their respective areas. These voluntary agencies are:

1. The New England Association of Colleges and Secondary Schools
2. The Middle States Association of Colleges and Secondary Schools
3. The North Central Association of Secondary and Higher Schools
4. The Southern Association of Colleges and Secondary Schools,
5. The Northwestern Association of Secondary and Higher Schools, and
6. The Western Association of Colleges and Secondary Schools.

In recent years some of the associations have established standards for elementary schools and now evaluate them. These voluntary regional accrediting associations have served well in setting standards for high schools and colleges and in so doing have aided in the gradual improvement of their programs. It should be noted that these associations do not operate in opposition to state standards or infringe on the

---

[14]National Commission on Teacher Education and Professional Standards, NEA, *New Horizons for the Teaching Profession*, (Margaret Lindsey, editor), Washington: The Association: 1961, p. 162.

state's rights to establish standards. Their prime purpose is to raise the standards of the public and non-public schools within their respective geographic areas.

If one studies the history of accreditation in the several professions, for example in certain of the publications listed at the end of this chapter[15], [16], it can be noted that the accrediting function is not the same among the professions or is it identical at all stages of a profession's development. In some cases stimulation appears to be largely the function whereas in others regulation seems to be more important.

Most of the professions other than teaching appear to have moved from regulation toward stimulation. In teaching, the opposite is the case. Accreditation of teacher education began with stimulation of a mild kind. It gradually moved toward greater reliance on stimulation, and has since placed its emphasis on regulation.

At present, the National Committee on Accrediting, originally consisting of representatives of five national organizations of institutions of higher education and now of six such groups[17], designates appropriate agencies to administer accreditation in the respective professional groups. The chief reason for such a body lies in the apparent need for giving leadership for unity in higher education and preventing division and fragmentation by special group pressures.

The National Council for Accreditation of Teacher Education, or NCATE, is the officially designated agency for accrediting teacher education institutions.

Accreditation of Teacher Education — 1927-1954

The year 1927 marks the beginning of standards for the accreditation of teacher education. In that year, the American Association of Teachers Colleges issued its initial list of members. A requirement for membership was that a college be approved, or pass an inspection, on the basis of standards set up or adopted by the Association. Since only teachers' colleges were included in the membership of this Association, a relatively small number of institutions were accredited. Actually a large

[15]U. S. Dept. of Health, Education and Welfare, Office of Education, *Accreditation in Higher Education,* Lloyd E. Blauch, editor, Washington, U. S. Govt. Printing Office, 1959.

[16]Wm. K. Selden, *Accreditation — A Struggle Over Standards in Higher Education.* New York: Harper and Brothers, 1960.

[17](1) American Association of Junior Colleges; (2) The National Association of State Universities; (3) The Association of American Universities; (4) The American Association of Land-Grant Colleges and Universities; (5) The Association of State Colleges and Universities; and (6) The Association of Urban Universities.

proportion of teachers, and especially high school teachers, have been prepared in higher institutions other than teachers' colleges.

By 1948, some liberal arts colleges and universities were being accredited as a result of the formation of a new organization, the American Association of Colleges for Teacher Education. This group was made up of departments of education in liberal arts colleges and schools of education in universities joining with teachers' colleges. This new association, the AACTE, set up a plan to visit all institutions in the organization within a four-year period. Such visitation was almost completed when the National Council for Accreditation of Teacher Education was formed in 1952.

Current Status.

NCATE began its work in 1954 by transferring the membership list of AACTE from that body to the new one. In 1957, NCATE structure was changed to broaden its base. Since that date, the Council has consisted of 19 members, all representatives of related organizations.[18]

The goal of the profession concerning accreditation appears to be that, to enter teaching, the candidate shall have completed an approved program of preparation in a higher education institution accredited by NCATE. Certainly accreditation by NCATE is an integral part of the professional standards movement.

It should be noted that there are persons who fear controls like those invested in such a body as NCATE and those implied in the whole professional standards movement. Some years ago, in 1927 to be specific, a prominent educator, Dr. Fred J. Kelly, then of the University of Minnesota, summarized the dangers in accreditation as he saw them in an address before a meeting of the Association of Urban Universities. These dangers were described as follows:

1. Standardization endangers public confidence in a profession by limiting the number entering the profession, and thereby increases fees for professional services;
2. Standardized schools extend a disproportionate influence, in their demands for curriculum adjustments and in their appeal for support for university funds; and

---

[18] 3 — Appointed by the National Commission on Accrediting.
 7 — Appointed by the American Association of College for Teacher Education.
 6 — Appointed by the National Education Association.
 1 — Appointed by the Council of Chief State School Officers.
 1 — Appointed by the National School Boards Association.
 1 — Appointed by the National Association of State Directors of Teacher Education and Certification.
 19 — Total

3. Agencies demand a uniformity in educational practice, which stifles experimentation and impedes progress.[19]

Since 1927, however, when these fears were expressed, we have seen tremendous gains in all of the professions. Certainly there has been little limit on experimentation if we are to judge by the experiments of the past decade in curriculum designs, organizational practices, and teaching methodology, to name a few! Perhaps it is appropriate to state that the chief limitations appear to lie within the profession itself and with individuals in the profession rather than in such controls as accreditation and certification!

The authors believe that the establishment of a national professional accrediting agency, the National Council for Accreditation of Teacher Education, is a most important move toward the enforcement of professional standards. In this connection, perhaps a fitting close for this section can be found in statements made in the conclusions of the New Horizons report in the section on accreditation.

A STEP UPWARD

> Standards employed by this (NCATE) must be cooperatively developed by the total teaching profession and based on sound theory and practical data. Once adopted, standards must be under constant review through research and analysis. Standards themselves must promote research and experimentation. Individuality of institutions and programs must be protected, indeed, individuality must be encouraged. If standards are to stimulate improvement in preparatory programs, they must be set beyond present practice and provide a challenge to institutional personnel.[20]

Professional Organizations for Teachers

A characteristic of the teaching profession is its many organizations. There are approximately 800 national, regional and state teacher associations. The exact number and names of the organizations can be found in the *Educational Directory* of the U. S. Office of Education, Federal Security Agency. The NEA Handbook issued each year currently indicates 65 state and 7,501 local affiliated associations![21] Apparently teachers are at the top in organizing and joining their associations!

---

[19]Lloyd Blauch, Editor, *op. cit.*, pp. 22-23.
[20]National Commission on Teacher Education and Professional Standards. *New Horizons for the Teaching Profession, op. cit.*, pp. 139-140.
[21]National Education Association, *NEA Handbook for Local, State and National Associations*, 1961-62 edition. Washington: The NEA, 1961, p. 2.

This should not be too surprising, however, for at least two reasons. First, the tremendous size of the teaching profession offers leeway for many associations. As of March 29, 1962, there were 1,545,549 teachers in service.[22]

In the second place, the American culture in general possesses much the same characteristics of "joining" and of widespread group association. Such widespread organization would seem to indicate a realization that much more can be accomplished by collective action than individually.

Other professionals do not face the same problem of selecting an organization or organizations. Beginning medical practitioners, for example, have no competing national groups. Their national organization is the American Medical Association. This is true for most other professions. Each has its one national organization with its affiliated state and local associations. There may be some special interest groups within other professions, but they cannot be compared with the multiplicity of organizations open to teachers!

Perhaps a strong reason why teachers have this problem is simply that as yet they do not have one national organization to which all belong and which all recognize as the main over-all association speaking for the entire profession.

Since beginning teachers as well as those in service need some basis for judging what associations are the most appropriate to join, some of the large national organizations and several types of local, state and regional associations will be discussed in this chapter.

National Education Association.

The National Education Association is the largest teachers' organization in the world; in fact, it is the largest of all professional organizations! It was organized in 1857 and chartered by a Congressional Act in 1906. As of June, 1963, its membership totaled more than 859,000, or about 52 per cent of the employed public school teachers in the nation. While this percentage is only slightly over one-half of the number of teachers in service, the current total is significant. As the figures in Table I indicate, NEA membership growth has been remarkable in recent years.

As Table I shows, the growtn was slow until the period following World War I. Since 1920, the growth has been tremendous. In 1920, the basic structure of the NEA was altered to provide for more repre-

---

[22]NEA Membership Report, No. 13, April 9, 1962. Washington: The NEA, 1962.

TABLE I

MEMBERSHIP IN NEA IN SELECTED YEARS*

Year	No. Belonging	Number of Teachers
1857	43	–
1870	170	200,515
1880	354	286,593
1890	5,474	363,922
1900	2,332	423,062
1910	6,909	523,210
1918	10,104	600,000 (est.)
1920	52,850	679,533
1930	172,354	854,263
1940	203,429	875,477
1950	453,797	967,602
1957	703,829	1,298,819
1958	616,707	1,366,473
1960	713,994	1,468,502
1961-2	815,000	1,545,549
1963	859,505	1,665,065

Source — NEA Handbook 1961- 2; 1960-61, 1959-60, 1958-59, 1957-58. NEA Membership Report — 5/10/62 and 6/14/63.

*T. M. Stinnett, *The Teacher and Professional Organizations,* Washington NEA 1956, p. 111.

sentation from affiliated state and local associations. (Figure 2 shows the organizational structure of the NEA.)

The student will note that 1958 marks a sharp decline in membership. In 1957 the annual active dues were raised to $10.00 from the former rate of $5.00. By 1960, however, the loss had been recovered, and in 1961-2 the membership rose above 800,000 for the first time. The NEA membership slogan is "A Million or More By '64." Members are hopeful that if recent gains are an indication, the goal will be reached. The organizational chart, Figure 2, page 136, indicates the great range and variety of activities of the National Eduction Association. As you note, there are 33 departments, 26 commissions and committees and 14 headquarters divisions. They carry on the many services to members and to education in general.

The representative assembly is the governing body. It determines the basic policies of the NEA through its annual meetings. It is composed of over 6,000 members who are delegates from affiliated state and local teachers' associations. As provided in the NEA By-Laws (Article VII), delegates are chosen on the following basis: each local

ORGANIZATION CHART

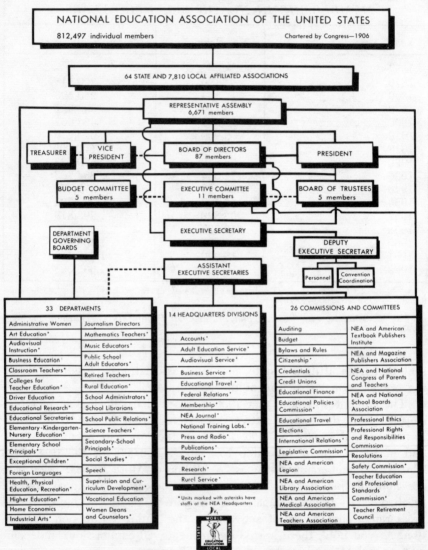

NATIONAL EDUCATION ASSOCIATION OF THE UNITED STATES

812,497 individual members   Chartered by Congress—1906

64 STATE AND 7,810 LOCAL AFFILIATED ASSOCIATIONS

REPRESENTATIVE ASSEMBLY
6,671 members

TREASURER   VICE PRESIDENT   BOARD OF DIRECTORS 87 members   PRESIDENT

BUDGET COMMITTEE 5 members   EXECUTIVE COMMITTEE 11 members   BOARD OF TRUSTEES 5 members

EXECUTIVE SECRETARY

DEPARTMENT GOVERNING BOARDS

DEPUTY EXECUTIVE SECRETARY

ASSISTANT EXECUTIVE SECRETARIES

Personnel   Convention Coordination

33 DEPARTMENTS

Administrative Women	Journalism Directors
Art Education*	Mathematics Teachers*
Audiovisual Instruction*	Music Educators*
Business Education	Public School Adult Educators*
Classroom Teachers*	Retired Teachers
Colleges for Teacher Education*	Rural Education*
Driver Education	School Administrators*
Educational Research*	School Librarians
Educational Secretaries	School Public Relations*
Elementary-Kindergarten-Nursery Education*	Science Teachers*
Elementary School Principals*	Secondary-School Principals*
Exceptional Children*	Social Studies*
Foreign Languages	Speech
Health, Physical Education, Recreation*	Supervision and Curriculum Development*
Higher Education*	Vocational Education
Home Economics	Women Deans and Counselors*
Industrial Arts*	

14 HEADQUARTERS DIVISIONS

Accounts*
Adult Education Service*
Audiovisual Service*
Business Service *
Educational Travel *
Federal Relations*
Membership*
NEA Journal*
National Training Labs.*
Press and Radio*
Publications*
Records*
Research*
Rural Service*

*Units marked with asterisks have staffs at the NEA Headquarters

JULY 1962

26 COMMISSIONS AND COMMITTEES

Auditing	NEA and American Textbook Publishers Institute
Budget	
Bylaws and Rules	NEA and Magazine Publishers Association
Citizenship*	
Credentials	NEA and National Congress of Parents and Teachers
Credit Unions	
Educational Finance	NEA and National School Boards Association
Educational Policies Commission*	
Educational Travel	Professional Ethics
Elections	Professional Rights and Responsibilities Commission
International Relations*	
Legislative Commission*	
NEA and American Legion	Resolutions
	Safety Commission*
NEA and American Library Association	Teacher Education and Professional Standards Commission*
NEA and American Medical Association	
NEA and American Teachers Association	Teacher Retirement Council

THE NATIONAL EDUCATION ASSOCIATION IS THE ONLY ORGANIZATION THAT REPRESENTS OR HAS THE POSSIBILITY OF REPRESENTING THE GREAT BODY OF TEACHERS IN THE UNITED STATES.

Reproduced by permission of the NEA.

FIGURE 2.

association is allowed one delegate for each 100 NEA members, or major fraction thereof; each state and territorial association may elect one delegate for each 100 NEA members, or major fraction thereof, up to 500 members. Hence, one delegate is allowed for each 500 NEA members.

The officers, board of directors, and board of trustees are elected by the delegates to the representative assembly. The functions of the assembly, which meets annually, are to determine policies of the Association, receive and approve the budget, create new committees and commissions as necessary, adopt resolutions, and receive reports of the various committees and commissions.

The executive secretary is the chief administrative officer. He is a national professional leader.

In performing its functions as a comprehensive professional organization, the NEA is the world's largest publisher of educational materials, carries on extensive research in and study of problems in education, and sponsors action programs in terms of legislation at the national level. It also leads in many programs for the improvement of education on all levels.

The NEA also publishes *The NEA Journal* monthly during the school year. The Journal is an outstanding publication for educators. Students preparing to teach will find in it many challenging ideas and worthwhile materials of practical use to them in the classroom.

NEA Research Bulletins are published quarterly. Research Reports are prepared and issued by the research division of the NEA. The Bulletins and Reports contain the latest available information on professional matters such as salaries, tenure, certification, legislation and related areas.

One of the most significant activities of the NEA in moving toward full professionalization is that of the Commission on Teacher Education and Professional Standards, or TEPS. This commission was established by the NEA Representative Assembly in 1946. In addition to the national commission, there are now, through national TEPS initiation, similar groups in all of the states except one. The nature of the work of the national and state bodies can be described briefly in terms of the charge given to the national commission by the representative assembly in 1946 — to develop and carry forward "a continuing program for the profession in matters of recruitment, selection, preparation, certification, and advancement of professional standards, including standards for institutions which prepare teachers."[23]

---

[23]National Education Association, NEA Handbook, 1961-2, *op. cit.,* p. 90.

The basic idea back of this work is that a profession determines its own standards and enforces them in improving and maintaining high quality in membership and in education generally.

Through state, regional and national meetings, the commission has worked to promote high professional standards. In the past three years, national TEPS meetings have drawn together representatives of many learned societies and professional organizations for consultation and cooperative planning. In this period, a major project has been undertaken in the "New Horizons in Teacher Education and Professional Standards." From this work has come a significant publication entitled "New Horizons for the Teaching Profession" referred to earlier in this chapter. This report of a TEPS Task Force of 36 prominent educators directed by Professor Margaret Lindsey of Teachers College, Columbia University, offers guidelines for action toward professional maturity. All students preparing to teach should familiarize themselves with this volume. The principal recommendations include sweeping proposals for teacher preparation, certification and accreditation of teacher education institutions. The commission is now "developing a formal statement of policies, goals, and plans of action, in each of its several areas of responsibility."[24]

TEPS publishes quarterly *The Journal of Teacher Education*, the only national journal devoted exclusively to teacher education. Reports of each annual national conference are published as yearbooks. A Newsletter also is published to aid in coordinating the work of state and local TEPS committees.

The American Federation of Teachers.

Some teachers belong to another national organization, The American Federation of Teachers, or AFT. Affiliated with organized labor, the AFT was chartered by the American Federation of Labor in 1916. There are some 500 local and state affiliates of the American Federation of Labor-Congress of Industrial Organizations (AFL-CIO) and 70,821 members as of 1962.[25] An important exception is that a large group, The Teachers Union of New York City, is unaffiliated.

The AFT publishes a monthly journal during the school year, *The American Teacher*. Unlike the NEA, the AFT admits only public school teachers to membership. School administrators are not permitted to join.

The programs of AFT locals deal generally with security and welfare provisions for their members such as salaries, tenure, academic

---

[24]National Education Association — NEA Handbook, 1961-2, *op. cit.*, p. 91.
[25]Carl J. Megel, report by the president to the convention of the American Federation of Teachers, Detroit, Michigan, 1962. p. 44.

freedom, leaves of absence, teaching load, and the like. Many of the locals are quite militant, as witness the New York City Teachers' Union in its moves to gain higher salaries and other benefits. The AFT is currently working for the following goals:[26]

1. A single salary schedule based on training and experience, starting at $6,000 and reaching $14,000 in eight annual increments for every teacher at the Bachelor's level, and an additional spread up to $500 for training above the Bachelor's, to more nearly equal the incomes of other professions requiring comparable education and training;
2. State tenure laws to protect teachers from being discharged without proven cause, after reasonable probation;
3. Elimination of overcrowding in classrooms, excessive class interruptions, and use of students as teacher substitutes;
4. State laws for free and uninterrupted lunch periods;
5. Better teacher retirement pensions supplemented by social security where feasible;
6. Adequate, accumulative sick leave pay, hospitalization and medical insurance paid for from school funds; severance pay, and
7. Recognition of the rights of teachers everywhere to organize, negotiate, and bargain collectively.
8. The AFT opposes . . . . the merit rating system of pay.

Except for the lack of emphasis on quality of membership, the goals of the AFT are quite similar to those of most professional organizations in the stages before maturity.

Some fear that the profession's prestige will suffer if it is affiliated with labor. Others argue that labor organizations are an accepted fact in our nation, however, and labor union membership is not of itself an indication of a lack of professional status or social responsibility.

At times the NEA and the AFT disagree over ideas or methods of procedure. Sometimes there is actual controversy between the two concerning specific issues. It should be pointed out, however, that the conflict between the two is not one between individual teachers in the respective groups. It is, rather, a disagreement over values and procedures.

In any event, teachers should belong to and be active in one or more professional organizations. NEA membership, together with local and state affiliation, is strongly recommended. If a teacher finds that he believes in the objectives and procedures of teachers' unions, he should feel free to join.

---

[26]AFT. *Questions and Answers* about the *American Federation of Teachers,* Chicago: The AFT, 1962, p. 4.

Some teachers may be effective in both organizations. As stated before, the AFT does not admit administrators to membership. Teachers' unions seem to identify administrators and supervisors with management, and claim that there is conflict of interest between teachers and administrators. On the other hand, the NEA denies any such conflict and contends that teachers and administrators have a common cause.

In the final analysis, it would seem that an association's value should be judged only in terms of its ability to perform the responsibilities of the total profession. On this basis, it would seem that the NEA with its affiliated state and local associations can better serve the widespread interests and needs of the teaching profession.

The NEA undoubtedly has weaknesses. The fact that its basic charter as granted by Congress cannot be amended except by permission of Congress would seem to be a rather serious limitation. The large and rather unwieldly size of the representative assembly (now approximately 6,700) makes it very difficult for many individuals to participate actively in the business of governing the Association. The large size does however make it possible for more people to be involved, and thus add to the possibility of the Association's reaching more teachers over the nation.

The simple facts that the NEA now has over 859,000 members, has close relationship with the 50 state associations, has built up a remarkable service for teachers in publications, is active on the international front, and strongly supports a growing student membership in colleges and high schools would seem to suggest the probability that it offers teachers their best chance for a strong, unified and universal professional organization.

State and Local Associations.

State and local teachers' associations are very important because education is controlled largely by state and local political units. Such organizations should be strong so as to speak effectively for teachers and their interests.

Each of the 50 states has a teachers' association. Most of them are relatively strong and are well supported. Generally, over 90 per cent of the teaching force in a given state joins the respective state association. Latest available membership figures are shown in Table II.

You may note certain facts relating to state association membership. The states with largest memberships are California with 114,000 and Texas and New York[27] each with approximately 85,000. Sixteen other

---

[27]New York has more than 90,000 members currently (1962), some of whom are not active at present.

states have 100 per cent or more in membership[28] The states with the smallest memberships are Alaska with 1,580, and Nevada with 2,325 members.

The state associations vary in structure and services. They play a major role in state legislation affecting teachers and public schools, particularly in matters of finance. Each state association publishes a journal which is distributed to all members, carries on research, and performs services of many kinds for the membership. Among them are those concerning group term insurance, educational films, credit unions, legal counsel, recreational camps, and in some cases, homes for retired teachers.

Actually, the NEA can be said to be an outgrowth of state associations as eighteen were established before the NEA was founded in 1857.

All state associations have membership dues. These vary from a low of $4.00 annually in Missouri to a high of $84.00 in Puerto Rico.[29]

Local associations, of which there are more than 7,800 affiliated with the NEA, are really the foundation of teachers' professional organizations. They make effective the work of state and national associations. The local groups aid state and national associations with financial support and membership. They carry out at the grass roots level state and national programs and projects. There is little question that they are the backbone of state and national legislative campaigns. At present, many local associations affiliate with their state organizations and with the NEA.

In recent years, local associations have assumed additional roles. Some of them aid in recruiting young people to enter teacher preparation programs. Often, they are very helpful to new and beginning teachers in providing an orientation program for the local school system.

Local groups also aid various community projects and drives. The local association may be largely a social group. This may be a legitimate function, but it certainly should not be the only one. Stinnett[30] summarizes the aims of local groups as follows: "It can be said that local teachers' organizations have at least four objectives: (1) social, (2) better salaries and improved working conditions for teachers in the system, (3) service to school and community, and (4) general advancement of the profession."

[28]Some college staff and private school members, in addition to public school teachers, belong to the respective state associations. This makes for a plus 100 per cent in some cases.

[29]Source — NEA Handbook, 1961-62.

[30]A. J. Huggett, and F. M. Stinnett. *Professional Problems of Teachers.* New New York: The Macmillan Company, 1956, p. 341.

TABLE II

MEMBERSHIP — NEA, STATE ASSOCIATIONS AND ESTIMATED NUMBER OF INSTRUCTIONAL STAFF IN PUBLIC ELEMENTARY, SECONDARY SCHOOLS

	*Estimated No. of Instructional Staff in public Elem. and Sec. Schools (March 29, 1962)	**Membership in state Associations (May 31, 1961)	*Membership in NEA (May 10, 1962)
Alabama	28,700	28,541	18,938
Alaska	1,960	1,580	1,550
Arizona	12,866	9,847	10,919
Arkansas	15,075	16,390	9,304
California	131,900	114,000	69,554
Colorado	17,992	16,934	12,395
Connecticut	21,775	17,428	6,059
Delaware	3,878	3,390	1,830
District of Columbia	4,825	3,515	3,343
Florida	41,832	40,451	20,559
Georgia	34,995	34,247	23,457
Hawaii	5,500	4,661	4,571
Idaho	6,675	5,742	6,170
Illinois	78,120	61,200	36,764
Indiana	38,700	37,760	21,095
Iowa	28,369	28,544	21,030
Kansas	23,703	22,985	22,717
Kentucky	25,210	25,989	18,892
Louisiana	28,453	26,808	1,364
Maine	8,435	8,529	5,091
Maryland	25,230	19,590	16,479
Massachusetts	38,670	28,238	8,155
Michigan	69,576	52,365	24,837
Minnesota	30,800	25,608	13,059
Mississippi	19,200	19,091	3,547
Missouri	32,780	35,461	22,079
Montana	7,483	6,055	6,163
Nebraska	14,735	13,902	6,948
Nevada	2,984	2,325	2,506
New Hampshire	4,578	4,968	2,425
New Jersey	49,150	46,100	24,142
New Mexico	9,657	10,019	8,048
New York (except NYC)	86,728	85,000	23,354
New York City	45,872	–––––	1,168

TABLE II (Continued)

	Estimated No. of Instructional Staff in public Elem. and Sec. Schools (March 29, 1962)	**Membership in state Associations (May 31, 1961)*	*Membership in NEA (May 10, 1962)*
North Carolina	40,080	40,074	33,710
North Dakota	7,000	7,558	4,270
Ohio	78,204	71,234	45,720
Oklahoma	22,000	24,850	15,460
Oregon	18,078	16,075	17,112
Pennsylvania	83,390	70,345	55,338
Puerto Rico	15,395	16,165	3,385
Rhode Island	6,040	4,200	563
South Carolina	21,595	21,147	9,501
South Dakota	8,495	8,917	3,435
Tennessee	29,531	30,359	23,958
Texas	88,050	85,860	30,563
Utah	9,170	9,775	9,021
Vermont	3,361	3,283	1,580
Virginia	33,700	34,827	19,438
Washington	27,250	25,000	25,157
West Virginia	17,425	15,161	16,017
Wisconsin	30,500	30,773	12,312
Wyoming	3,988	4,362	3,621
Overseas Dep. Schools	5,891	3,612	2,369
Foreign and others	——	——	1,073
TOTAL (U.S.)	1,545,549	1,380,640	812,115***

*Source: NEA Membership Report — No. 13, April 9, 1962, and Special Report of May 10, 1962.
**Source: NEA Handbook — 1961-62, p. 315.
***815,000 as of September, 1962 and 859,000 as of June, 1963.

Currently, a major emphasis concerning teacher organizations is on unified local, state and national association membership, with the NEA national goal of "A Million or More by '64" in the forefront. We can be sure that local associations will need to play an important role. To those who believe in the value of a strong, united professional organization, it would seem that active membership in their local and state associations is highly desirable. The next step is to top this with membership in the NEA. "A Million or More by '64" teachers can be a strong force in upgrading their professional status and welfare.

Student National Education Association.

A significant movement in education is the establishment of the Student National Education Association. This organization, hereafter referred to as Student NEA, is an outgrowth of the Future Teachers of America, known familiarly as the FTA. The FTA movement was born in 1937 as a result of the work of Joy Elmer Morgan. At this time, FTA clubs were formed in both high schools and colleges. In 1955, the National Commission on Teacher Education and Professional Standards (NCTEPS) accepted responsibility for FTA and its development. In 1957, the representative assembly of the NEA established Student NEA, and at this time, the name FTA was given exclusively to chartered high school clubs. Student NEA is the name given to chartered college chapters. Since NCTEPS assumed the administration of the program, the growth of FTA high school clubs and Student NEA college chapters has been rapid. In 1955, there were 528 college chapters with about 25,000 members, and 2,441 high school FTA clubs with approximately 62,000 members. In 1961, there were 845 college chapters wtih a total membership of over 72,000 and 5,115 high school FTA clubs with total membership of over 163,000.[31]

The purposes of Student NEA are to aid students in gaining a better understanding of professional problems; to offer them opportunity to develop leadership skills and to demonstrate ability to participate with effectiveness as group members; to understand and follow a student professional code of ethics; and to have opportunity for personal and professional activities and for participation in professional activities at all levels.

Members also have the opportunity to learn the ethics, history, and program of the organized teaching profession, and particularly the professional standards movement and the New Horizons project. Active participation in Student NEA chapters is essential for students who wish to become teachers.

Student NEA college chapter members receive the *NEA Journal* and the official journal of their state association. In addition, each chapter receives through NCTEPS copies of the *Journal of Teacher Education,* the *TEPS Newsletter, NEA News,* and *Student NEA News* as well as other publications and materials. Each student NEA chapter has membership dues. These are largely nominal, with the major cost of the publications being provided by the parent organizations in the interest of early professional orientation of incoming members.

---

[31]Source: NEA Handbook, 1961-62, *op. cit.,* p. 93.

Other National Associations

There are many national associations for teachers. In addition to those described, the following are listed:

American Teachers Association — an organization of Negro teachers in Southern and Middle Atlantic states.

American Education Fellowship — the successor to the Progressive Education Association.

American Asssociation of University Professors — an association of professors in colleges and universities.

Pi Delta Kappa — a national honorary education fraternity for men.

Kappa Delta Pi — a national honorary fraternity for both men and women.

The Association for Childhood Education — International — or ACEI, as it is more familiarly known, can be called a special interest group in that its members are interested primarily in the growth and development of children from two to twelve. The official journal of ACEI is *Childhood Education,* an excellent magazine dealing with problems and articles on child growth, needs of children and teaching methods.

The National Council of Teachers of English or NCTE is another large special interest association. It is composed primarily of persons engaged in the teaching and supervision of English. It was founded in 1911 for the primary purpose of improving the quality of teaching of English at all school levels. It also encourages research and experimentation. The organization's governing body is the council composed of representatives of three sections — elementary, high school and college. Three monthly journals are published by NCTE. They are the *Elementary English Review,* the *English Journal,* and *College English.* NCTE holds an annual convention to conduct business and programs dealing with English teaching.

Through the years, the NCTE has sponsored a great deal of research and publication. A few examples are: *English: Past, Present and Future; Basic Issues in The Teaching of English,* and *Issues, Problems and Approaches in Teaching English.* NCTE also produces teaching aids such as recordings, films and filmstrips. The council sponsors achievement awards annually for excellence in writing in high schools. The executive office of NCTE is in Champaign, Illinois. You can secure information about this organization from your English professors.

There are many other large organizations primarily of the nature of special interest to teachers in their various fields. They are departments and commissions of NEA. Space does not permit discussion of these groups. Their names are indicated on the NEA Organization Chart on page 136. The student will find quite detailed discussions of these groups in the latest *NEA Handbook*.

You were referred earlier in the chapter (p.126) to codes of ethics. On the following pages, the two codes mentioned (the medical code and the NEA code for teachers) are reproduced for your study. Note similarities and differences. What is significant to you in each of the codes?

PRINCIPLES OF MEDICAL ETHICS[32]
OF THE AMERICAN MEDICAL ASSOCIATION

PREAMBLE. These principles are intended to aid physicians individually and collectively in maintaining a high level of ethical conduct. They are not laws but standards by which a physician may determine the propriety of his conduct in his relationship with patients, with colleagues, with members of allied professions, and with the public.

SECTION 1. The principal objective of the medical profession is to render service to humanity with full respect for the dignity of man. Physicians should merit the confidence of patients entrusted to their care, rendering to each a full measure of service and devotion.

SECTION 2. Physicians should strive continually to improve medical knowledge and skill, and should make available to their patients and colleagues the benefits of their professional attainments.

SECTION 3. A physician should practice a method of healing founded on a scientific basis; and he should not voluntarily associate professionally with anyone who violates this principle.

SECTION 4. The medical profession should safeguard the public and itself against physicians deficient in moral character or professional competence. Physicians should observe all laws, uphold the dignity and honor of the profession and accept its self-imposed disciplines. They should expose, without hesitation, illegal or unethical conduct of fellow members of the profession.

SECTION 5. A physician may choose whom he will serve. In an emergency, however, he should render service to the best of his ability. Having undertaken the care of a patient, he may not neglect him; and unless he has been discharged he may discontinue his services only after giving adequate notice. He should not solicit patients.

SECTION 6. A physician should not dispose of his services under terms or conditions which tend to interfere with or impair the free and complete exercise of his medical judgment and skill or tend to cause a deterioration of the quality of medical care.

SECTION 7. In the practice of medicine a physician should limit the source of his professional income to medical services actually rendered by him, or under his supervision, to his patients. His fee should be commensurate with the services rendered and the patient's ability to pay. He

---

[32]Published by the American Medical Association, 535 N. Dearborn Street, Chicago 10, Illinois. Reprinted by permission of AMA.

should neither pay nor receive a commission for referral of patients. Drugs, remedies or appliances may be dispensed or supplied by the physician provided it is in the best interests of the patient.

SECTION 8.   A physician should seek consultation upon request; in doubtful or difficult cases; or whenever it appears that the quality of medical service may be enhanced thereby.

SECTION 9. A physician may not reveal the confidence entrusted to him in the course of medical attendance, or the deficiencies he may observe in the character of patients, unless he is required to do so by law or unless it becomes necessary in order to protect the welfare of the individual or of the community.

SECTION 10. The honored ideals of the medical profession imply that the responsibilities of the physician extend not only to the individual, but also to society where these responsibilities deserve his interest and participation in activities which have the purpose of improving both the health and the well-being of the individual and the community.

CODE OF ETHICS[33]
OF THE NATIONAL EDUCATION ASSOCIATION
OF THE UNITED STATES

As a guide for the teaching profession, the members of the National Education Association have adopted this code of professional ethics. Since all teachers should be members of a united profession, the basic principles herein enumerated apply to all persons engaged in the professional aspects of education — elementary, secondary, and collegiate.

FIRST PRINCIPLE: The primary obligation of the teaching profession is to guide children, youth and adults in the pursuit of knowledge and skills, to prepare them in the ways of democracy, and to help them to become happy, useful, self-supporting citizens. The ultimate strength of the nation lies in the social responsibility, economic competence, and moral strength of the individual American.

In fulfilling the obligations of the first principle the teacher will —

1. Deal justly and impartially with students, regardless of their physical, mental, emotional, political, economic, social, racial, or religious characteristics.

2. Recognize the differences among students and seek to meet their individual needs.

3. Encourage students to formulate and work for high individual goals in the development of their physical, intellectual, creative, and spiritual endowments.

4. Aid students to develop an understanding and appreciation not only of the opportunities and benefits of American democracy but also of their obligation to it.

5. Respect the right of every student to have confidential information about himself withheld except when its release is to authorized agencies or is required by law.

6. Accept no remuneration for tutoring except in accordance with approved policies of the governing board.

---

[33]Adopted by the Representative Assembly of the NEA, Detroit, 1952. Reprinted by permission of the NEA.

SECOND PRINCIPLE: The members of the teaching profession share with parents the task of shaping each student's purposes and acts toward socially acceptable ends. The effectiveness of many methods of teaching is dependent upon cooperative relationships with the home.

In fulfilling the obligations of this second principle the teacher will —

1. Respect the basic responsibility of parents for their children.

2. Seek to establish friendly and cooperative relationships with the home.

3. Help to increase the student's confidence in his own home and avoid disparaging remarks which might undermine that confidence.

4. Provide parents with information that will serve the best interests of their children, and be discreet with information received from parents.

5. Keep parents informed about the progress of their children as interpreted in terms of the purposes of the school.

THIRD PRINCIPLE: The teaching profession occupies a position of public trust involving not only the individual teacher's personal conduct, but also the interaction of the school and the community. Education is most effective when these many relationships operate in a friendly, cooperative, and constructive manner.

In fulfilling the obligations of this third principle the teacher will —

1. Adhere to any reasonable pattern of behavior accepted by the community for professional persons.

2. Perform the duties of citizenship, and participate in community activities with due consideration for his obligations to his students, his family, and himself.

3. Discuss controversial issues from an objective point of view, thereby keeping his class free from partisan opinions.

4. Recognize that the public schools belong to the people of the community, encourage lay participation in shaping the purposes of the school, and strive to keep the public informed of the educational program which is being provided.

5. Respect the community in which he is employed and be loyal to the school system, community, state, and nation.

6. Work to improve education in the community and to strengthen the community's moral, spiritual, and intellectual life.

FOURTH PRINCIPLE: The members of the teaching profession have inescapable obligations with respect to employment. These obligations are nearly always shared employer-employee responsibilities based upon mutual respect and good faith.

In fulfilling the obligations of this fourth principle the teacher will —

1. Conduct professional business through the proper channels.

2. Refrain from discussing confidential and official information with unauthorized persons.

3. Apply for employment on the basis of competence only, and avoid asking for a specific position known to be filled by another teacher.

4. Seek employment in a professional manner, avoiding such practices as the indiscriminate distribution of applications.

5. Refuse to accept a position when the vacancy has been created through unprofessional activity or pending controversy over professional policy or the application of unjust personnel practices and procedures.

6. Adhere to the conditions of a contract until service thereunder has been performed, the contract has been terminated by mutual consent, or the contract has otherwise been legally terminated.

7. Give and expect due notice before a change of position is to be made.

8. Be fair in all recommendations that are given concerning the work of other teachers.

9. Accept no compensation from producers of instructional supplies when one's recommendations affect the local purchase or use of such teaching aids.

10. Engage in no gainful employment, outside of his contract, where the employment affects adversely his professional status or impairs his standing with students, associates, and the community.

11. Cooperate in the development of school policies and assume one's professional obligations thereby incurred.

12. Accept one's obligation to the employing board for maintaining a professional level of service.

FIFTH PRINCIPLE: The teaching profession is distinguished from many other occupations by the uniqueness and quality of the professional relationships among all teachers. Community support and respect are influenced by the standards of teachers and their attitudes toward teaching and other teachers.

In fulfilling the obligations of this fifth principle the teacher will —

1. Deal with other members of the profession in the same manner as he himself wishes to be treated.

2. Stand by other teachers who have acted on his behalf and at his request.

3. Speak constructively of other teachers, but report honestly to responsible persons in matters involving the welfare of students, the school system, and the profession.

4. Maintain active membership in professional organizations and, through participation, strive to attain the objectives that justify such organized groups.

5. Seek to make professional growth continuous by such procedures as study, research, travel, conferences, and attendance at professional meetings.

6. Make the teaching profession so attractive in ideals and practices that sincere and able young people will want to enter it.

* * *

It should be noted that NEA, through its Committee on Professional Ethics, has issued a new proposed draft of a basic code. This new draft was issued to members following the July, 1962, NEA Convention at Denver, with the request that local associations give high priority to its study in the fall of 1962. Criticisms, comments and suggestions for revision were requested. The new draft is not reproduced here because of space limitations; however, you can read the results of this effort in 1963 issues of the NEA JOURNAL.

TOPICS AND QUESTIONS FOR STUDY AND DISCUSSION

1. Try to formulate definitions of the following terms: profession, trade, code of ethics, association, professional standards, professional autonomy. Illustrate.
2. What similarities and differences do you find in your study of the illustrative codes of ethics reproduced in this chapter?
3. Find codes of other professional organizations and compare them with the NEA Code.
4. Should administrators be permitted to join teachers' professional organizations? Why?
5. Should membership in professional organizations be voluntary or required? Why?
6. Should teachers join a teachers' union affiliated with organized labor? Why?
7. Discuss the relative merits of teachers' professional organizations and teachers' unions.
8. Make a study of the National Commission on Teacher Education and Professional Standards. What is its major work?

SELECTED REFERENCES

Brown, K. R., "Indispensable Guides for the Profession," *California Teachers Association Journal,* 56:10-11 (April 1960).

Chamberlain, Leo M., and Leslie W. Kindred, *The Teacher and School Organization,* Englewood Cliffs, N. J.: Prentice-Hall, Inc., 3rd ed., 1958.

Chandler, B. J., *Education and the Teacher.* New York: Dodd, Mead and Company, 1961.

Corey, A. F., "Key to Professional Status: Higher Standards," *California Teachers' Association Journal,* 54:15, (April 1958).

Cressman, G. R., and H. W. Benda., *Public Education in America,* New York: Appleton-Century-Crofts, Inc., 2nd ed., 1961.

Drake, W. E., "Challenge of Professionalization," *School and Community.* 45:14-16, Sept. 1958.

Gregory, E. T., "Our Professional Responsibilities," *Kentucky School Journal,* 38:13 ff. (Feb. 1960).

Huggett, Albert J., and T. M. Stinnett, *Professional Problems of Teachers,* New York: The Macmillan Co., 1956.

Hughes, J. M., *Education in America,* Evanston, Ill., Row, Peterson and Co. 1960.

Kinney, L. B., and Walter E. McPhie, "Professional Autonomy in Education," *Journal of Teacher Education,* 10:285-90, (Sept. 1959).

Lieberman, Myron, *Education As a Profession.* Englewood Cliffs, N. J.: Prentice-Hall, Inc., 1956.

——. *The Future of Public Education.* Chicago: The University of Chicago Press, 1960.

Lindsey, Margaret. "New Horizons in Teacher Education and Professional Standards," *Wisconsin Journal of Education,* 92:7-11 (April 1960).

Murra, Wilbur F., "The First Century of the National Education Association," *School and Society,* LXXXV (May 11, 1957).

National Commission on Teacher Education and Professional Standards. *New Horizons for the Teaching Profession.* (Editor — Margaret Lindsey) Washington, D. C.: The National Education Association, 1961.

National Education Association. *NEA Handbook for Local, State and National Associations.* Washington, D. C.: The Association, 1961. (The handbook is published annually.)

National Society for the Study of Education. *Education for the Professions.* Chicago: The University of Chicago Press, 1962. (61st Yearbook of the Society, Part II.)

Stevenson, Margaret, "Improving the Educational Quality by Improving Conditions of Work," *NEA Journal,* (January 1960).

Stinnett, T. M., *The Teacher and Professional Organizations.* Washington, D. C.: National Education Association, 3rd ed., 1956.

———. "New Horizons in Teacher Education and Professional Standards," *Journal of Teacher Education,* 10:387-9 (December 1959).

Thomas, L. G., Lucien B. Kinney, A. P. Colardarci, and Helen A. Fielstra, *Perspective on Teaching, An Introduction to Public Education,* Englewood Cliffs, N. J.: Prentice-Hall, Inc., 1961.

Wynn, Richard, *Careers in Education,* New York: McGraw-Hill and Co., Inc., 1960.

Yeager, H. V., "Profession Anyone?" *Journal of Teacher Education,* 11:460-3 (Dec. 1960).

7 Chapter

Teachers' Salaries
And Related Factors

"A fair day's wages for a fair day's work."
Thomas Carlyle

There are many factors affecting teacher welfare and security. One of the most significant is salary. Teacher supply and demand also is of significance to teachers and the public as well. The purpose of this chapter is to present basic information and some interpretation of the foregoing matters.

The authors believe that students preparing to teach as well as teachers in service should be fully aware of all matters affecting their welfare. Such awareness should enable them to participate more effectively in the improvement of conditions affecting their status.

Teachers' Salaries and Economic Status

Most citizens in the United States realize that good education is critically important to the survival of democracy in the world and its improvement at home. But education has become an enormous, complex enterprise, and it costs more money than many people want to pay.[1] This statement from the New Horizons Report underscores a problem which is related closely to teachers' salaries. The economic status of teachers is highly significant to teachers themselves, to local districts and the nation. Good schools require good teachers, and quality in education as in anything else tends to be expensive.

[1]NEA, New Horizons for the Teaching Profession, *Ibid.*, p. 9.

Though teachers' salaries have risen steadily in recent years as pointed out in Chapter 6, page 126, and as shown in Tables IV and V following, the history of the profession has been one of almost constant struggle to lift the level of teacher status from that of mere subsistence. A current national average total instructional staff salary of $5,716 as reported in Chapter 6 may appear to be fairly adequate. When one considers the current rate of federal and state taxes and the average salaries of other professional groups, however, the salaries of teachers seem hardly adequate! Further, the gains in teachers' salaries of more than 185 per cent over the past three decades have been largely offset by the inflationary spiral of the same period.

When one considers the history of teachers' remuneration, he should not be too surprised at the present state of affairs! In New York, for example, a high-salary state, at about the mid-nineteenth century period, teachers' salaries were at a low point. According to one account,[2] the average salary for men was approximately $13.00 to $14.00 per month and for women approximately $6.00 to $7.00. These figures are exclusive of board which made up a large portion of the typical teachers' remuneration. Indeed, salaries were so low that men teachers quite often took other kinds of jobs during summers in which they could earn more money than teaching!

Some 34 years ago, when one of the authors began his teaching career in a little midwestern village, he received the sum of $60.00 per month. Countless others who have taught for twenty-five or more years can cite similar figures.

When viewed in the light of the foregoing, teachers' salaries of the present may seem more favorable than some think they are. Quite obviously, however, they are not high enough even now to attract the most capable and talented people, and they are not high enough to compete with other professional salaries. All studies of comparative salaries show that teachers' salaries are lower than those of most of the professions and lower than even some skilled trades.

Some Factors Influencing Teachers' Salaries

Many factors influence the salaries of teachers. Full delineation of this complex problem would require an exhaustive study. Within the scope of this chapter only a brief survey of some of the most significant

---

[2]L. F. Hodge, and D. Emma Wilbur Hodge, *A Century of Service to Public Education,* Albany: NYSTA, 1945, p. 39.

factors is possible. The student is referred to the references at the close of the chapter for more detailed study.

Supply of and demand for teachers is an important factor in determining rate of pay. There exists considerable opinion which holds that to a large degree the gains in teachers' salaries in recent years can be attributed to teacher shortages and the greatly increased school enrollments. There is little actual proof of this belief in terms of research; however, the familiar law of supply and demand would seem to work here with respect to teachers' salaries as well as with the cost of an item of merchandise.

Economic conditions in general also influence salaries of teachers. In prosperous periods such as that following World War I and the more recent period since 1939, teachers' salaries have tended to rise along with those of other groups. In periods of economic depression teachers' salaries tend to go down, but not as fast nor as far as workers in general. The salaries of other professional groups such as physicians, lawyers and dentists follow the same general pattern except that the level of income for these groups is much higher than that of teachers.

Table III reveals specific salary comparisons.

TABLE III

AVERAGE EARNINGS OF TEACHERS AND CERTAIN OTHER GROUPS
(Selected Years)

Year	°Teachers Calendar Year Est. Avg. Salary	All Persons working for wages or salaries	Employees in Manu-facturing	Civilian Employees of Fed. Gov't	Non-Salaried Professional Practitioners		
					Dentist	Lawyers	Physician
(1)	(2)	(3)	(4)	(5)	(6)	(7)	(8)
1929	$1,400	$1,405	$1,543	$1,933	$4,267	$5,534	$5,224
1934	1,235	1,091	1,153	1,717	2,391	4,218	3,382
1939	1,420	1,264	1,363	1,843	3,096	4,391	4,229
1943	1,640	1,951	2,349	2,628	5,715	5,945	8,370
1948	2,710	2,795	3,040	3,168	7,039	8,003	11,327
1953	3,645	3,587	4,049	4,226	8,500	9,392	15,000
1955	4,019	3,847	4,351	4,595	12,480	----	18,122
1956	4,221	4,036	4,584	4,808	----	----	----
1957	4,467	4,205	4,781	4,971	----	----	----
1958	4,781	4,346	4,939	5,514	14,311	----	20,000
1959	5,004	4,557	5,215	5,682	15,000	----	22,100
1960	5,240	4,705	5,342	5,946	----	----	----
1961	5,538	4,857	5,503	----	----	----	----

Source: (1) Columns 2, 3, 4, and 5. National Education Association, Research Division — "Economic Status of Teachers in 1961-62." Washington, D. C., The NEA May 1962, p. 21 (Table 7) adapted. (2) Columns 6, 7, and 8 — NEA Research Division — "Economic Status of Teachers in 1960-61." Washington, D. C. The NEA. March 1961, p. 41 (Table 3) adapted.

°"Teachers" refers to total instructional staff.

In addition, while the amount of salary you receive is significant, you must remember that the real worth of what you receive in salary is determined by what it will buy. An inflationary period will reduce the purchasing power of a dollar, as we have seen in recent years. In rural or non-city areas living costs are generally lower than in wealthy urban areas. A moderate salary in the low-cost area thus may represent more real money than a higher income in higher cost area. Such a factor may well play considerable part in your choice of a teaching position.

Here it should be pointed out that the authors consider it highly desirable that teachers be concerned or become more concerned — that is, intelligently concerned — with salary matters. The public has never been very clear as to where teachers should be placed on the economic scale. Are teachers to be considered as wage earners or as professionals, and paid accordingly? This question has never been answered very satisfactorily. The data presented in Table III showing the rather close relation between teachers' and all wage earners' salaries, and the great disparity between teachers' income and that of other professionals, points up the seriousness of this condition. It would seem that you as a teacher and your professional organizations have a public relations role to play in improving the public image of the teacher. As has been pointed out elsewhere in this book, professional organizations, particularly the NEA and affiliated state associations, have done much in recent years to improve teacher status, and continued efforts are anticipated as increasing numbers of teachers participate more actively in the associations' work.

Another factor affecting teachers' salaries is the relative conditions of preparation of teachers and other professionals. Historically, other professions, such as medicine and law, arrived at the status of high standards of preparation earlier than has the profession of teaching. Considerable disparity continues to exist The recent rise in standards of selection and preparation of teachers, however, sparked largely by teachers' professional associations, may help in making the public more aware of the importance of and strong need for highly qualified and well prepared teachers.

Teachers' salaries are also affected by factors such as the length of the school year and school day. Some people argue that since teachers work only nine or ten months of the year, and from "nine to three" daily for five days each week, and thus have time free for work at other jobs particularly in the summer, they do not deserve to be paid on the same scale as other professionals. Of course, this attitude overlooks or ignores several important aspects of the teacher's life and work. Teachers have to live the entire year on their nine or ten months of income. Many *do* work in summer months at local district recreational programs or on other types of school work. In some school systems, too, teachers are not permitted to hold part-time jobs at other kinds of work.

It is the considered judgment of the authors that teachers really do not have time for part-time work. The demands on them are such that with their teaching and the attendant study and preparation required if they are to do the most effective work, they must give full time to their regular jobs and should be rewarded accordingly in their incomes. It is quite common practice for teachers to participate in various kinds of community service which require time and energy. In addition, many teachers must spend their summer months in professional and academic study doing graduate work or renewing their certificates. Such attendance costs money which generally must come from their nine or ten months' income.

As to the so-called teaching day, all qualified and sincere teachers know that the teacher's work starts before pupils come to school and ends long after they are gone! Indeed, many evening hours are spent by teachers in preparing lessons, reading papers and other forms of pupil work, and in general study. Teachers, too, must have some time for recreation. The teaching profession will do well to inform the public of the many services and aspects of the work of teachers. Some of this information should be directed, of course, toward correcting public opinion relative to these matters.

Current Status of Teachers' Salaries

Tables III, IV, V, and VI all afford information from which you can gain some idea of current strengths and weaknesses as well as future possibilities in the salary picture for teachers. In consulting the tables, you are cautioned not to draw too many definite conclusions. It should be noted particularly that the "average" salary may conceal wide variations in actual salaries received. For example, while the "average" salary for a given state may be low as in Arkansas ($3,675 in 1961-62), in all probability there are many higher and many lower salaries paid in that state.

Some of the more significant facts regarding current salary levels are:

1. There has been a steady rise in teachers' salaries in recent years. As a matter of fact, they have been rising rather steadily since early in this century. Between 1953 and 1961, the average yearly increase has been $232.

TABLE IV

AVERAGE SALARY OF INSTRUCTIONAL STAFF IN PUBLIC SCHOOLS IN SELECTED YEARS AND RANK OF THE SEVERAL STATES — 1953-54; 1957-58; 1960-61

(1) State	Rank	(2) 1953-54	Rank	(3) 1957-58	Rank	(4) 1960-61
U. S. AVERAGE	—	$3,825	—	$4,702	—	$5,449
Alabama	44	2,783	40	3,489	39	4,300
Alaska	1°	5,016a/	1°	6,546a/	2°	7,000
Arizona	4	4,401	8	5,193	9	5,900
Arkansas	49	2,286	48	3,174	49	3,398
California	2	4,787	3	6,010	1	7,025
Colorado	26	3,640	26	4,457	23	5,300
Connecticut	7	4,275	5	5,382	4	6,177
Delaware	15	4,042	4	5,602	8	5,994
Florida	23	3,785	15	4,971	25	5,214
Georgia	41	2,862	37	3,692	42	4,200
Hawaii	9	4,172a/	25	4,522a/	18	5,540
Idaho	31	3,350	32	4,021	36	4,538
Illinois	5	4,353b/	9	5,132c/	6	6,109
Indiana	13	4,086	19	4,836	13	5,760
Iowa	39	2,897	41	3,482	32	4,721
Kansas	33	3,258	30	4,145	29	4,792
Kentucky	47	2,526	49	3,102	43	4,200
Louisiana	29	3,504	23	4,654	24	5,230
Maine	48	2,427	47	3,190	40	4,289
Maryland	11	4,148	14	4,989	10	5,880
Massachusetts	17	4,006	20	4,782	15	5,750
Michigan	18	3,999	6	5,319	5	6,125
Minnesota	25	3,687	22	4,655	21	5,425
Mississippi	50	1,864	50	2,698	50	3,561
Missouri	35	3,188	31	4,129	31	4,765
Montana	27	3,530	34	3,875	30	4,775
Nebraska	38	2,922	43	3,404	41	4,225
Nevada	22	3,786	11	5,080	11	5,866
New Hampshire	38	3,252	33	3,967	33	4,654
New Jersey	8	4,271	10	5,119d/	7	6,065
New Mexico	12	4,127	12	5,039	17	5,634
New York	3	4,658	2	6,071	3	6,800
N. Carolina	30	3,354	35	3,862e/	35	4,310
N. Dakota	45	2,659	44	3,365	45	4,100
Ohio	16	4,012	17	4,845	19	5,450
Oklahoma	32	3,271	29	4,196	28	4,904
Oregon	10	4,163	13	5,028	12	5,774
Pennsylvania	14	4,074	18	4,840	20	5,441
Rhode Island	20	3,881	16	4,935	16	5,700

TABLE IV (Continued)

(1) State	Rank	(2) 1953-54	Rank	(3) 1957-58	Rank	(4) 1960-61
S. Carolina	43	2,815	46	3,209	48	3,762
S. Dakota	46	2,638	45	3,238	47	3,850
Tennessee	40	2,875	42	3,471f/	44	4,137
Texas	19	3,886	24	4,527	34	4,621
Utah	24	3,746	21	4,732	28	5,100
Vermont	42	2,820	38	3,691	35	4,540
Virginia	36	3,082	36	3,829f/	37	4,520
Washington	6	4,334	7	5,199	14	5,750
W. Virginia	37	3,058	39	3,634	46	4,100
Wisconsin	21	3,840g/	27	4,454	22	5,330
Wyoming	28	3,512	28	4,302	27	5,185

Source: Columns 2 and 3 from U. S. Office of Education, U. S. Department of Health, Education and Welfare. Column 3 from estimates of the NEA Research Division. (Both as reported in NEA Research Memo 1962 -1, January, 1962.

*Alaska's average salary and rank are much lower in terms of the purchasing power of the dollar. According to NEA Research Division Reports, the higher living costs in Alaska require a reduction of about 25 per cent in all dollar amounts to make them roughly comparable with costs in the other states. Hence, on this basis, Alaska's "real" salary average ranks about twenty-third or twenty-fourth or approximately $5,250 for 1960-61.

a/ Not included in U. S. average
b/ Includes teachers in junior colleges
c/ Includes administrators
d/ Includes clerks
e/ Includes administrators except full-time superintendents
f/ Includes attendance personnel
g/ Excludes vocational schools

2. There is wide variation among the states in teachers' salaries. In 1961-62, thirteen states paid an average salary of $6,000 or above and thirty-three paid the average of $5,000 and above. This contrasts sharply with the year 1957-58, for example, when only three states paid $6,000 and above and thirteen paid $5,000 and above. On the other end of the salary scale, four states were below $4,000 in average salary paid and eighteen were below $5,000. A range in average salary of $7,000 or above as in Alaska, California and New York to below $4,000 as in South Dakota, South Carolina, Arkansas and Mississippi indicates a serious problem in education in general.

The reference is to the ability to pay for education. Studies[3] have shown clearly that the differences in revenue provided for the support

[3]For example — Johns, R. L. "Ability and Effort of the States to Support the Public Schools." NEA — Discussion of Legislation and Federal Relations — April, 1958.

of public education are due to ability (or lack of it) rather than from willingness. The inescapable fact is that variations in ability among the several states is so great that there is definite need for federal support for public education. Only the federal government can alleviate the inequalities which affect so greatly the lives of children and youth as well as teachers and the communities they serve.

3. Tables IV and V point to the fact that whatever the salary level is in a state, there is a general tendency for it to retain its rank or to remain near its rank from year to year. For example, New York has been second or third in average salary since 1953-54 while Mississippi and Arkansas at the other end of the salary scale rank forty-eighth to fiftieth. You can check other states to note this general tendency. In some cases you will note some variation, but this is hardly enough to invalidate the general conclusion.

4. While it is difficult to make direct comparisons of teachers' salaries with those of other professionals, it can be noted from Table III

TABLE V

ESTIMATED AVERAGE ANNUAL SALARIES OF TOTAL INSTRUCTIONAL STAFF 1961-62 (PRELIMINARY ESTIMATES)

Rank (1)	State (2)	Average Salary Instructional Staff (3)	Est. Average Salaries of Classroom Teachers		
			Elem. (4)	Secondary (5)	Total (6)
	U. S. (50 States & D. C.)	$5,716	$5,327	$5,800	$5,527
1	°Alaska (18th—$5,661)	7,650	7,200	7,550	7,300
2	California	7,325	6,600	7,375	7,025
3	New York	7,000	6,450	6,985	6,700
4	Connecticut	6,400	6,050	6,350	6,150
5	Michigan	6,362	6,065	6,300	6,162
6	Illinois	6,327	5,951	6,585	6,156
7	New Jersey	6,295	5,990	6,310	6,104
8	Maryland	6,180	5,900	6,000	5,940
9	Arizona	6,150	5,800	6,575	6,000
10	Delaware	6,125	5,750	6,150	5,950
11	Indiana	6,081	5,750	6,250	5,924
12	Washington	6,065	5,750	6,095	5,915
13	Nevada	6,000	5,768	6,157	5,900
14	Oregon	5,970	5,650	6,050	5,775
15	Massachusetts	5,900	5,625	5,975	5,775

TABLE V (Continued)

Rank (1)	State (2)	Average Salary Instructional Staff (3)	Est. Average Salaries of Classroom Teachers		
			Elem. (4)	Secondary (5)	Total (6)
16	Rhode Island	5,900	5,715	5,900	5,800
17	Ohio	5,800	5,288	5,845	5,530
18	New Mexico	5,765	5,500	5,790	5,650
19	Pennsylvania	5,639	5,433	5,545	5,470
20	Hawaii	5,575	5,405	5,465	5,430
21	Colorado	5,550	5,300	5,550	5,425
22	Minnesota	5,550	5,225	5,700	5,450
23	Wisconsin	5,540	5,010	5,850	5,400
24	Florida	5,497	5,250	5,375	5,303
25	Wyoming	5,425	5,110	5,550	5,252
26	Texas	5,300	5,125	5,330	5,205
27	Louisiana	5,260	4,910	5,350	5,075
28	Utah	5,217	5,000	5,100	5,006
29	Missouri	5,200	4,950	5,370	5,080
30	Oklahoma	5,100	4,930	4,980	4,950
31	North Carolina	5,087	4,820	4,998	4,877
32	Iowa	5,042	4,490	5,572	4,922
33	Kansas	5,036	4,628	5,197	4,872
34	Montana	4,900	4,490	5,360	4,760
35	New Hampshire	4,886	4,652	5,007	4,800
36	Vermont	4,715	4,400	4,975	4,625
37	Idaho	4,700	4,350	4,850	4,585
38	Virginia	4,700	4,450	4,700	4,550
39	Maine	4,600	4,250	4,850	4,450
40	Alabama	4,500	4,275	4,630	4,435
41	Georgia	4,450	4,250	4,550	4,325
42	West Virginia	4,450	4,050	4,700	4,325
43	Nebraska	4,375	3,750	4,950	4,160
44	North Dakota	4,300	3,800	4,850	4,150
45	Kentucky	4,250	3,985	4,400	4,125
46	Tennessee	4,050	3,863	4,298	4,013
47	South Dakota	3,900	3,550	4,650	3,850
48	South Carolina	3,850	3,650	3,925	3,760
49	Arkansas	3,675	3,441	3,820	3,614
50	Mississippi	3,675	3,390	3,830	3,560

Sources: (1) National Education Association — Research Division. "Ranking of the States, 1962" Washington. D. C. The NEA, January 1962. p. 25. Table 25. (2) National Education Association — "Teaching Career Fact Book." 1962, adapted from information on pages 21 to 25 and Table 8.

*Alaska's average salary and rank are much lower, in terms of purchasing power of the dollar, than is the case in the remaining 49 states. Hence, a figure of $5,661 and an approximate rank of 18 are more appropriate. This is computed by the NEA Research staff.

that dentists, lawyers and physicians earned in recent years from three to four times as much as teachers. Teachers' salaries compare very favorably, on the other hand, with all persons working for wages, employees in manufacturing, and civilian employees of the federal government. In fact, in 1961 the average teacher's salary was higher than the average for all employees receiving wages and for employees in manufacturing. One may seriously question, however, whether teachers' salaries are anywhere near a professional level!

5. There is a rather steady trend toward the establishment of state minimum salary laws. As of September, 1962, thirty-two states had minimum salary laws. Ten were in the $4,000 or better class with Alaska leading with $5,150. Sixteen were in the $3,000 to $3,800 class, with the remaining six having mandated beginning salaries of under $3,000. It is recognized that to be effective such laws must be raised frequently. There are at least ten states, however, that have not revised their salary laws for four or more years. Table VI reveals the general status with respect to state prescribed beginning salaries for teachers

TABLE VI

LEGAL STATE MINIMUM SALARIES FOR BEGINNING TEACHERS — 1962-63				
(1)	*(2)* Bachelor's	*(3)* Degree	*(4)* Master's	*(5)* Degree
State	*Minimum Salary*	*Increase over 1959-60*	*Minimum Salary*	*Increase over 1959-60*
*Alaska	$5,150[5]	$500	$5,500[5]	$700
**New York	4,500	500	4,800	500
California	4,500	500	4,500[3]	300
Massachusetts	4,500	900	4,500[3]	900
Delaware[1]	4,200	600	4,600	600
Washington	4,200	1,800	4,200[3]	1800
Texas	4,014	810	4,239	810
Illinois	4,000	600	4,200	600
Rhode Island	4,000	800	4,000[3]	800
Wisconsin	4,000	——	4,000[3]	——
New Jersey	3,800	——	4,000	——
Ohio	3,800	100	4,200	100
Oregon	3,700	——	4,000	——

TABLE VI (Continued)

(1) State	(2) Bachelor's Minimum Salary	(3) Degree Increase over 1959-60		(4) Master's Minimum Salary	(5) Degree Increase over 1959-60
North Carolina	3,607	661		4,079	739
Indiana	3,600	---		3,800	---
Kentucky	3,600	990		3,870	990
Maryland	3,600	400		3,600[3]	400
Oklahoma	3,600	---		3,800	---
Pennsylvania	3,600	---		3,600[3]	---
Georgia	3,600	600		3,900	600
Louisiana	3,400	---		3,600	---
Vermont	3,400	---		3,700	---
Virginia[1]	3,400	750		3,400[3]	750
Florida	3,240	180		3,645	180
West Virginia	3,135	345		3,420	360
Maine	3,000	---		3,200	---
Mississippi	2,900	250		3,175	300
Tennessee[4]	2,850	200		3,120	200
Arkansas	2,700	---		3,000	---
Idaho	2,370	---		2,570	---
South Carolina					
Lowest grade	1,485	378	(lowest)	2,889	621
Highest grade	2,988	---	(highest)	3,366	---
Iowa[2]	810[2]	---		810[2]	---

Sources: NEA Research Report, 1962-R12, "State Minimum-Salary Laws and Goal Schedules for Teachers, 1962-63." (Cols. 1, 2, and 4). NEA Research Bulletin, Vol. 40, No. 1, Feb., 1962 (Cols. 3 and 5).

*Alaska's dollar value is computed as worth about 74 cents (NEA Research Division) as compared with prices in large cities in the other states. On this basis, a salary of $5,150 would be about $3,811 and $5,500 would be about $4,070.

**In New York State in schools with fewer than eight teachers, the minimum is a flat rate amount of $4,500.

[1]Adopted salary schedule not fully in effect in 1962-63.

[2]Law currently obsolete; all salaries higher than stated minimum.

[3]No separate minimum for master's degree (flat rate).

[4]Schedule applies to certificated teachers only.

[5]Alaska has separate minimum schedules by districts; $5,150 and $5,500 apply to the Southeastern Senate District; in the South Central Senate District, the respective minimum salaries are $5,550 and $5,900; in the Central and Northwest Senate Districts, the salaries are $5,850 and $6,200 respectively.

as of 1962. You will note that at least twenty states enacted laws in 1961-62 raising the beginning levels of 1959-60 by amounts ranging from $100 to $1,800 with an average raise for the twenty of approximately $500.

6. A consideration of more importance than "average" salary is that of the number of teachers receiving salaries at or near low levels and at or near the higher levels. The NEA reports[4] that for 1961-62, 6.4 per cent of the nation's teachers received salaries of below $3,500 and only 8.6 per cent received salaries of $7,500 or more. In the same year there were 18 states, chiefly in the northeast, middle Atlantic and western areas, that had no teachers receiving less than $3,500, and fifteen of these states had relatively small percentages of teachers who received salaries below $4,500. In Alaska and California no teacher received less than $4,500 and only 2 per cent in New York were in the "below $4,500" class.

At the lower end of the scale, in seven all rural and southern states, one third or more of the teachers received less than $3,500. In Arkansas and Mississippi 55 and 56 per cent respectively of their teachers received salaries of below $3,500, and in the two states combined only 2 per cent of their teachers received more than $5,500. None were in the $6,500 and above class!

7. Over the years teachers' salaries have been higher in urban areas than in smaller districts. This is still true, but the margin of difference

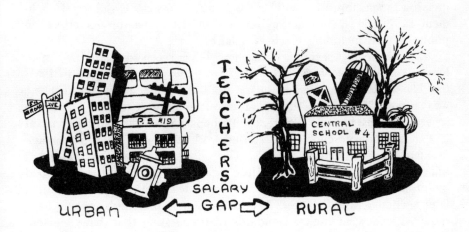

---

[4]NEA, *Teaching Career Fact Book*, Washington, D. C., The NEA, 1962, p. 22.

has lessened. The variation in favor of urban areas is due to a number of factors. The valuation of urban areas for tax purposes usually has been large enough to enable the authorities to raise money for school purposes without undue pressure on the people. Rural areas, in many cases, have not had adequate tax resources for school purposes. Urban area teachers have been able, through stronger organization than is possible in rural areas, to present their case to the public. They have been able to keep the urban population better informed generally on school needs. A serious problem resulting from the salary level variation has been that of higher turnover in rural areas as teachers migrate to larger centers.

The NEA and state associations have been concerned, as have state education authorities, over the problem of providing equal educational opportunities to all children and youth, rural as well as urban.

Fortunately, the gap in teachers' salaries between urban and rural areas has been closing. NEA Research Division studies show this trend. It can be summarized as follows:

> From the earliest salary studies of the NEA Research Division in 1923, salaries have been substantially higher in the large districts than in the small ones. However, just as rural and urban are coming closer together, so are salaries in the larger and smaller urban school districts. Also the differences among the larger districts are lessening.[5]

In addition, in the last few years large metropolitan areas have faced growing financial problems. This has resulted, in some cases, in retrenchment in public spending. Such retrenchment is having its effect on public schools including teachers' salaries.

8. Historically, secondary teachers have received more pay than have elementary teachers. Table V reflects this difference even in 1961-62. The nationwide average salary in 1961-62 for secondary teachers was almost $500 more than that of elementary teachers. There are several reasons for this difference. Perhaps one of the most important is that secondary schools are staffed with a much larger percentage of men than elementary schools. The public has always paid higher salaries to men than women. Here again, the profession has helped by promoting the single salary schedule idea. This is discussed in a later section of this chapter. Another reason is that high schools have required somewhat higher standards of preparation than have elementary. This difference is rapidly decreasing, as elementary certification standards have risen, particularly since about 1947. It is in this period

---

[5]NEA Research Division. Research Bulletin, Vol. 37, No. 3, October 1959, p. 69.

that the NEA through its TEPS Commission and state associations have placed increasing emphasis on higher standards.

Another reason of decreasing importance, fortunately, has been an attitude on the part of teachers themselves that to move from teaching in elementary school up the ladder to teaching in junior high and high school represented "promotion." If elementary teachers attached no great importance to their positions they hardly could have expected the public to hold a different view!

Salary Schedules

Historically, teachers' salaries were determined largely by a kind of bargaining between boards of education or trustee and the prospective teacher. This has never been very satisfactory. Such practices as "undercutting" on salaries, favoritism and the like eventually brought on a rising tide of opinion for a more suitable way of determining salaries. As a result there came the gradual development of a more orderly method known as the single salary schedule, beginning about the close of World War I. Such a plan has now become a generally accepted practice. The definite salary schedule idea has developed for a number of reasons such as to overcome the abuses of earlier practices; to improve teacher morale, and to give the teacher a definite idea as to what he can expect in salary over the years.

Single salary schedules are advantageous also to boards of education and school administrations in that they simplify some of the complex problems of budgeting. Boards know by means of definite salary schedules what they can anticipate in expenditures, what they need to raise in taxes, and how they can plan ahead.

The Research Division of the NEA regularly prepares many significant studies on the status of teachers including teachers' salaries, salary schedules, merit pay, and the like. If you wish to be informed on current status of salaries and salary schedules and their development, you should consult these studies, many of which have been referred to in this chapter. From them we learn that salary schedules for teachers are now in operation in most school systems throughout the nation. By the early 1950's, more than 97 per cent of school districts using the schedule idea had adopted the single salary schedule principle, and by 1957 the NEA reported it was used almost universally in urban school districts throughout the United States.[6]

---

[6]NEA Research Division, "Salaries and Salary Schedules of Urban School Employees — 1956-57" Bulletin No. 35, 2, April 1957, p. 68.

The salary schdeule plan most widely used, then, is the single salary type. It is based on the two factors of preparation and experience without regard for race, sex, teaching level, marital status, number of dependents or any other limiting factor.

It usually contains from two to four columns and twelve or thirteen steps. The columns represent preparation levels, the steps experience levels. Preparation levels are generally the bachelor's degree, the master's degree and/or thirty semester hours of credit above the bachelor's degree, the sixth year and the Ph.D. or Ed.D. The steps, also indicating increments, are for experience, as one year, two years, and the like. They also contain minimums, maximums, and increments for each of the preparation classes.

Illustrations of the single salary type are given in the sample schedules in Figures 3, 4, and 5. All samples indicate classifications determined by preparation levels. In all cases, too, yearly increments are given from a minimum to a maximum amount. They differ slightly in number, but all are in the range of from eleven to fourteen in the bachelor's degree class.

The sample in Figure 3 is fairly typical of New York State in 1962. It indicates uneven yearly increments with the largest coming in the ninth to twelfth year of service.

Salary Steps Increment by Years		Bachelor's Degree	Bachelor's + 30 s.h.	Bachelor's + 60 s.h.	Master's Degree	Master's + 30 s.h.	Doctor's Degree
1	(beginning)	$4,800	$5,100	$5,400	$5,200	$5,500	$5,800
2	($200)	5,000	5,300	5,600	5,400	5,700	6,000
3	($200)	5,200	5,500	5,800	5,600	5,900	6,200
4	($210)	5,410	5,710	6,010	5,810	6,110	6,410
5	($220)	5,630	5,930	6,230	6,030	6,330	6,630
6	($220)	5,850	6,150	6,450	6,250	6,550	6,850
7	($230)	6,080	6,380	6,680	6,480	6,780	7,080
8	($240)	6,320	6,620	6,920	6,720	7,020	7,320
9	($260)	6,580	6,880	7,180	6,980	7,280	7,580
10	($260)	6,840	7,140	7,440	7,240	7,540	7,840
11	($270)	7,110	7,410	7,710	7,510	7,810	8,110
12	($280)	7,390	7,690	7,990	7,790	8,090	8,390

Note: In the Bachelor's degree class — plus $60.00 for each additional 6 semester hours earned to a total of 30 semester hours. In the Bachelor's +30 and the Master's degree classes — plus $100 for each additional 10 semester hours earned to a total of 30 semester hours in each case.

Salary Schedule for 1962-1963

FIGURE 3. "Up-State" New York

Salary Steps Increment by Years	Bachelor's Degree	Bachelor's + 30 s.h.	Master's Degree	Master's + 30 s.h.	Doctor's Degree
1	$5,100	$5,400	$5,500	$5,700	$5,900
2 ($200)	5,300	5,600	5,700	5,900	6,100
3 ($300)	5,600	5,900	6,000	6,200	6,400
4 ($400)	6,000	6,300	6,400	6,600	6,800
5 ($300)	6,300	6,600	6,700	6,900	7,100
6 ($300)	6,600	6,900	7,000	7,200	7,400
7 ($200)	6,800	7,100	7,200	7,400	7,600
8 ($200)	7,000	7,300	7,400	7,600	7,800
9 ($200)	7,200	7,500	7,600	7,800	8,000
10 ($200)	7,400	7,700	7,800	8,000	8,200
11 ($200)	7,600	7,900	8,000	8,200	8,400
12 ($400)	8,000	8,300	8,400	8,600	8,800
13 ($200)	8,200	8,500	8,600	8,800	9,000
14 ($200)	8,400	8,700	8,800	9,000	9,200
15 ($400)	8,800	9,100	9,200	9,400	9,600
16		(300) 9,400	(300) 9,500	(300) 9,700	(300) 9,900
17		(300) 9,700	(400) 9,900	(400) 10,100	(400) 10,300
18					(400) 10,700

Note: In the Bachelor's class — plus $100 for additional 6 semester hours; In Bachelor's + 30 class — plus $200 for additional 6 semester hours.

Salary Schedule for 1962-63

FIGURE 4. "Down-State" New York

The principle of providing increments of sufficient amount to double the beginning salary is violated in the sample. Such is the case in many schedules in operation today.

Figure 4 illustrates a single salary schedule, somewhat rarer than that shown as Figure 3, but fairly typical of richer districts. You will note that increments in this case are not uniform except for the "plateau" of the seventh through eleventh year. The highest increment ($400) comes at the fourth, twelfth and fifteenth years in the bachelor's class. In this sample, the beginning salary at the "bachelor's degree" level is doubled in the "doctor's degree" class in the seventeenth year. It is almost doubled in the seventeenth year of the "master's degree plus 30 semester hours" class.

Figure 5 illustrates a schedule with a beginning minimum at the level recommended by the NEA, with uniform increments throughout of 7 per cent of the beginning base; master's degree and sixth year salaries are 10 per cent higher than the preceding level. The doctor's

Salary Step	Bachelor's Degree	Master's Degree	Sixth Year MA + 30	Doctor's Degree
1	$ 6,000	$ 6,000	$ 7,200	$ 8,100
2	6,420	7,020	7,620	8,520
3	6,840	7,440	8,040	8,940
4	7,260	7,860	8,460	9,360
5	7,680	8,280	8,880	9,780
6	8,100	8,700	9,300	10,200
7	8,520	9,120	9,720	10,620
8	8,940	9,540	10,140	11,040
9	9,360	9,960	10,560	11,460
10	9,780	10,380	10,980	11,880
11	10,200	10,800	11,400	12,300
12	10,620	11,220	11,820	12,720
13	11,040	11,640	12,240	13,140
14		12,060	12,660	13,560
15				13,980

Note: All increments are uniform, figured at 7 per cent of the bachelor's degree minimum. Master's degree and sixth year schedules are 10 per cent above base for each additional year of preparation. The doctor's degree is 15 per cent above the sixth year base.

Single Salary Schedule 1962-63

FIGURE 5. "Hypothetical" USA Salary Schedule

degree level is 15 per cent higher than the preceding class. In addition, the basic starting salary is doubled in each of the three higher preparation classes — in the fourteenth year in the master's degree and sixth year classes, and in the eleventh year in the doctor's degree class. The uniform increments and the specific percentages of difference between the classes are typical of what is called an Index Salary Schedule plan, which is briefly described later in this chapter.

The specific features of salary schedules vary from state to state and even within the same state. Some schedules are quite weak and show very little imagination. Others are quite strong. What are the basic factors you should consider with reference to salary schedules? You certainly will desire an adequate beginning salary. Consider the maximum salary. Does it go high enough to double the basic salary? How long will it take you to reach the maximum salary? What differences are there between the preparation levels? Are they sufficiently large in amount to warrant the extra expense involved in earning additional credits? Finally, how much can you earn in your professional career or lifetime under the schedule? Since salary schedule details may vary in some degree from school to school, you should attempt to find answers to such questions.

Some schedules award higher increments in the early years, leveling off with smaller amounts in the later years. Others give uniform increments throughout from minimum to maximum. Some begin with relatively small increments in the early years and gradually build up to larger amounts in the later years. Still others award relatively small increments in the probationary period with a larger increment accompanying the first year of tenure. Thereafter, the increments may be uniform or may gradually build to slightly higher amounts as the maximum is reached. Others may follow any one of the patterns indicated and grant "superior service" increments above the normal maximum. In addition, many school systems have policies which provide that an increment may be withheld in any year in which service is in some way unsatisfactory. Regardless of the specific plan or policy concerning salary scheduling, all aspects should be thoroughly explained to all staff members.

You are encouraged to study the various patterns mentioned. Each represents a philosophy of the school system which adopts it. Large increments in the beginning years assume that the greatest growth occurs early in the teacher's career. This pattern likely will result in larger total lifetime or minimum to maximum earnings. Uniform increments are an expression of the idea that growth takes place gradually and uniformly. Small increments in the early years with large amounts in the years near the maximum assume that experience is the factor of most importance or that a teacher is worth more as he acquires years of experience.

Small increments in the probationary period indicate that the district believes the teacher must prove himself. With tenure gained, the greatly increased amount rewards effective service.

The "superior service" extra increment idea is a form of paying salaries on a merit basis, as determined by the administration or the administration and staff. It recognizes that teachers differ in their effectiveness and service and should be paid accordingly.

As you begin your career, or if you have had several years of experience, you should be aware of the various patterns of salary scheduling. It may help you in making decisions regarding the school system seeking to employ you or that you may wish to enter.

There are some supplemental features to or variations from the straight "preparation-experience" single salary schedule plan.

A few schedules provide extra increments for teachers with dependents. Some pay men more than women, though this practice is steadily diminishing. A variation that appears to be growing is that of paying additional amounts for work outside the regular classroom assignment. A football coach, for example, who also teaches classes regularly, may be paid an extra amount for coaching. Added payments are made in similar fashion for other so-called "extra" duties. If such a plan is cooperatively developed by the whole staff it has some merit. It is used in a number of school systems.

SOME SCHOOL SYSTEMS GIVE SALARY CREDIT FOR MILITARY SERVICE

Some school systems give credit for military service in the form of an extra increment or amount. Supplementary amounts are given in some school systems because of increases in the cost of living. Occasionally this award is given as a bonus.

There are still a few examples of the "position" type of schedule. This was more popular until the general acceptance of the single salary schedule. In this plan, the board of education or chief administrator decides what each position is worth in relation to others and pays accordingly. Still current is the idea that the positions of superintendent, principal, supervisor and other specialists are worth more than classroom teacher positions and are paid higher salaries accordingly.

With the wide acceptance of the single-salary schedule, particularly in recent years, classroom teachers' salaries have risen at a faster pace than administrators' salaries. In general, the trend appears to be toward reducing the differences in salaries paid for "positions." Obviously, there are many exceptions to this. Large urban school systems pay relatively much higher salaries to chief administrators than to teachers. Perhaps a main problem caused by this great disparity between administrative and teacher salaries is that it weakens the motivation toward *teaching* as a career.

Another variation which seems to be developing in recent years is that of granting extra increments for extended service beyond the normal maximum salary in the various classes of a district's salary schedule. This recognizes the career teacher, and, of course, rewards those who remain in service in the district.

In discussing the salary schedule depicted in Figure 3, reference was made to some aspects of its similarity to the index salary schedule.

According to the NEA Research Division,[7] for more than a decade many school districts have been using indexes or ratios to determine amounts for administrators and supervisors beyond the teachers' schedule. More recently a small but growing number of districts have been using the index idea for teachers' salary schedules.

The index or ratio schedule ordinarily uses the bachelor's degree on first classification in the first year as the base of 100.0 or 1.0. The index schedule is thought to be desirable in that it seeks to set up appropriate salary step relationships before dollar amounts are adopted and to establish relationships which remain constant if dollar amounts change. In this plan, if the base is raised, all increments increase and the relative differences are maintained throughout the schedule. It can be easily revised, and the relationship between increments and classes can be ascertained quickly.

According to the NEA Research Division[8] four state education associations (Arizona, Connecticut, Minnesota and Wyoming) expressed their goal schedules for teachers in terms of indexes or ratios in 1961. According to the same report, many variations of the index schedule plan exist; however, all plans use the bachelor's degree with no experience class as the base (100.0 or 1.0).

Since school district use of the index or ratio schedule technique appears to be growing, it may be worthwhile for you to study it carefully. You can start by consulting the reference cited in footnote 7.

The NEA and state associations for years have vigorously promoted the idea and practice of the single salary schedule. At the same time they have even more vigorously pressed for higher salaries.

Since the 1958 meeting of the NEA Representative Assembly, the profession, as represented by NEA, has recommended a $6,000 minimum salary for beginning qualified teachers with a range to $13,000 and higher on the basis of certain principles as they have been developed through the years.

The most recent statement of such principles by the NEA is contained in the Resolutions of the Representative Assembly held at

---

[7]NEA Research Division — "Research Bulletin," Vol. 39, No. 4, Dec. 1961, pp. 108-112.

[8]*Ibid.*, p. 109.

Denver, Colorado, in July, 1962. The following statement is from Resolution #6.[9]

> A professional salary schedule should —
> a. Be based upon preparation, teaching experience, and professional growth.
> b. Provide a beginning salary adequate to attract capable young people into the profession.
> c. Include increments sufficient to double the beginning salary, followed by continuing salary advances.
> d. Be developed cooperatively by school board members, administrators and teachers.
> e. Permit no discrimination as to grade or subject taught, residence, creed, race, sex, marital status, or number of dependents.
> f. Recognize experience and advanced education, through the doctor's degree.
> g. Recognize by appropriate salary ratios, the responsibilities of administrators and other school personnel.
> h. Be applied in actual practice.
>
> The Association believes that it is extremely important that teachers' salaries compare favorably with incomes of persons in other professions and in industry.

The Resolution goes on to point up the importance of raising beginning salaries for teachers to meet the competition for the services of the most able young college people. It also recommends that salary increments recognizing successful teaching experience should be adjusted to any increases in beginning salaries. Finally, it repeats the recommendation made for the last five years of a beginning salary of at least $6,000 ranging to $13,000 and above.

The principles are quite well known by professional educators. Not all are fully implemented in practice. In fact, many salary schedule ranges from minimums to maximums do not provide large enough increments to double the beginning salary. With a trend toward higher beginning salaries and more adequate schedules, however, this problem may be solved eventually.

One item of particular importance is teacher participation in salary scheduling. Since teachers are most directly affected by salary policy, it would seem that they should have a share in policy making. Over the years there has been considerable public opposition to teachers taking part in salary making. Some exists presently but there is a trend toward their participation. Much credit for this trend is due their professional associations. As the professional standards movement moves

---

[9]NEA Handbook for 1962, pp. 6-7.

to maturity, it offers much promise in this and other areas of teacher interest. One of the NEA priorities adopted at its Denver Convention in July, 1962, was that of professional negotiation. It called for the establishment of "formal procedures by which professional organizations and governing agencies can reach agreement on conditions of work including salaries; and to provide for appeal through educational channels."[10]

The growth in teacher participation in salary scheduling demands growth in teacher understanding of financial problems. Teachers should be aware of the finances of school districts including such things as tax rates, school budgets and general operating costs. A good understanding of basic economics is essential if teachers are to participate intelligently in salary negotiations. Professional associations can be of much help in such matters in supplying information and personal service.

Merit Rating

The single salary schedule is strongly backed by the professional associations, as pointed out previously. It is in wide use throughout the nation as reported by the Research Division of the NEA. It has merit in that it eliminates discrimination against women teachers and between elementary and secondary teachers and is relatively easy to administer, but it does not settle all aspects of the salary problem.

Scarcely anyone will insist that all teachers are alike in their efficiency and effectiveness. Although essential, preparation and experience are not necessarily measures of merit. Despite such facts, merit rating in determining salaries of teachers, or recognizing superior service of teachers and paying accordingly, has been a controversial subject for most of the twentieth century.

With perhaps a few exceptions, most of the demands for recognition of superior service has come from the public rather than the profession. School board members and many other segments of the public have from time to time urged the adoption of merit features in salary schedules. Recently the report of the President's Commission on National Goals stated that merit pay should be universally adopted with adequate safeguards to insure fair treatment.

In theory, the idea of recognition of superior service of teachers sounds entirely reasonable, and many pages have been written and more words have been spoken in support of the idea. At the same time, there are perhaps a like number of pages and words pointing out how

---

[10]NEA Handbook, *Ibid.,* p. 70.

difficult it is to put merit rating for determining teachers' pay into actual practice. There are also many reports from teachers and professional associations indicating that merit rating for determining salaries is unsatisfactory and undesirable.

What is the current situation regarding merit pay? It is difficult to determine, but the following may shed some light.

It should be noted that at least two states adopted laws requiring state-wide plans of merit pay only to repeal them after a few years of use. Delaware adopted the plan in the 1930's and dropped it in 1947. New York established its plan in 1947 and repealed it in 1955. In both cases there arose widespread dissatisfaction with the ratings and general administration of the plans. Teachers and administrators opposed the plans. As opposition grew, the professional associations joined in securing repeal.

Another state, Florida, has recently enacted a plan of merit pay on a state-wide basis. The plan was made effective in 1960-61. In 1961, the Florida Education Association called for the plan to be made optional rather than mandatory with the school districts.[11]

The Research Division of the NEA has carried on studies of the status of merit pay provisions in teachers' salary schedules for the last twenty-five years.

In 1938-39, a study of schedules received from 225 districts of 30,000 or more population revealed that 20.4 per cent included a superior service maximum. In 1958-59, a study based on schedules from 539 school districts in the 30,000 or more class showed only 6.2 per cent included provisions for rewarding superior service.[12]

Chief reasons for abandoning the merit-pay plan appear to be unsatisfactory evaluations, the creation of dissensions, low morale, poor administration of the plan, and opposition of teachers' organizations.[13] While this representation is not large enough to enable one to identify definite trends, it would appear that many school districts are moving away from merit rating in teachers' salary schedules. Further, many school systems that have adopted such schedules do not actually operate them.

It should be understood here that rating of teachers may have several purposes. One, of course, is that of providing a base for salary. Another, perhaps of as much or more importance, is that of evaluation of teacher

---

[11]NEA Research Bulletin, Vol. 39, No. 2, May 1961, p. 63, Washington, D. C. The NEA, 1961.

[12]*Ibid.*, p. 61.

[13]*Ibid.*, p. 62.

performance for the purpose of improving instruction. On this latter point, the NEA has several times taken the position that the teaching profession has a responsibility for evaluating the quality of its services. One of the most recent statements was that made by the Department of Classroom Teachers of the NEA in a report of the Teachers' Salary Committee.[14] Continued research was called for to discover methods of objective evaluation of teaching performance for the purpose of improving instruction.

Teachers have been rated also for reappointment in the probationary period of service and to determine whether to grant tenure status. You will doubtless find other purposes and uses for rating if you will search the literature.

In this chapter, the primary concern is with merit rating as a means of paying teachers' salaries. As pointed out, it is a highly controversial subject. Teachers and professional associations generally oppose merit rating for salary schedules even though they may support the principle of merit rating or evaluation for improving instruction and other aspects. The public appears to prefer, and at times has demanded, that "good" teachers be rewarded and "poor" teachers be paid less or eliminated. What are the reasons for teacher opposition and, on the other hand, general public acceptance?

Research reports on merit rating and the literature generally[15] indicate that some of the chief reasons for teacher opposition are:

1. There are no reliable instruments or means of evaluating teacher performance for salary purposes. There is little agreement on what constitutes merit.
2. Merit rating for salary purposes tends to create dissension, cause worry and discouragement and lower teacher morale.
3. Merit rating is inconsistent with the nature of the work of the teacher. Teaching is essentially cooperative rather than competitive.
4. Merit rating introduces "politics" and "apple polishing."
5. Too many who do the rating are unable to do it objectively.
6. Too many plans for merit schedules have been poorly administered.
7. Merit rating hinders the proper relationship between administrators and supervisors on the one hand and teachers on the other.

---

[14]NEA, The Dept. of Classroom Teachers and the Research Division. "The Teachers' Salary Committee and Its Work." Washington, D. C., The NEA, 1957, pp. 50-51.

[15](1) NEA — Research Report, "Why Have Merit Plans for Teachers' Salaries Been Abandoned?" 1961 — R3, Washington, D. C. The NEA, March, 1961. (2) New York State Teachers Association, "Teacher Merit and Teacher Salary," Report of Special Committee on Merit Payments, Albany, N. Y. 1957, pp. 40-45.

MERIT RATING INTRODUCES POLITICS AND "APPLE POLISHING"

8. Too many plans for merit schedules were introduced too hastily, without adequate study, and without teacher participation or approval.

On the other hand, those who favor merit rating for salary purposes claim that:

1. It is a fair way to determine salaries. It is a sound principle.
2. It keeps the best teachers in service.
3. It discourages poor teaching, and may eliminate the poorer teachers.
4. Teachers are stimulated to be critical of their own work.
5. It stimulates improvement in service.
6. It adds to the prestige of the profession.
7. Merit schedules are flexible. They can be applied to the exceptional teachers and at the same time provide a minimum base salary with increments for years of service and preparation.
8. A merit schedule assures the public, and the taxpayer in particular, of value received.

Whatever the situation may be in the immediate future or over the years regarding merit in salary payments, past experiences seem to indicate that certain principles have evolved which must be seriously considered in any realistic attempt to relate teachers' salaries to quality of service.[16] They are:

1. Teacher acceptance and cooperation must be achieved in advance.
2. The basic purpose must be to help teachers succeed and improve their work.
3. The school authorities must sincerely intend to make the salaries available and be just in implementing the plan.
4. The district must adhere to the merit principle in selection and retention of all employees.
5. A merit salary plan cannot be used for correction of the failure to apply the merit principle in selection and retention of staff in earlier years.
6. Teachers must be provided with a good basic salary program.
7. The reward (for quality or merit) should be large enough to be worth the effort.
8. Only administrative officers should rate for salary purposes. (This, of course, involves appropriate preparation of school administrators to be instructional leaders.)
9. The plan must be administratively feasible and adequate staff must be added for its administration. (This will probably add considerably to the school cost.)
10. All teachers must thoroughly understand the plan and procedure to be followed.
11. Appeals from teachers must be provided for.
12. Merit should be only one of the factors in granting salary increments.

The authors would add that it seems necessary to have an adequate supply of fully certificated, fully qualified teachers to make possible any reasonable chance of success in developing and operating a satisfactory plan of merit pay.

Summary

It is well known that salary is a major factor in determining one's choice of career. It is also a fact that our nation can afford any amount or quality of education, including the rate of teachers' salaries, it wishes to have.

---

[16]*Ibid.* Teacher Merit and Teacher Salary, pp. 45-48. (See this reference for a a fuller discussion of these principles.)

Our tremendous national expenditures for luxuries, automobiles, recreation, for defense in peacetime and in support of our various wartime efforts all attest to the fact that as a people we can afford whatever we value highly.

For longer than the authors wish to think, the matter of support of education including teachers' salaries has been one of policy rather than of national wealth. Individual teachers as well as professional associations will do well to call for a reappraisal of our values!

Teacher Supply and Demand

As has been pointed out, a factor in determining teachers' salaries, and particularly the general level of salaries, is supply and demand. The relatively short supply of teachers for more than a decade has greatly influenced the rise in salaries in that period.

Another consideration of vital importance is that of the general welfare of our society as a whole. Any serious disparity in either direction tends to work to the disadvantage of teachers and society. It would seem proper that both interests should be served.

The teaching profession has long contended that a fair balance between teacher supply and demand together with high professional standards in selection and admission of candidates as well as high standards of preparation, are in the best interests of both society and teachers.

For at least the last three decades, the nation has faced either an oversupply or a shortage of qualified teachers. During the depression

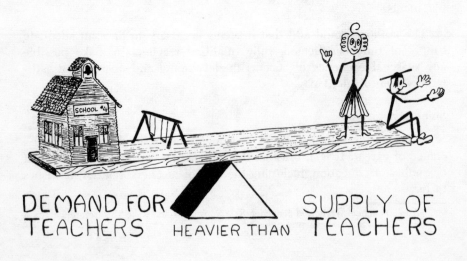

DEMAND FOR TEACHERS   HEAVIER THAN   SUPPLY OF TEACHERS

period of the 1930's there was an actual oversupply. Salaries of teachers were low, and many could not find suitable employment. Since the early 1940's and particularly during and since World War II a serious shortage of teachers has existed. As indicated in Table VII, there presently is a shortage which is likely to continue to be a serious problem in the decade ahead.

TABLE VII

SUMMARY OF THE DEMAND FOR AND THE SUPPLY TEACHERS IN PUBLIC SCHOOLS, 1962		
Demand	*Teachers Needed*	
1. To replace those leaving	125,000	
2. To serve increasing enrollments	35,000	
3. To relieve overcrowding and eliminate part-time sessions	30,000	
4. To provide instructional and other services not now provided	25,000	
5. To replace the unprepared	25,000	
6. TOTAL TEACHERS NEEDED		240,000
Supply		
Number of college graduates completing certification of requirements in 1962:		
7. Elementary graduates 54,499 Not likely to teach (16.8%) 9,156 Net supply 45,343		
8. Secondary graduates 88,048 Not likely to teach (31.6%) 27,823 Net Supply 60,225		
9. TOTAL NET SUPPLY		105,568
10. SHORTAGE (Net Estimated) (Item 6 minus item 9)		134,432

The total figure for elementary teachers certified was 57,076 which included an additional (2,577) 30- 60- and 90-semester hour people.

1. Based on percentage of graduates certified to teach in elementary schools in 1961 and who actually entered the profession (83.2%)
2. Based on percentage of graduates who received certificates to teach in secondary schools in 1961, and who actually entered the profession (68.4%) (An average of all secondary school teaching fields combined.)

Source: NEA Research Division, "Teacher Supply and Demand in Public Schools, 1962," Washington, D. C. The NEA, 1962. Adapted from (pp. 21, 30, 31).

According to studies made by the NEA Research Division and reported in 1962, the number of new teachers needed for our public schools totalled 240,000, and the supply of graduates in teacher education in 1962 was 142,547. Of this number of qualified teachers, it was estimated by the NEA Research Division that 106,000 would enter teaching. Hence, the total teacher shortage in 1962 was estimated at 134,000.[17]

Table VII shows the estimates of supply and demand for 1962. The NEA studies, in terms of supply, are based solely on the graduates of colleges meeting certification requirements. Since new teachers come from a number of sources, a complete assessment of supply is difficult. It is known, for example, that many new teachers enter the field from the general population. Some leave other areas of employment, perhaps attracted by advancing salaries or other factors in teaching. Others return to teaching, particularly women, after rearing a family or during stages of that process. Some, retiring early from other fields, then enter teaching. The actual supply thus was somewhat higher than that reflected in Table VII since it deals only with college graduates of 1962.

It appeared likely that at least two of the areas of need would be met. Generally, it can be assumed that these will be met in any year in some fashion. They are (1) the replacement of those teachers leaving the service, and (2) increased enrollments. In 1962 this was a large requirement as you can note by referring to Table VII. The total need for these two areas was 160,000.

The number of teachers leaving the profession each year is quite high. The Research Division of the NEA, the most reliable source of annual studies of teacher supply and demand, estimates the annual loss to be a minimum of 8.5 per cent. This is considered conservative because other sampling studies show the loss to run as high as 10.9 per cent.[18] The chief reasons for teachers' leaving the service are retirement, death, entering other occupations, marriage (women teachers), entering military service, returning to college, and simply withdrawing from gainful occupation. There are other reasons, but the NEA studies do not include those individuals transferring from one teaching position to another.

The estimate of a need for 35,000 new teachers to serve increasing enrollments in 1962 is also conservative. For the past decade, public school enrollments have been increasing annually by one million or more

---

[17]NEA Research Division, "Teacher Supply and Demand in Public Schools, 1962." Washington, D. C., The NEA, p. 21.
[18]*Ibid.*, p. 19.

pupils. By checking census figures and/or NEA Research Division studies on annual live births, you can readily understand why enrollments in our schools have risen so much. Birth rates since the early 1940's have moved steadily upward from 2 1/2 million to more than 4 million annually in the years 1954 to the present. Elementary school enrollments as well as those in high schools therefore will continue to soar. Simply to staff the nation's classrooms likely will require each year some 75,000 to 100,000 or more new elementary teachers and from 50,000 to 60,000 or more new secondary teachers. Even these numbers will not completely relieve overcrowding and part-time sessions, provide additional needed services, or replace the unprepared or so-called substandard teachers.

You will note in Table VII that a total of 57,000 new elementary teachers and 88,000 secondary graduates received certification in 1962. It thus is apparent that efforts must be strengthened to recruit many more qualified candidates for the profession.

According to NEA Research Division reports[19] as well as the foregoing presentation, there was in 1962 no sign of relief in the teacher shortage. In addition, there continued to be an imbalance in the division of the new supply of elementary and secondary teachers.

The elementary school need is the most urgent in the entire profession, and likely will continue for years. At the same time, the distribution of new supply in the secondary field is out of balance with demand, though increases in recent years in the areas of greatest shortage are encouraging. Prospective increases in foreign language and in sciences are favorable though more teachers are needed in these fields as well as in mathematics and English. Demand in the social sciences and men's physical education is somewhat exceeded by current supply.

There is a variation in demand for teachers in different parts of the country. Urban areas often have acute demand while there may be an oversupply in areas which are losing population.

With rising college enrollments, there is a shortage of qualified instructors. The needs in higher education are not likely to be met for some years.

What can be done to balance teacher supply and demand? Obviously, the real problem now and in the years ahead is to increase the supply of qualified teachers for our elementary schools and in fields of greatest need in our secondary schools.

Among possible means for increasing the supply of qualified teachers, of chief importance are raising salaries toward the NEA recommen-

---

[19]*Ibid.*, p. 5.

dation of a beginning salary of $6,000 and improving retirement systems and conditions of work generally.

Certainly the high standards approach in the selection of candidates entering teacher preparation institutions is desirable. It seems to attract persons of high capability. Teachers themselves should join vigorously in the professional standards movement promoted by the NEA and state associations. As described in Chapter 6, this involves a continuing program of upgrading standards of recruitment, selection and preparation of candidates, certification, and retention of qualified personnel. Other possible means are to:

1. Provide more college scholarships for able students who for financial reasons are not attending college. The federal government, state governments, and industries, all of which provide some scholarships, should be encouraged to do more in this area.
2. Continue to promote the development of student professional organizations: FTA Clubs in high schools and Student NEA associations in colleges.
3. Develop stronger public relations programs. One aspect should be the development of favorable publicity to attract more high quality persons to the profession.
4. Continue to experiment with some of the new media such as TV, radio and other audio-visual devices.
5. Provide more clerical aid to relieve teachers of many of the non-teaching duties current in most schools.

TOPICS AND QUESTIONS FOR STUDY AND DISCUSSION

1. For each of the following terms, provide an illustration, or definition, or both:

Salary schedule	Index salary schedule
Continuing contract	Teacher demand
Merit rating	Teacher supply

2. If a school board member or other citizen should state that teachers' salaries are too high, how would you answer him?
3. Why are teachers not paid as well as those in some other professions — dentistry, medicine, law, engineering?
4. What are the advantages of the single-salary schedule? What are the disadvantages?
5. Should the salary schedule have uniform increments? Why or why not?
6. If your answer is "No" to question five, what plan of schedule arrangement would you recommend? Try to justify your position.
7. Should teachers be paid extra for extra service such as coaching athletic teams or sponsoring the school newspaper? Why or why not?
8. Should teachers with dependents receive extra pay? Why or why not?

9. Can you think of reasons, in addition to those given in the text, why secondary school teachers have received higher salaries than have elementary teachers?
10. Compare teachers' salaries in your state with the salaries paid in states in the same geographical area. Are your state salaries higher? Why or why not?
11. What are the chief arguments for merit rating for payment of teachers' salaries? What the chief arguments against merit rating for salary purposes?
12. Is the NEA recommendation of a minimum beginning salary for all qualified teachers reasonable? Try to think of as many reasons why or why not as you can.
13. Make a salary schedule. Try to include all the elements or variables which you think are justifiable.
14. What are the advantages of the Index plan of salary scheduling?
15. Study the hypothetical salary schedule in the text. This is set up on the Index-Schedule basis. Does it have advantages over the other schedules in the text?

Selected References

Association for Supervision and Curriculum Development, *Better than Rating*, Washington, D. C.: The NEA, 1950.

Beecher, Dwight, *The Evaluation of Teaching*, Syracuse, N. Y.: The Syracuse University Press, 1949.

Burrup, Percy E., *The Teacher and the Public School System*, New York: Harper and Brothers, 1960.

Chamberlain, Leo N., and Leslie W. Kindred, *The Teacher and School Organization*, third edition, Englewood Cliffs, N. J., Prentice-Hall, Inc., 1958.

Cressman, George R., and Harold W. Benda, *Public Education in America*. New York: Appleton-Century-Crofts, second edition, 1961.

Eastmond, Jefferson N., *The Teacher and School Administration*, Boston: Houghton Mifflin Co., 1959.

Gould, George, and Gerald Alan Yoakam, *The Teacher and His Work*. New York: Ronald Press Co., 1954.

Kearney, Nolan C., *A Teacher's Professional Guide*, Englewood Cliffs, N. J.: Prentice-Hall, Inc., 1958.

Lieberman, Myron, *Education As A Profession*, Englewood Cliffs, N. J.: Prentice-Hall, Inc., 1956.

Lueck, William R., *An Introduction to Teaching*, New York: Holt, Rinehart and Winston, 1953.

NEA Department of Classroom Teachers and the Research Division, *The Teachers' Salary Committee and Its Work*, Washington, D. C.: The NEA, 1957.

NEA Handbook for 1962, Washington, D. C.: The NEA, 1962.

National Education Association, National Commission on Teacher Education and Professional Standards, *New Horizons for the Teaching Profession*, (Ed. Margaret Lindsey). Washington, D. C.: The NCTEPS, 1961.

National Education Association, *Teaching Career Fact Book,* Washington, D. C.: The NEA, 1962.

NEA Research Division: Washington, D. C.: The NEA.

Economic Status of Teachers in 1961-62, May, 1962.

Economic Status of Teachers in 1960-61, March, 1961.

Advance Estimates of Public Elementary and Secondary Schools for the School Year, 1954-55, Nov. 1954.

Ranking of the States, April, 1959.

Ranking of the States, May, 1960.

Ranking of the States, January, 1961.

Ranking of the States, January, 1962.

Salaries and Salary Schedules of Urban School Employees, 1956-57. Bulletin #35-2, April, 1957.

Why Have Merit Plans for Teachers' Salaries Been Abandoned? — 1961.

Teacher Supply and Demand in Public Schools, 1962.

State Minimum — Salary Laws and Goal Schedules for Teachers, 1962-63.

NEA Research Bulletin:

Volume 40, No. 1, February, 1962.

Volume 37, No. 3, October, 1959.

Volume 39, No. 4, December, 1961.

Volume 39, No. 2, May, 1961.

Volume 39, No. 3, October, 1961.

New York State Teachers Association, *Teacher Merit and Teacher Salary,* Report of Special Committee on Merit Payments, Albany, N. Y.: 1957.

Reeder, Ward G., *A First Course in Education,* New York: The Macmillan Co., fourth edition, 1958.

Richey, Robert W., *Planning for Teaching,* New York: McGraw-Hill Book Co. Inc,, second edition, 1958.

Rogers, Virgil M. (Ed.), *Do We Want "Merit" Salary Schedules?* Syracuse University School of Education, Syracuse: Syracuse University Press, 1960.

Van Dalen, Deobold B., and Robert W. Brittell, *Looking Ahead to Teaching,* Boston: Allyn and Bacon, Inc., 1959.

Yauch, W. A., Martin H. Bartels, and Emmet Morris, *The Beginning Teacher,* N. Y.: Henry Holt Co., 1955.

Chapter 8

There Are Other Factors
Affecting Teacher Welfare and Security

"If you do not think about the future, you cannot have one."

John Galsworthy

In addition to salary, there are other factors such as certification, tenure, retirement, social security, insurance, credit unions, and leaves of absence which have significance for teacher welfare. It is the purpose of this chapter to provide prospective teachers with basic information related to each of the areas mentioned. Such information should help make them aware of choices open to them and to make proper choices. It should also enable them to participate actively in working for improved conditions in the teaching profession.

Certification

What Is It?

You are familiar with the necessity for licenses to permit you to do certain things like fish or hunt or drive an automobile. You may not be as familiar with licenses to practice an occupation or profession. Society through its laws has provided that you as a teacher, like the person who wishes to practice medicine or law, must qualify for a license indicating that you meet certain professional standards. In effect, that is what you are now doing in your teacher preparatory program

185

— qualifying for a license to teach. Licensing of teachers is referred to as certification.

Licensing or certification is a legal requirement enacted by the state as a guarantee that children and youth in our schools shall be taught by qualified teachers. Educators are quite generally agreed that certification possesses the following purposes or values in addition to the one mentioned:

1. It serves as a protection for the state or society against incompetent or inadequately prepared persons.
2. It protects qualified teachers against unfair competition.
3. It makes for conditions under which the teacher in service finds it profitable to advance himself professionally.
4. It affords a control by the state through which it can effect professional improvement.
5. It yields information on which a continuous inventory of teachers and their qualifications can be based.

Legal Basis of Certification

Public education is a legal function of the state. Its basis was established early in our national life by our Federal Constitution in Article 10 which reserves to the states and to the people all powers not expressly delegated to the United States nor prohibited by it to the states. This means that each of the fifty states may prescribe all measures necessary to provide public education. Under this power, the state therefore may prescribe the qualifications necessary for its school teachers. Licensing is now exercised by each of the states and territories, and since each state acts independently it is not surprising that we find a great deal of variation among them regarding certification.

The certificate is not a guarantee of employment; it is not a contract. It is basically a permit to follow or practice a profession. In addition, the certificate does not limit a school district and its board of education. A board may set higher standards than the minimum set by the states. The certificate merely assures that minimum qualifications have been met. Many of the better districts actually set requirements of more professional preparation than that guaranteed by the state's license.

Brief Background

The first licensed teacher in America as far as we know today was Adam Roelantsen, licensed by the Reformed Dutch Church in Holland to teach on Manhattan Island about 1637 or 1638 for the

West India Company of the New Netherlands. Since that time, we have witnessed various certification practices ranging from little or no training requirements to the present four years of college requirement in the majority of the states.

Most of the real gains in certification standards have come in the present century. In early periods the candidate possessed little preparation and often won his job in an interview by the employing official. This examination was the certifying act. Later written examinations, often prepared and rated by local boards or the school or county superintendent, were the mode. Often these examinations were little more than formalities, and few were standardized. As a result, there were many objections by teachers and others. Examination procedures eventually were improved by granting the examining and certifying authority to a state agency.

It is only since the 1920 to 1926 period that certification requirements for beginning teachers have improved. The improvement has been slow but steady. In the same period, the second and third year normal schools have become four year teacher education institutions.

State departments of education now set the certification standards and usually accept for certification the graduates recommended by teacher-education institutions within the state concerned.

Table I is an attempt to summarize the general trend in certification requirements over the past thirty-six years. It can be noted, for example, that thirty-six years ago (1926) no states required more than three years of college for the lowest elementary certificate. Only twelve states required four years of college for the secondary certificate in 1927.

The number of states requiring a minimum of four years of college gradually increased from five in about 1937 for elementary teachers to forty-four in 1962. As of September, 1960, all states but one require four or more years of college for the secondary certificate. Three have the fifth year requirement for the permanent certificate. The gains in the 1950's are especially noteworthy, for this is the period of the worst or most critical teacher shortage in our history!

Current Status of Teacher Certification

Though the several states are rapidly approaching a common minimum of four years of preparation for a teaching certificate, they vary greatly in other aspects. Some of these are the amount of general and professional education required, length of the period of practice teaching, and semester hours required.

TABLE I

SUMMARY OF ACADEMIC REQUIREMENTS FOR TEACHING
CERTIFICATES IN THE SEVERAL STATES — 1926-1962

Years of college preparation required for lowest certificate	Elementary				Secondary		
	Number of States				Number of States		
	1926 (1)	1937 (2)	1951 (3)	1962 (4)	1927 (5)	1931 (6)	1962 (7)
5 years	0	0	0	0	0	4	3
4 years or bachelor's degree	0	5	17	44	12	38	48
2-3 yrs.	4	19	19	5	18	4	1
1 yr.-2 yrs.	9	16	11	3	1	1	0
No state req.	15	8	1	0	—	1	—
Totals	23	48	48	52	21	48	52

Cols. 1 and 2 — Adapted from Benjamin W. Frazier, *Development of State Programs for the Certification of Teachers*, U. S. Office of Education Bulletin, 1938, No. 12, Washington (Government Printing Office, 1938), p. 73.

Cols. 3 and 6 — W. Earl Armstrong and T. M. Stinnett, *A Manual on Certification Requirements for School Personnel in the U. S.*, National Commission on Teacher Education and Professional Standards, NEA, Washington, D. C. — The Association 1961 Edition.

Cols. 4 and 7 — *NEA Research Memo* — 1960-2, January, 1960, Washington, D. C. (Research Division).

Col. 5 — Adapted from E. J. Ashbaugh, "Need of Uniformity in Certification of High School Teachers," *School Life*, 12: 154-55, April, 1927.

Table II, page 189-190, indicates several aspects of specific requirements by states.

Standards for high school teachers are considerably higher and more uniform than for elementary teachers. (See Table II.) More specifically, the semester hours of professional education required ranges from eight in one state (Nebraska) to thirty-six in four others (Mississippi, New York, Pennsylvania and New Jersey), for elementary teachers. For secondary teachers, the range is less extreme from twelve hours in three states (Arkansas, Maine and Masschusetts) to twenty-nine in Puerto Rico.

The practice teaching semester hour requirement also varies considerably, or from three to twelve semester hours for elementary teachers and from none to eight semester hours for high school teachers.

There are many other requirements for the teacher candidate in

TABLE II

MINIMUM REQUIREMENTS FOR THE LOWEST REGULAR TEACHING CERTIFICATE AS OF SEPTEMBER, 1961

		Elementary			Secondary		
		1. Degree or no. sem. hrs. req.	2. Prof. educ. req.	3. Prac. tea. sem. hrs. req.	1. Degree or no. sem. hrs. req.	2. Prof. educ. req.	3. Prac. tea. sem. hrs. req.
1.	Alabama	B	30	3	B	24	3
2.	Alaska	B	24	C	B	18	C
3.	Arizona	B	18	6	5 yrs.	18	6
4.	Arkansas	60 - (a)	12	3	60 - (1)	12	3
5.	California	B	24	8	5 yrs.	22	6
6.	Colorado	B	AC	AC	B	AC	AC
7.	Connecticut	B	30	6	B	18	6
8.	Delaware	B	30	6	B	18	6
9.	District of Columbia	B	24	6	5 yrs.	18	6
10.	Florida	B	20	6	B	20	6
11.	Georgia	B	18	6	B	18	6
12.	Hawaii	B	18	AC	B	18	AC
13.	Idaho	B	20	6	B	20	6
14.	Illinois	B	16	5	B	16	5
15.	Indiana	B	30	6	B	18	5
16.	Iowa	B	20	5	B	20	5
17.	Kansas	B	24	5	B	20	5
18.	Kentucky	B	24	8	B	17	8
19.	Louisiana	B	24	4	B	18	4
20.	Maine	96	AC	AC	B	12	0
21.	Maryland	B	26	8	B	16	6
22.	Massachusetts	B	18	2	B	12	2
23.	Michigan	B	20	5	B	20	5
24.	Minnesota	B	30	6	B	18	4
25.	Mississippi	B	36	6	B	18	6
26.	Missouri	B	20	5	B	10	5
27.	Montana	64 - (b)	AC	AC	B	AC	AC
28.	Nebraska	40	B	B	B	18	3
29.	Nevada	B	18	4	B	18	4
30.	New Hampshire	B	AC	6	B	21	6
31.	New Jersey	B	36	6	B	14	6
32.	New Mexico	B	24	6	B	18	6
33.	New York	B - (c)	36	12	5 yrs.(2)	18	6
34.	North Carolina	B	18	3	B	18	3
35.	North Dakota	64	16	3	B	16	3
36.	Ohio	B	28	6	B	17	6
37.	Oklahoma	B	21	6	B	21	6
38.	Oregon	B	20	4	B - (3)	24	6
39.	Pennsylvania	B	36	6	B	18	6
40.	Puerto Rico	68	53	6	B	29	5
41.	Rhode Island	B	30	6	B	18	6
42.	South Carolina	B	15	3	B	20	5
43.	South Dakota	60	15	3	B	20	5
44.	Tennessee	B	24	4	B	24	4
45.	Texas	B	24	6	B	24	6

TABLE II (Continued)

	Elementary			Secondary		
	1. Degree or no. sem. hrs. req.	*2. Prof. educ. req.*	*3. Prac. tea. sem. hrs. req.*	*1. Degree or no. sem. hrs. req.*	*2. Prof. educ. req.*	*3. Prac. tea. sem. req. hrs.*
46. Utah	B	30	8	B	22	8
47. Vermont	B	18	6	B	18	6
48. Virginia	B	18	6	B	15	4-6
49. Washington	B - (d)	AC	AC	B - (4)	AC	AC
50. West Virginia	B	20	5	B	20	5
51. Wisconsin	64	26	8	B	18	5
52. Wyoming	B	20	C	B	20	C

AC Approved Courses
C   Course
a.   Bachelor's degree required in 1963 (Arkansas)
b.   Standard certificate based on degree program (Montana)
c.   Five year program will be required after September 1, 1966 (New York)
d.   Five years required for standard certification (Washington)
1.   Bachelor's degree required in 1963 (Arkansas)
2.   A non-renewable 5-year certificate is issued for the academic fields on the basis of the bachelor's degree. A permanent certificate is granted on completion of 5th year. (New York)
3.   Provisional Certificate; 5 years required for standard certification (Oregon)
4.   Provisional Certificate; 5 years required for standard certification.

Sources: NEA Research Memo — 1960 (2), January, 1960 — Washington, D. C., NEA Research Division, the NEA
Armstrong, W. Earl, and T. M. Stinnett, Manual on Certification Requirements for School Personnel in the United States, 1961 Edition.
National Commission on Teacher Education and Professional Standards, NEA.

the several states: Thirty-one states require U. S. citizenship or first papers; forty-one require a recommendation from a preparatory institution or employing school officer; twenty-six require an oath of allegiance or loyalty to the United States and to the state; thirty-four have a minimum age requirement; twenty-three require a health certificate; twenty-eight have an application fee; eleven require that the candidate have a position secured prior to issuance of the certificate and fifteen have special course requiremnts. Specific state requirements can be found in Armstrong and Stinnett.[1] Another good source is the booklet published annually by Woellner and Wood,[2] *Requirements for*

---

[1]W. Earl Armstrong and T. M. Stinnett, *A Manual on Certification Requirements for School Personnel in the U. S.*, NEA, Washington, 1961, op. cit. — p. 24.
[2]Robert C. Woellner and M. Aurilla Wood, *Requirements for Certification of Teachers, Counselors, Librarians, Schools, and Junior Colleges*, University of Chicago Press, Chicago, Ill. (Revised annually).

Certification of Teachers et al. You will find these two reports helpful in planning for teaching. The state department of education located in the capital of the state in which you wish to teach will also send you, without charge, information on state and local requirements.

In addition to the foregoing and despite the variations among the several states, the following practices, in general, are current:

1. Certificates are issued for specific subject fields in secondary education, and in a number of states for grade areas in elementary education.
2. Certificates must be renewed periodically. The several states have varying requirements for maintaining and renewing them. These may be additional course work in an approved program within a certain period of time or some other kind of in-service requirement such as travel, educational research, or professional activity other than classroom teaching.

   For example, New York has had for a number of years the course requirement for renewal of the so-called permanent certificate of six semester hours in approved courses in a ten-year period. In March, 1960, however, the regent's rules were modified to eliminate the requirement. At present, the requirements for the elementary teacher in New York are the satisfactory completion of a four-year program in an approved collegiate institution and at least one year of actual teaching in each five-year period by the holder of a certificate. As of September 1, 1966, the elementary teaching requirement will be raised to a 5-year program, and the prospective elementary teacher must earn at least 24 semester hours in any academic field. Secondary teachers in New York are granted provisional certificates, good for five years from date of issue. The licenses are made permanent on completion of an additional or fifth year of study. Further, in New York State, the State Education Department has moved steadily in the direction of approved college programs for the preparation of teachers.
3. Authority for certification is centralized in the state education departments.

The certification of teachers in our nation has existed in some form in our public schools for over a century. It has passed through a number of stages from local and county authority for issuing certificates to the present situation in which all states exercise legal authority and require that all or most teachers' certificates be issued by the central state agency. That central agency is the state department of education. A few states diffuse this authority to some extent. In seven, certain cities are authorized to issue local certificates and in four states cer-

over a century

100 years

teacher certification

tification authority is shared with state colleges. The four states are Colorado, Missouri, North Dakota and Washington.

Some Problems and Issues.

Temporary and Substandard Certificates. One of the more serious problems in the area of teacher certification has been and still is that of issuing temporary and substandard certificates to teachers who cannot qualify for the regular certificate. Of course, World War II had a serious effect upon teacher certification requirements. Because qualified teachers were lost to the war effort, many states resorted to the practice of issuing emergency certificates or "letters of authorization." According to the NEA Research Division[3] estimates of emergency teachers ranged in 1948-49 from about 105,000, or a one in eight ratio to the total number of teachers, to about 95,000 in 1958-59, or a ratio of one in thirteen. The years between the two mentioned fluctuated from about 95,000 to about 70,000. Needless to say, figures as large as these which represent a ratio of one emergency teacher in each ten to fourteen of all classroom teachers is serious. This situation has far-reaching bad results such as the slowing down of an upgrading process in teacher certification requirements and the development of a complacent public attitude. If someone is in every classroom no matter what, the public becomes oblivious to the fact of the real teacher shortage. In addition, lowering requirements seems to diminish the prestige of teaching and to attract fewer able people to the profession. It would seem only proper to raise or at least to maintain requirements, and to issue letters of authorization to fill the gaps still remaining in our public schools. This would mean a continuation of the drive to improve certification standards.

---

[3]Research Division of the NEA, *Estimates of School Statistics*, 1958-59, Washington, NEA, 1958.

Multiplicity of Certificates. Another problem is that of the multiplicity of certificates for teachers. As recently as 1949, the states were issuing as many as 1,000 separate name certificates. Though there is some multiple certification in the professions generally, standard practice in the professions other than teaching is to issue one certificate to all practitioners regardless of their kind or degree of specialization.

"A Chicken in Every Pot" . . . .

"A Fully Certified Teacher in Every Classroom"

Educators generally agree that the multiplicity of certificates for teachers is undesirable and yet there seems to be reluctance to reduce drastically the number of certificates and move definitely toward one or a very few standard certificates. There is a trend toward reduction of separate name certificates. Twenty-eight states still issue the life certificate generally based on additional preparation above the bachelor's degree and experience. There is a trend away from this type, however, toward the long-term renewable certificate.

As pointed out, there are as yet significant differences between the certification levels of secondary school teachers and those of elementary teachers. Though the trend is toward greater uniformity, as long as the differences exist sound personnel policies are difficult to administer. How can uniform salaries be justly paid, for example, to teachers with widely varying certification attainments?

Another problem has to do with the mobility of teachers from state to state. In the interest of the children and youth of the nation, as well as of teachers themselves, it would seem desirable to have complete reciprocity. This could come through agreements among the states. Notable among reciprocity agreements are the Eight-State Reciprocity Compact involving the New England states, New York, and New Jersey (now an eleven-state agreement including Delaware, Maryland and Pennsylvania in addition), and the Central States Conference of state departments of education involving twelve midwestern states. There have been other regional attempts at reciprocity in the north central and southern state areas, however, much remains to be developed and put into actual practice. Perhaps the most promising recent development in this respect is the move toward national reciprocity. At the 1958 conference of the National Commission on

Teacher Education and Professional Standards at Bowling Green, Ohio, a tentative agreement was reached by thirty-five states to accept any teacher graduating from a college or university fully accredited by the National Council for Accreditation of Teacher Education. This interest by the profession in certification standards is a most encouraging development.

All teachers should be familiar with the two professional organizations mentioned or become so as soon as possible. They are described in Chapter 6. The prime purpose of the National TEPS Commission is to work toward improvement of standards of selection, preparation and certification of teachers. Established by the teaching profession, the Commission has led in professional standards movements for the past twelve or fourteen years. The significant advances in certification described undoubtedly have been greatly influenced by its work. The second is the National Council for Accreditation of Teacher Education, or NCATE, as it is familiarly known in the teaching profession. Made operative in 1954, this body is now the recognized accrediting agency for teacher education institutions. These two professional organizations promise much, in the opinion of the authors, for continued improvement of professional standards.

Trends In Teacher Certification.

The significant advances in teacher certification have been made in recent years, and certainly in large part as the profession itself has become more sensitive to and interested in the problems and issues of teacher selection, preparation and certification.

Some of the trends have been developing throughout most of the current century. Among these long-time trends are:

1. The raising of preparation levels. This has been a slow but steady trend with the profession itself largely influencing recent developments.
2. The gradual addition of professional courses in education in teacher preparation programs.
3. The gradual elimination of the life certificate.
4. The assumption of licensure by state departments of education. It should be noted, however, that the idea of legal sanctions for professional boards is taking force. Again the profession is leading this move.
5. Certification by examination which developed early, waned, and then assumed added importance. This is indicated by such things as the National Teachers' Examination as a guide to higher institutions and the use of qualifying examinations by city school systems.

6. Placing more emphasis on subject matter or academic content in teacher preparation programs. This is a more recent development, although there has been interest for a long time by some segments of both the public and the profession in such a move.

    Other trends, several of which have been discussed are:

7. The action of the teaching profession itself to raise its own standards through such groups as NCTEPS and NCATE, and the NEA generally, as well as the state teachers' associations. An example of such action is the increase in reciprocity agreements among the states in certification matters.

8. The reduction in the number of certificates issued by the states. Though there are still too many differently named certificates (some 800 in 1957), this does represent considerable decrease. There seems to be a trend toward the establishment of two basic types of certificates. One is the probationary or provisional type issued for short periods of three to five years. The other is the permanent or long-term renewable type which would be granted after successful experience and added professional work.

9. A minor trend in the direction of requiring state licensing of teachers in private and parochial schools. At present twelve states have such a requirement. This is a recent development.

The student is reminded that certification at best can do no more than enforce minimum standards for all teachers. In the main, these standards are expressed only in quantitative terms. Certification cannot produce excellence in teachers and teaching! Quality and excellence must be the responsibility largely of teacher education institutions. The public and the profession also have large stakes in bringing quality into teaching. The colleges must provide challenging programs — programs planned and executed by the total faculties. They must be more highly selective in admissions policies, for quality teaching demands superior persons. Poor prospects must be eliminated as soon as the colleges discover them. Finally, it would seem that educational institutions have a responsibility for more intelligent follow-up of their graduates. Such follow-up might lead to improvement of teachers in service as well as to improved programs of preparation.

The public has a responsibility for properly recognizing the teacher as an important member of society. Recognition would include adequate pay.

The profession must move more rapidly toward greater assumption of responsibility for quality performance of its members as well as enforcement of ethical practices.

Certification will continue to afford minimum protection as indicated, but real quality in teaching can come only from those sources capable of bringing it about!

Teacher Tenure

> *"Performance of tenure is necessary to make the position of teacher one of dignity and independence."*
>
> *Charles Eliot*

Historically, teachers were dismissed at will and teaching was in general a journeyman's occupation. Where contracts existed, they were for less than a year, often a month or two in duration, prior to the beginning of the twentieth century. The idea of the annual contract came into being largely as the nation moved from a rural to an urban status. Even so, in many school systems teachers rarely stayed more than about a year in the same place, particularly small towns and rural areas.

Gradually, as teachers became better prepared and as professional associations grew stronger, the annual contract became more nearly universal. This protected the teacher for at least a year. Then came the continuing contract principle which may take several forms. It may provide for employment for an indefinite period or it may be issued after a probationary period. Another alternative is the "spring notification" type in which the teacher holds his position unless notified (usually in March or early April) that his services are not to be continued in the following year.

The law of contracts is a very complicated area of the law. It involves two or more legally important persons who agree voluntarily to offer or accept something. Money is often involved. The teacher offers to teach for a certain sum for one year and the board of education accepts, or the board offers the job at a certain salary and the teacher accepts. With teachers a valid certificate is involved as far as the law is concerned. Probably the most satisfactory kind of continuing contract is one which is granted after a probationary period or from one to three years.

The final stage in the road to permanency or relative permanency of position is known as tenure status. Tenure is defined in various ways. Here the term is used to mean a status based on law which affords the teacher full protection in his position and continuance in that position as long as he is efficient, competent and conducts himself properly, both professionally and morally.

The appropriateness of tenure is based on the idea that a teacher free from worry and emotional stress over the possibility of losing his job can be a more effective teacher. Further, freedom in his position, though he may not belong to the "right" political party or agree with school authorities and others of influence in the community on issues unrelated to the work for which he is employed, is highly important to the teacher citizen in our democracy. It is important to education and to society as well.

The main reasons for tenure are well stated by the NEA Committee on Academic Freedom. This committee stated the following reasons:[4]

1. To protect classroom teachers and other members of the teaching profession against unjust dismissal of any kind — political, religious or personal.
2. To prevent the management or domination of the schools by political or non-educational groups for selfish and other improper purposes.
3. To secure for the teacher employment conditions which will encourage him to grow in the full practice of his profession, unharried by constant pressure and fear.
4. To encourage competent, independent thinkers to enter and to remain in the teaching profession.
5. To encourage school management, which might have to sacrifice the welfare of schools to fear and favor, to devote itself to the cause of education.
6. To set up honest, orderly, and definite procedures by which undesirable people may be removed from the teaching profession.
7. To protect educators in their efforts to promote the financial and educational interests of public school children.
8. To protect teachers in the exercise of their rights and duties of American citizenship.
9. To enable teachers, in spite of reactionary minorities, to prepare children for life in a democracy under changing conditions.

Under an adequate tenure law, a teacher usually is granted tenure after serving a satisfactory probationary period, commonly three years of service. After being placed on tenure, he continues to hold his position permanently as long as he meets the requirements of work and conduct. Finally, if dismissal is sought of a teacher on tenure, the charges must be based on the specified reasons (improper conduct, inefficiency or incompetency, or disability), and the teacher in question, accompanied by counsel, is entitled to a hearing before the board. If desired by the

---

[4]NEA — Committee on Tenure and Academic Freedom, "Analysis of Teacher Tenure Provisions: State and Local," Washington, D. C. June, 1944.

teacher, an appeal may be taken to the chief state school officer and finally to the courts.

THERE IS A DIVIDED OPINION AMONG VARIOUS SEGMENTS OF OUR
SOCIETY AS TO THE WORTH OF TENURE

There is divided opinion among various segments of our society, including teachers, as to the worth of tenure. The case for tenure is well stated in the words of the NEA Committee on Tenure and Academic Freedom.

The opposition bases its case on the following. (These are among the chief reasons generally given):

1. Competent teachers do not need tenure protection.
2. Tenure laws force retention of poor teachers while they protect the competent.
3. Tenure laws provide too much security and teachers become indifferent to improvement and progress.
4. Some boards take advantage of the situation by releasing teachers in the probationary period before tenure status can be achieved. This contributes to teacher insecurity and operates against the best interests of pupils and the school.
5. Tenure interferes with the proper authority of the school administration.

On the basis of experience with tenure and studies of its effects, it would seem that most of the foregoing reasons have little validity.

The profession has never insisted that incompetents be retained. Tenure does not mean that a teacher cannot be dismissed. It does mean that such dismissal must be within the scope of the tenure law, and carried out in an orderly way.

Current Status of Tenure Laws.

There are basically three kinds of teacher contracts. They are state-wide tenure, continuing contract, and annual contract. There are how-ever many variations in practice among the states. Table III shows status relative to tenure as of 1960.

As Table III indicates, for the 1960-61 school year, 37 states and the District of Columbia had tenure laws on a state-wide basis with some variations or in certain designated areas only. Six states operated on the spring notification basis. The remaining seven states had laws providing for annual or long-term contracts.

There are many other variations among the states with respect to employees covered, areas or types of school systems covered, causes of dismissal, the probationary period, and marital status. A few local dis-tricts even had clauses providing for dismissal of women teachers who marry.

It would appear that while many gains have been made in the past three decades, there is much room for improvement in tenure legisla-tion. With 13 states having no tenure laws, and other states needing laws to strengthen or modify those already enacted, much work remains to be done if the objectives of sound tenure laws for all teachers are to be realized.

Tenure is a very complicated subject, and it is beyond the scope of this book to attempt an exhaustive treatment. Teachers should study their tenure laws carefully and join with professional associations in seeking appropriate legislation.

Teacher Retirement

Though teachers' salaries have risen in recent years, they are hardly adequate to provide for current living needs and savings in sufficient quantity to care for future needs. The same is true for countless other workers in public employment and in industry generally. Retirement and pension plans thus have become quite general for teachers as well as for millions of other workers. In addition, the federal government

TABLE III

TYPE OF STATE TENURE OR CONTRACT PROVISIONS IN EFFECT, 1960

STATES WITH TENURE LAWS		STATES WITHOUT TENURE LAWS
1. *State-wide*		3. *State-wide Continuing Contract or Spring Notification*
Alabama	Maine	
Alaska	Maryland	Arkansas
Arizona	Massachusetts	Nevada
California[1]	Michigan[1]	North Dakota
Colorado[1]	Minnesota	Oklahoma
Connecticut[2]	Montana	South Dakota
Delaware	New Hampshire	Virginia
District of	New Jersey	
Columbia	New York[3]	
Florida[2]	New Mexico	
Hawaii	Ohio	4. *Annual or Long-Term Contracts*
Idaho	Pennsylvania	Mississippi
Illinois[3]	Rhode Island	North Carolina
Indiana[3]	Tennessee	South Carolina
Iowa	Washington	Texas
Kentucky	West Virginia	Utah
Louisiana		Vermont
2. *In Certain Places Only*[4]		Wyoming
Georgia	Nebraska	
Kansas	Oregon	
Missouri	Wisconsin	

[1]Subject to local option in small districts in California and Colorado; subject to local adoption throughout Michigan.

[2]Separate local tenure laws govern cities or counties.

[3]Illinois and New York exclude small districts; Indiana excludes township schools. Illinois and Indiana provide spring notification continuing contracts in non-tenure areas.

[4]In non-tenure areas in Georgia and Kansas, annual contracts are the usual practice. Non-tenure areas in Missouri, Nebraska, Oregon and Wisconsin are controlled by continuing laws of the spring notification type.

Source: NEA Research Bulletin, Vol. 38, No. 3, October, 1960, page 83, Washington, D. C. The NEA, 1960.

provided, through social security legislation, a compulsory plan that applies to millions in many fields of employment.

Probably you are like most other young people. You are naturally more concerned with beginning a career than with ending one. You may not see the need for retirement plans. Financial responsibilities will increase shortly as you assume family obligations, however, and the years slip by all too fast. You have a real stake in a retirement system. An adequate salary, a sound retirement plan and tenure in service provide a good basis for reasonable security. Actually a retirement system is a cooperative affair requiring the active interest of as many of its members as possible, both the young and the old. All members have the same goal and the same responsibility for taking any legitimate action indicated for improving the plan in the interest of all.

In addition, even though you do not remain in teaching, your contributions are not lost. A good retirement system allows withdrawal of your contributions plus interest if you leave the profession of teaching.

A retirement system for teachers has a number of purposes. One is to provide an adequate retirement income for the career teacher. Another can be called an educational one — that of helping to secure good teachers for children and society by making teaching attractive and keeping good teachers in the profession.

Retirement systems are of relatively recent origin. Early plans originating in the late 1800's were largely mutual help societies organized by groups of teachers in the larger cities. Such cities as New York, Baltimore, Boston, Cincinnati, Philadelphia, and Washington, D. C., were among the first to establish some kind of voluntary old-age plan. The first state-wide system was enacted into law in New Jersey in 1896. Since that time, and particularly in the last four decades, many local and state-wide systems have been established and greatly improved.

Current Status of Retirement Systems for Teachers.

At present, every state has in operation a state-wide teacher retirement system. There are still a number of cities and a few local units that maintain separate retirement systems for their teachers.

There are basically two types of plans for teacher retirement. They are (1) pension plans, and (2) joint-contributory plans leading to a retirement allowance. Among the states and local units there is some variation from these, but they remain the basic plans.

Two states currently operate on the basis of the pension plan. They are New Mexico and Delaware. All the rest have the joint-contributory plan.

A joint-contributory system is a plan financed by two parties — the employer and the employee. In the state teacher retirement systems,

TABLE IV

SUMMARY OF SELECTED STATISTICS OF TEACHER RETIREMENT SYSTEMS, 1961			
Item	*Number of Systems*		*Other*
	State	*Local*	*Data*
Total Active Membership	44	20	1,851,247
Total Living Retired Membership	40	20	201,387
Total Reserves	36	11	$6,812,525,347
Annual Income:			
Public Funds	42	19	$ 583,225,323
Members' Contributions	42	20	$ 491,251,706
Investments	41	18	$ 414,984,438
Total — All Sources	42	20	$1,532,785,947
Disbursed to Retired Teachers			
and Beneficiaries	43	20	$ 359,619,479
Total Disbursements	43	19	$1,514,594,420
Investments:			
In U. S. Govt. Securities	41	19	$3,494,598,533
In Corporate Bonds	34	16	$2,388,177,069
Total — All Investments	41	19	$7,294,344,791
Number of Members Covered			
by Social Security	30	11	990,483
Medians of Average Allowances:			
Paid Last Year (1959-60)	36	18	$ 1,748
Over-all Average	39	18	$ 1,313

Source: NEA Research Division, Research Report. 1961-R16, "Systems of Retirement to Which Teachers Belong," Oct., 1961, Washington, D. C. The NEA, 1961. Adapted from Table 2, p. 8.

the contributors are the state and the teacher. This is the most widely used plan in the nation.

A pension is a plan financed entirely by the employer or state.

The term "retirement allowance" describes the amount paid to a retired member of a joint-contributory system. It consists of two parts — a pension from state funds and an annuity based on the member's contributions.

You will also note the terms "actuary" and "actuarial standards" in the literature concerning retirement systems. An actuary is a financial expert who determines insurance premiums and risks. If a retirement system is based on actuarial standards, it simply means that payments made into the fund are sufficient to meet all possible circumstances of life expectancy. The actuary bases his study of needs on mortality rates, sex differences and economic conditions.

Joint-contributory plans can be further classified in terms of the type of financing involved. There are (1) pay-as-you-go or cash-disbursement joint-contributory systems, and (2) reserve joint-contributory systems.

In the first plan, employer and employee funds paid currently are used to pay current retirement allowances to retired teachers. It is similar to the plan used by some state and city governments of paying the cost of governmental services entirely with current taxes or what is sometimes referred to as paying-as-you-go, or spending as you receive the money.

The reserve system is that in which reserves are built up from contributions by employer and employees over and above current obligations. Implied is a guarantee of future payments generally based on actuarial standards.

The most widely used plan is the reserve joint-contributory system.

The current status of state and local systems is reflected in the selected statistics summarized in Table IV. Covered are returns from 44 state and 20 local systems for the years 1959 and 1960.

As you may note, there were over 1,850,000 members in the 64 systems and over 200,000 who had retired. A total of over two million people thus are directly involved. This is an indication of the service offered by retirement systems.

With investments in sixty-two systems totalling $7.3 billion in government securities, corporate bonds, stocks, mortgages, school bonds, and other sources, it is apparent that retirement systems play a significant part in the economy of the nation. Annual income and total annual disbursements of over $1.5 billion each are also indicative of the economic significance of retirement systems.

Nearly a million members in forty-one systems were covered by social security.

The retirement allowance paid in terms of the median of average payments indicates need for continued improvement of retirement systems. The median average retirement allowance paid in 1959-1960 to retired teachers was $1,748. In the current period of high living costs, this amount is hardly satisfactory. As pointed out in the study referred to for this summary, the averages are deceiving. Included in this group are persons who were not career teachers and teachers who retired early and with few years of service. Since many receive social security in addition, the average of $1,748 may be a bit more adequate. Not shown in the table is the fact that annual allowances ranged from $439 to $3,918.

All of the foregoing figures indicate some progress over previous years, but the professional goal of one-half of the teacher's final salary has not been achieved by all of the systems.

Member Contribution, Age and Service Requirement.

After studying the foregoing statistics and information, you are perhaps wondering how retirement systems affect you personally upon entering teaching.

The several state and local systems have a variety of contribution rates and age and service requirements.

The NEA report referred to previously indicates the specific data.[5]

In the 62 state and local systems included in the report for 1959-60, the most common contribution rates were 5 per cent and 6 per cent, with a range of from 2 per cent to 8 per cent.

You may be doing a bit of mental arithmetic about now. It may run something like this — "Five per cent or 6 per cent for retirement — 3 per cent more for social security, and then there will be tax deductions! Is it really a bargain?"

If such is your view, you are not alone. It appears to the authors that teachers pay too much for benefits under current policies. Other employees, particularly governmental, military and the like receive more benefits than teachers for less personal cost. The profession should consider seriously the issues involved. One possible solution would be to have more adequate provisions from public funds for teacher retirement programs, thus cutting the cost to teachers. This would place teachers more on a par with other professions and employees.

----

[5]*Ibid.*, p. 13.

What are the age and service requirements for retirement? The NEA Research Division reports[6] that as of 1960 twenty-seven state and all local systems had compulsory age limits for retirement ranging from age 65 to 72. On othe other hand, seventeen states had no age limits, reflecting the view which is coming to be more generally accepted: that retirement is a matter for the local district to decide rather than the retirement system.

The ages 60 to 65 are the most common retirement ages specified. Five systems set age 65 for normal retirement and require up to 20 years of service. Seven permit normal retirement at age 65 regardless of years of service. Twelve use age 60 for normal retirement and require up to 20 years of service. Eleven systems set age 60 regardless of years of service. Twelve systems set normal retirement at age 60 and require from 20 to 35 years of service. Five use age 65 and the same range of service years.

Three provide alternatives, while using ages of 60 and 65. One, for example, set normal retirement at age 60 with 20 years of service or any age with 35 years of service.

Benefits.

What would you receive in retirement allowance or pension if you were retiring now? Currently, there is a variety of practices among the several states and local plans.

The NEA Research Division reports that in 1959-60[7] there were two primary types of benefit formulas. The so-called fixed benefit formula, typical of 27 state and 16 local systems, is a plan in which the retirement allowance is figured as a total amount, usually a fraction or a per cent of final average salary multiplied by the total number of years of service.

The other plan is one involving a money purchase type of formula. Currently, 14 state and two local systems use this plan. The retirement allowance is computed in two parts: (1) an annuity based on the member's accumulated contributions, and (2) a pension derived from public funds. The pension part may be fixed at a certain amount or rate, or equal to the annuity part.

There are a great many disability formulas for retirement allowance in case of disability of the member. Usually the amount is a portion of the normal retirement allowance with a limitation of minimum years

---

[6]*Ibid.*, pp. 9-16.
[7]*Ibid.* — NEA Research Division, "Statistics of Retirement Systems," pp. 48-55.

of service. Sixteen systems have a service limitation of five years or less. The remaining systems vary all the way up to 20 years, with 10 years and 15 years of service the most common.

You are urged to study carefully the retirement system in your state. A Retirement Primer or Handbook is issued by a number of systems. You are reminded that just as retirement plans have been improved greatly in the past two decades, it is entirely likely future improvements will afford members even better retirement benefits.

Some improvements are indicated in the following list of essentials or criteria of sound and effective retirement systems quite generally agreed upon by the experts or authorities. Items one through twelve list the essentials currently operative in a number of retirement plans. The remaining items, while common to a few plans, are considered by the authors as necessary to the achievement of a sound system, as well as one that provides appropriate benefits for all teachers.

1. The system should be a joint-contributory plan.
2. The system should be a reserve plan.
3. All funds and investments should be safeguarded by legislation.
4. Membership should be required of all new teachers and be optional with those in service at time of adoption.
5. All benefits specified should be guaranteed by law.
6. All deposits or payments should be concurrent with teacher service.
7. Options should be available at time of retirement.
8. Actuarial tables should be modified to meet changing conditions. The plan should be adjustable to meet cost-of-living changes.
9. The system should be democratically administered with representation on the governing board of all interested groups.
10. Member contributions to the fund should be returnable plus interest in an equitable manner in case the member leaves the system.
11. Retirement benefits should be based on full salaries of members.
12. Credit should be allowed for past service.
13. Provision for disability retirement should be made after a reasonable period of service (not more than five years with choice of options).
14. Members should have vested rights after a reasonable period of service (not more than five years).
15. Reciprocity among the several state systems should be achieved.
16. The costs of the plan for teacher members should be reasonable, (probably lower than 5 per cent of pay), with the state assuming most of the cost.
17. Social security benefits should be in addition to the retirement plan benefits, and not in lieu of any portion of them.

Admittedly, reciprocity may be difficult to achieve since a nation-wide plan would require legislative changes to provide for it in all or nearly all of the states. (The retirement law in New York State has a clause providing for reciprocal transfer to other state systems having a like provision).

The lack of reciprocity is a barrier to the mobility or free flow of teachers from state to state. If reciprocity were provided among all the states, it would be possible for a retired teacher to receive benefits from two or more state systems. Obviously, some reasonable limit on years of service in a given state should be set, probably ten.

As stated previously, recent history of leigslation on state retirement systems indicates that most changes have been such as to improve existing plans. You should know, however, that though courts have held a retirement system is a contract that cannot be revoked for present members, changes can be made for future members. A legislature might even abolish a plan for all save present members, though this is considered highly unlikely.

All teachers should become as familiar as possible with their retirement systems and should work cooperatively with their respective state associations for needed improvements. It should be noted that the NEA and state associations for years have led the fight to secure strong and equitable teacher retirement plans.

Social Security for Teachers

In addition to teacher retirement allowance and pension plans in all of the states, social security coverage is now available to them under amendments to the Federal Social Security Act passed in 1950. However, these amendments extended coverage to only those teachers not covered by a state or local retirement system. Several states abandoned their retirement plans in the 1951-54 period to enable teachers to become eligible for social security. After teachers in these states were covered by social security, all but one, South Dakota, restored their retirement systems. South Dakota followed suit in 1959.

In 1954, the Social Security Law was again amended by Congress to permit members of retirement systems to be covered by social security provided the members, or any division of members, of a given state system voted to accept it. For example, public school teachers were permitted, under the act, to vote separately from college teachers. Amendments to the federal law were enacted again in 1956. These amendments extended the possibility of benefits to additional states. As of 1962 some or all of the teachers in 38 states in public schools were covered by social security, according to a NEA Research Division report.[8] This included between 50 and 60 per cent of all public school teachers in the nation.

Social security is not generally considered an adequate substitute for retirement systems. It does however have an advantage in the survivor benefit, which is not included in many retirement plans. This is significant to the teacher with dependents. There is no problem of reciprocity with social security since it is under federal law and applies throughout the nation.

Currently, individuals contribute on the following basis with the employer matching the percentage:

1962	3 1/8%	1966-67	4 1/8%
1963-65	3 5/8%	1968 and after	4 5/8%

The tax is based on $4,800 of the person's salary, the present salary limit for social security taxes.

When an individual earns 40 quarters of coverage, he is fully insured for life. This equals a ten year period but since service time may be made retroactive, generally considerably less than ten years is required.

Currently, the maximum total monthly benefit possible for an individual at age 65 is $127; the maximum monthly family benefit is $254. Members may retire at age 62 also with reduced monthly benefits, or 80 per cent of the normal maximum.

Since each session of Congress may bring changes in social security laws, you should study the current provisions of the act. Information is available at the local social security office.

Insurance for Teachers

Like tenure, retirement procedures and social security, insurance is not easy to understand. It requires careful study, and a great deal more information than the amateur ordinarily can elicit from insurance salesmen. You would do well to study individual and group insurance plans

---

[8]NEA Research Division — Report No. 24, Retirement Income Series (Prepared for the National Council on Teacher Retirement by the NEA Research Division, Washington, D. C. The NEA, March, 1962.)

and to check the libraries, both college and public. For many years, teachers have been considered good risks by insurance companies and many group and individual plans have been available to them.

Health (or sickness) insurance plans, life insurance plans, income protection plans, and accident insurance are available to teachers on both an individual and a group basis.

Originally, teachers paid the entire cost of the premiums for their insurance even in group plans, some of which involved the teachers of an entire district. Other plans were state-wide. As has been the case with so many other welfare benefits for teachers, urban school systems have led in the development of group insurance plans while rural districts generally have lagged far behind.

Currently group insurance, including life, sickness and accident, and income protection plans are fairly common in institutions of higher education.

The general popularity of Blue Cross illness and hospitalization and Blue Shield surgical plans has probably influenced many boards of education to become more interested in providing health insurance for their teachers. Many urban districts and an increasing number of rural districts have such plans in effect or are in the process of developing them. In addition, some districts are paying all or part of the cost of some insurance plans.

An NEA Research Division survey[9] in 1960-61 revealed that in 621 urban districts of 30,000 or more population, 22 per cent paid in part for the premiums for group health and medical insurance. Sixteen per cent of the urban districts involved paid in part for group life insurance premiums. Only 10 per cent of the districts paid part of income protection insurance. In all of the categories, relatively more of the larger than the smaller districts assumed part of the cost of premiums.

The foregoing represents a distinct gain over previous years, and in the present period of a highly competitive market for teachers, such non-salary benefits as are represented by the various kinds of insurance plans are likely to increase. Some state education associations have group insurance programs for their members and the NEA has recently inaugurated a group term life insurance membership plan. Effective in December, 1961, for the first time this life insurance plan offered to all members of the NEA and the affiliated state associations the following insurance amounts at the cost indicated:

---

[9]NEA Research Bulletin, Vol. 39, No. 3, October 1961, pp. 92-93.

NEA LIFE INSURANCE*				
Age	Amount Before Dec. 1, 1962	Amount Beginning Dec. 1, 1962 or one year after beginning policy	Annual Cost	
Less than 50	$4,000	$5,000	Less than 30	$ 9.10
50 to 59	2,000	2,500	30 or over	$22.60
60 to 69	1,200	1,500		

This insurance plan is underwritten by the Prudential Insurance Company of America. The insurance terminates at the age of 70, or it may be converted within the two calender months after termination to an individual policy without furnishing evidence of insurability.

The chief requirement for this insurance, in addition to maintenance of premium payments, is that the teacher be a member of the NEA and the affiliated state association. You can obtain information about this plan from your student NEA chapter or from the NEA Insurance Trust, P. O. Box 2013, Washington 13, D. C. The administration office, where all questions about payments, beneficiary options, claims, and the like should be sent, is NEA Insurance Trust, P. O. Box 888, Newark 1, New Jersey.

It seems likely to the authors that group insurance plans of various kinds will become more generally available to teachers in the next few years. Currently, some state associations hold that work for increased salaries is of first importance. With this many teachers will agree. In any event, the trend seems to be toward advancement along all lines.

You will do well to study carefully group and individual insurance plans since you soon may be in a position to make decisions about them.

Credit Unions for Teachers

Teachers can help themselves through credit unions. You may find early in your career or even later that you need to borrow money. If the

---

*As of March 31, 1963, new benefits were added to the plan. Plan A adds a monthly disability income payment of $100 monthly at age less than 50, and $50 monthly at ages 50 to 59 (after being totally disabled for more than 9 months). These added benefits are at the same cost as indicated above. Plan B doubles the life insurance benefits and adds an accidental death benefit (or double indemnity) with the same monthly disability income benefits as indicated above. The costs of Plan B are just double those indicated above, or $18.20 for those of ages less than 30, and $45.20 for ages over 30.

school system in which you teach has a credit union, your problem may be simplified. High rates of interest on money borrowed from the usual sources, and particularly in the case of the average commercial loan company, can be avoided if you can borrow from your teachers' credit union. If you are fortunate enough to have money to invest, the credit union may provide a good opportunity.

The credit union is a corporation authorized by and operating under the laws of a given state. Such laws provide the basis necessary for protecting investments of the union.

There is a national organization of local credit unions and state credit union leagues known as the Credit Union National Association, or CUNA. Through CUNA, members have an insurance company, the CUNA Mutual Insurance Society of Madison, Wisconsin. Some unions insure their members through CUNA. Others have their own insurance programs.

NEA has a standing committee on credit unions. The committee serves to keep the teaching profession informed about the need for and value of credit unions. It also seeks to make credit union services available to all schools, and to encourage teacher credit unions to broaden their field of membership. According to the NEA through this committee,[10] in 1961-62 there were over 1,300 school and college credit unions in the nation, and many local groups were reported as expressing interest in forming new credit unions.

Teacher Leaves of Absence

There are several types of leave for teachers. In the main, they are leaves for illness and/or disability, maternity leaves, and professional leaves (for study, sabbaticals, professional conferences, and the like).

The most common type of leave in school districts throughout the nation is sick leave. This is a natural development since a person who is ill, regardless of his kind of work, is less effective and even a hazard to those around. In addition, teaching is a type of work that taxes both physical and mental health. This is not always realized by the public, but nevertheless it makes necessary a reasonable policy on sick leave.

It should be pointed out that the teaching profession, like other professions and occupational groups, has within it some persons with unprofessional attitudes. Some have taken advantage of sick leave plans by being absent without just cause. Such unprofessional attitude, of

---

[10]NEA Handbook of Local, State and National Association for 1962-63, p. 109. Washington, D. C. The NEA, 1962.

course, retards progress. As the profession matures, we can expect improvement in this respect. This would seem to be an area, along with many others involving personal conduct, in which the profession itself can be more effective in policing its own ranks.

A 1961 survey[11] of legal provisions on leaves of absence made by the NEA Research Division indicates that 33 states and the District of Columbia have legislation dealing with sick leave for teachers. Several other states have provisions, such as state board of education regulations and various kinds of permissive legislation, relative to sick leave. Leaves are authorized both with and without pay. Twenty-five of the states and the District of Columbia have specific state-wide mandatory provisions for fully paid sick leave for teachers.

It appears that as the NEA and state associations together with other interested groups, continue to press for more adequate sick leave policies, steady gain in mandatory state legislation is resulting. Since 1957, for example, at least four states have joined the list of those with state-wide mandatory sick leave laws.[12]

In addition, many districts throughout the nation have adopted local sick leave plans without the prompting of state law. A vast majority of urban districts have sick leave policies, with rural districts lagging behind as is usual in terms of salary and welfare matters in general. As implied before, however, the number of teachers covered by sick leave plans is growing. With a majority of all districts having some kind of sick leave plan, we can expect this coverage to grow in the immediate years ahead.

The amount of sick leave varies from state to state and from district to district, but ten days of paid leave per year is most common. Another fairly common practice is to provide for accumulation of unused days of sick leave from year to year to a specified maximum or total.

You should check on local district sick leave policy in seeking a position. The authors believe that a policy of at least twenty days paid sick leave per year, cumulative to at least a half or full year in a five- to seven-year period, is reasonable at present. You likely will not find such a plan in effect currently in many districts. Obviously, costs are involved. As more adequate ways of financing public education are developed and accepted they will aid in this and many other areas of school and teacher need.

---

[11]NEA Research Division, Research Bulletin, Vol. 39, No. 3, October, 1961: Washington, D. C. The NEA, 1961, pp. 94-95.

[12]*Ibid.*, p. 94.

Maternity leaves, while not nearly as common as sick leave plans, appear to be increasing as more married women teachers are being retained and even recruited. As we continue to face teacher shortages in most levels and areas, we have real need for all qualified personnel regardless of marital status. With continued rising birth rates, this need appears to be an indefinite one for at least many years.

Again, urban areas have had maternity-leave plans for some time, with rural areas lagging behind. Studies by the NEA and state associations indicate some gains in recent years in implementing maternity-leave policies.

Since maternity leave demands longer periods of time than sick leave, there are some problems involved. Among them are progress on the salary schedule, tenure rights, and retirement credit and payment.

It would seem that a reasonable maternity-leave plan would be flexible and simple. Details that would impinge on family privacy or limit the rights of teachers to live normal lives seem entirely unnecessary.

A flexible plan would allow for mutual agreement of teacher and employer as to when the leave begins and when it ends without fixed rules. Laws probably would have to be changed with respect to retirement credits and payments. It would seem reasonable that an arrangement could be made to count maternity-leave time in the service years for retirement purposes. The matter of teacher contributions presents a difficulty since there are normally no salary payments from which to make the usual retirement deductions. This simply could be omitted for the period of leave with resumption on return to service.

The matters of salary progression and tenure rights could be worked out by the local district. Needed are rules that state that salary progression resumes at the step level achieved when the teacher left, and that maternity leave does not disturb tenure rights.

Sabbatical leaves and other kinds of professional leaves are quite common. On the college and university level, sabbatical leaves are almost universal. This probably has influenced the gradual development of such leaves for public school teachers. Temporary absence to attend professional meetings or to visit other schools is provided for to some extent, but it is far from universal.

The purpose of such professional and sabbatical leaves is educational — to enable the teacher to improve himself so that his contribution in service to his school and his pupils or students can be increased.

Sabbatical leaves are based on the traditional college plan of the seventh year. Where provided, such leaves are from one-half year to a year in length. In institutions of higher education they are granted with half to full pay. Half-pay is most common.

The situation varies greatly among public school systems, but some gains can be expected as the profession matures and ways and means of financing education improve. A few states have enacted laws in recent years giving local districts the right to grant professional and sabbatical leaves.

You are encouraged to investigate professional leave provisions in local district plans. They may be indicative of an enlightened policy or adequate finance or both.

TOPICS AND QUESTIONS FOR STUDY AND DISCUSSION

1. Study the changes in the certification requirements in your state over the past decade. What are the most significant developments?
2. Are teachers' certificates or licenses necessary?
3. Before one can practice law, he must pass the state bar examination. Would a like requirement for teachers be desirable?
4. Define or explain the following terms: provisional certificate, permanent certificate, emergency certificate.
5. Is the large number of certificates issued by the several states desirable? Why or why not?
6. Would it be desirable for all states to have the same requirement for a teaching certificate?
7. Should all emergency certificates be eliminated now? Why or why not?
8. What are some of the chief barriers to reciprocity among the states in certification? Why is reciprocity desirable?
9. What are the chief features of the tenure laws in your state?
10. What are the advantages and disadvantages of tenure for teachers?
11. Define the following terms:
    Retirement allowance   Pension
    Joint-contributory plan   Annuity
12. How does the retirement or pension system for teachers in your state compare with the systems now effective in neighboring and other states?
13. Does the retirement plan in your state meet the profession's goal of at least one-half or more of final average salary as an allowance at time of retirement?
14. What do you consider to be the chief essentials of a good retirement plan for teachers?
15. What particular advantages does social security offer over prevailing state retirement plans?
16. Does social security coverage supplement the retirement plan in your state? If not, what is the arrangement?
17. If you do not have social security coverage of teachers in your state, what can you do to help gain it?
18. Is social security coverage of teachers desirable? Explain.

19. Secure the latest copies of social security information, booklets and leaflets at your local post office or other government building. Can you figure your social security allowance at retirement time? What will be your costs in monthly contributions?
20. Investigate insurance plans available to teachers in your state. It is suggested that you check the plans available in an urban district and in a rural or central school district.
21. Why should you be very careful about purchasing both individual and group insurance plans? What are the chief essentials to be considered in evaluating insurance plans?
22. Why are teachers considered to be "good" insurance risks? Should this play a part in getting insurance bargains?
23. What are the chief values of credit unions for teachers?
24. Could you and your colleagues form your own credit union? Could you form your own group insurance plan?
25. What are the essentials of a desirable "leave" plan for a local district or for a state mandated plan?
26. Check the latest NEA Research Division reports and bulletins for information on teacher certification, tenure, retirement, group insurance and leaves of absence.
27. Secure the latest issue of the Retirement Handbook or Primer describing your state plan. What information does it afford?

SELECTED REFERENCES

Armstrong, W. Earl, and T. M. Stinnett, A Manual on Certification for School Personnel in the U. S., Washington, D. C. The NEA, 1961.

Burrup, Percy E., The Teacher and the Public School System, New York: Harper and Brothers, 1960.

Chamberlain, Leo N., and Leslie W. Kindred, The Teacher and School Organization, Englewood Cliffs, N. J.: Prentice-Hall, Inc., Third Edition, 1958.

Cressman, George R., and Harold W. Benda, Public Education in America, New York: Appleton-Century-Crofts, Inc., Second Edition., 1961.

Eastmond, Jefferson N., The Teacher and School Administration, Boston: Houghton-Mifflin Co., 1959.

Elsbree, Willard S., The American Teacher, New York: American Book Co., 1939.

Elsbree, Willard S., and E. Edmund Reuttar, Jr., Staff Personnel in the Public Schools, New York: Prentice-Hall, Inc., 1954.

Gould, George, and Gerald Alan Yoakam, The Teacher and His Work, N. Y.: Ronald Press Co., 1954.

Grieder, Calvin, and Stephen Romine, American Public Education — An Introduction, New York: The Ronald Press Co., Second Edition, 1955.

Kearney, Nolan C., A Teacher's Professional Guide, Englewood Cliffs, N. J.: Prentice-Hall, Inc., 1958.

Moore, Harold E., and Newell B. Walters, Personnel Administration in Education, New York: Harper and Brothers, 1955.

NEA Handbook, 1962-63, Washington, D. C.: The NEA, 1962.
NEA Research Division, Washington, D. C.: The NEA
Estimates of School Statistics, 1958-59.
Systems of Retirement to Which Teachers Belong, October, 1961.
The Teacher and the Law, Monograph, 1959-M3, 1959.
NEA Research Bulletin
Volume 38, No. 3, October, 1960.
Volume 39, No. 3, October, 1961.
New York State Teachers Association, *Teacher Merit and Teacher Salary*,
Report of Special Committee on Merit Payments, Albany, N. Y.: 1957.
Reeder, Ward G., *A First Course in Education*, New York: The Macmillan
Co., Fourth Edition, 1958.
Richey, Robert W., *Planning for Teaching*, New York: McGraw-Hill Book
Co., Inc., Second Edition, 1958.
Thomas, Lawrence G., Lucien B. Kinney, Arthur P. Coladarci and Helen A.
Fielstra, *Perspective on Teaching*, Englewood Cliffs, N. J.: Prentice-Hall,
Inc. 1961.
Van Dalen, Deobold B., and Robert W. Brittell, *Looking Ahead to Teaching*,
Boston: Allyn and Bacon, Inc., 1959.
Wahlquist, John T., and Patrick J. Ryan, *An Introduction to American Edu-
cation*, New York: The Ronald Press Co., Second Edition, 1958.
Woellner, R. C., and Aurilla Wood, *Requirements for Certification*, Chicago:
University of Chicago Press, 1958-59.
———. *Requirements for Certification*, Chicago: University of Chicago Press,
1959-60.
Wynn, Richard, *Careers in Education*, New York: McGraw-Hill Book Co.,
Inc., 1960.
Yauch, W. A., Martin H. Bartels, and Emmet Morris, *The Beginning Teacher*,
N. Y.: Henry Holt Co., 1955.

Chapter 9

Securing A Teaching Position

*Blessed is he who has found his work; let
him ask no other blessedness.*

> Thomas Carlyle
> *Past and Present*
> *Book III Chap. II*

Once you have completed your college preparation for teaching you
are confronted with the problem of job selection. In some respects job
selection is analogous to launching a missile. If the guidance system
miscalculates the course of the missile by a single degree its entire
mission may be destroyed. This seemingly small miscalculation is greatly
magnified throughout the duration of the missile's flight. It is vital to
get the missile off to a "good" start. For your own future, it is equally
as important for you to get off to a "good" start in your profession. A
seriously large number of beginning teachers leave the teaching profession at the close of their first year of teaching. Many have become
disillusioned or discouraged as a result of poor job selection.[1] They
generalize about *all* teaching situations on the basis of one unhappy
experience. Actually no teaching situation is "good" or "bad" from the
vantage point of a teacher, excepting as the teacher himself conceives
it. While one teacher may view a particular classroom setting as a
depressing or even hopeless situation, another may view the same

[1]Lou Kleinman, "A New Dimension In Teacher Education," *Journal of Ed.
Sociology*, Vol. 34, Sept., 1960, pp. 24-33.

classroom setting as an exciting challenge. Selecting a teaching position therefore becomes a matter of compiling an accurate description of the job and then "matching" the candidate with the job. This matching process involves attaining congruency between the professional and personal expectations and aspirations of the teacher candidate and the characteristics of the teaching position. The process is not one-sided. Thoughtful job selection benefits not only the teacher candidate but the school, community and profession as well. Most job procurement agents, such as college placement offices and commercial employment agencies, attempt to match teacher and position to the best of their ability. You can make the job of such agencies much easier by attempting to crystallize your own thinking in relation to the type of teaching position you desire. Student teaching will assist you a great deal in this as it offers a firsthand opportunity to view the components of a total school program.

Perhaps the results of the following one-item questionnaire[2] will help shed some light upon your deliberations:

Question: What *two* elements do you consider to be of greatest importance in selecting your first teaching position?

The authors recognize that this questionnaire is subject to all of the limitations, frailties and weaknesses inherent in this type of research device. The questionnaire also employs a small and restricted sampling. These shortcomings notwithstanding, the responses point to some interesting conclusions. One statistic gleaned from this questionnaire is that the freshmen education majors placed little importance upon the educational philosophy of a school but seniors relegated prime importance to it. This could be interpreted to mean that the intervening three years of college training serve to point up its importance.

A second obvious fact is that the education majors placed prime importance upon salary. The authors feel this to be a wholesome attitude. Certainly it can be blown out of proportion, but it is a facet of the profession which has long been neglected. Teacher candidates who are vitally concerned about receiving a salary commensurate with their college training and vital service to the community can serve only to strengthen the entire salary picture. Teaching, likened to any other major profession such as medicine or law, should be financially very well supported.

---

[2]Neil Howard and Alvin Westcott, unpublished survey. Syracuse and Oswego, New York, 1959.

RANDOM SAMPLE

		Answers
45 Syracuse University Seniors	(Ed. majors) (SUs)	90
113 State University of New York –(Seniors– College at Oswego	Ed. majors) (Os)	226
42 State University of New York — (Freshmen — College at Oswego	Ed. majors) (Of)	84

Elements Stated	Per cent of total responses		
	SUs	Os	Of
1. General character of the community	10	10.1	7.1
2. Special professional services and teachers available — art, music, psychology P. Ed.	7.7	2.6	0
3. Educational philosophy of the school	32.2	30.1	4.7
4. Physical facilities of the school	8.8	3.9	5.9
5. Grade level	4.4	4.8	3.5
6. Location of the school geographical)	4.4	7	29.7
7. Salary	15.5	20.7	32.1
8. Rate of turnover of teachers on the staff	1.1	1.3	0
9. General characteristics of the school fac.	1.1	3.5	9.5
10. Availability of educational resources — films, textbooks audio-visual materials	3.3	3.9	0
11. Over-all work load of the teacher	4.4	3	0
12. Curriculum content and development procedures	1.1	1.7	0
13. Opportunity for professional growth	2.2	1.7	7.1
14. Class size	3.3	2.2	0
15. Grouping of children within the school	0	2.6	0

In studying the choices made by these education majors on this questionnaire you may identify with other ideas which are important to you.

The placement of a new teacher in a teaching job is analogous to fitting a precious gem to a setting. The two elements can detract from or enhance one another in terms of the total effect or end result. Decide what type of teaching position will best suit your personality and talents and persist until you acquire it.

Many vehicles or avenues are at the disposal of the teacher candidate who is seeking employment. The three most commonly used are the college or university placement office, a commercial employment agency or personal contact. The results of a questionnaire sent out by the New York State Teachers Association gives some indication of the agency utilization picture. How did 1,161 classroom teachers in New York State locate their original teaching position or relocate to another teaching position?

State-wide Summary of Teacher Placement Sources[3]

	Per Cent Reporting Use of Source by			
ITEM	Teachers in Original Positions Who Have		Teachers Who Have Relocated and Have	
	−10 yrs. Exp.	10 or +yrs. Exp.	−10 yrs.	10 or +yrs.
Total Replies	312	99	−476	274
Placement Source:				
1—Personal Contact (with)	48.8%	50.5%	64.2%	73.4%
—administrator	29.5	28.3	44.3	43.4
—a teacher	9.3	2.0	9.2	8.0
—a board member	1.6	10.1	3.6	11.7
—a friend	4.5	5.1	3.8	2.6
—other persons	1.9	5.0	3.3	7.7
2—College or University Placement Service	40.0	24.2	14.7	6.2
—teachers college	25.3	19.2	9.0	3.3
—other	14.7	5.0	5.7	2.9
3—Commercial Agency	4.2	7.1	7.4	12.8
4—All other Sources	8.9	18.2	13.7	7.6

The authors feel that these percentages are not atypical of the general national picture.

It's a Port In the Storm.

The college placement office is probably the first employment agency with which you will have contact as a beginning teacher. The personnel which man this "port" are well trained in helping teacher candidates to secure a suitable teaching position. Most college placement offices adhere closely to the principles and practices set forth by The College Placement Council, Inc.[4]

---

[3]New York State Teachers Association, "Public Education Research Bulletin," Albany, New York, Oct., 1960.

[4]The College Placement Council, Inc., "The Principles and Practices of College Recruiting," 35 E. Elizabeth Ave., Bethlehem, Pa.

Your college placement office will have specified procedures for helping you with job procurement. Help them to help you by being professionally ethical in all of your dealings. College placement services are free of charge to graduates of the particular college in which the office is maintained.

Commercial Employment Agencies.

These agencies provide the same basic functions that the college placement office provides. Since they are commercial ventures their services are supported by fees. The agency charges to clients vary in terms of the services desired. The amounts also vary with reference to whether the contract is for a flat fee or a per cent of the salary obtained.

If a teacher moves about by changing teaching jobs periodically, then he may either lose contact with or not be geographically located near his college placement office. Here is another instance where a commercial agency can be of particular value. The services of the commercial agency have unique attraction to the teacher candidate who is attempting to locate a teaching position a great distance from home base. Some of the larger agencies maintain regional offices throughout the country.

There is a standard code of operational ethics to which most commercial employment agencies subscribe. In general these agencies do provide a highly utilitarian service.

The names and addresses of commercial employment agencies can be found through their advertisements in professional teachers' journals (such as the professional journal of your state teacher's association or the NEA) as well as in newspapers, magazines and the yellow pages of telephone directories. If all else fails you can write to the National Association of Teachers' Agencies, 620 Case Building, 82 St. Paul St., Rochester 4, N. Y., to secure the name of the agency nearest to you.

Have You Considered These?

You will not be eligible immediately for most teaching positions described in the following few paragraphs if you are a beginning teacher, since teaching experience is usually required. You may want, however, to tuck away the following job opportunities for future investigation.

The United States Department of Health, Education and Welfare has some very fine positions available periodically in the field of education. Such positions as Education Research and Program Specialist or Education Specialist (in various subject matter fields) are often available. The salaries presently range from $6,435 to $13,730 per year depending upon your qualifications. For information regarding these and other positions contact your regional civil service office or write to: Executive Secretary, Board of U. S. Civil Service Examiners, Office of Education, Department of Health, Education and Welfare, Washington 25, D. C.

Another source of good positions in the educational field is your state education department. Here again special requirements in terms of academic preparation and field experience are usually keys to the job. Descriptions of the various job vacancies can be obtained by writing to your state education department.

Bon Voyage! If you seek foreign travel as one of your personal ambitions and would like to couple it with some professional experience, then you should consider the foreign teacher exchange program[5] or a United States Government Dependent School. The armed services maintain overseas dependent schools and hire teachers who have had two or more years of teaching experience. While the salaries of these positions are not highly attractive, transportation is provided free of charge and there are many other valuable fringe benefits. For further information write to:

> Navy Overseas Employment Office
> Headquarters, Potomac River Naval Command
> Washington 25, D. C.
>
> or,
>
> Civilian Personnel Officer
> Brooklyn Army Terminal
> 58th St. & 1st Ave.
> Brooklyn 50, New York
>
> or,
>
> Chief of Overseas Employment Branch
> Overseas and Field Affairs Division
> Directorate of Civilian Personnel
> Department of the Air Force
> Washington 25, D. C.

---

[5]U. S. Department of Health, Education, and Welfare, *Teacher Exchange Opportunities,* Educational Exchange and Training Branch, Teacher Exchange Section, Washington, 25, D. C., 1963-4.

Perhaps you would like to secure capsuled information relative to teaching positions open in UNESCO and the Peace Corps in addition to the three armed services. If this is the case then you may want to secure a copy of:

Teaching Opportunities Overseas
Hill International Publications,
P.O. Box 79, East Islip, N.Y.

Included in this booklet is a list of private schools overseas together with one of American firms employing teachers abroad.

A Job In Another State.

Some first year teachers desire to secure a teaching position in a state other than the one in which their teachers' college is located. This means obtaining a teaching license (certification) in another state and sometimes necessitates job hunting on a long distance basis. To determine the requirements for a teacher's license in another state you can write to the education department (teacher certification division) of the state government that is involved. Sometimes reciprocity is permitted or perhaps you may have to take some addiitonal academic courses to become licensed. Check the certification section of Chapter 8 for further details.

The other problem that often arises is how to locate a suitable teaching position in a state which is not at all familiar to you. For example, you have graduated from a teacher training institution in New Jersey. You have been recently married and your husband's work requires you to move to California. How can you locate a suitable teaching position in California in advance of your arriving there? Very often the state teachers' organization can supply you with information. Howard Chandler and Company publishes a series of booklets related to teaching in various states. You might find the one entitled "Teaching In California" of particular help.[6] For a complete listing of this series write to the address in the footnote below.

Another alternative would be to write letters of inquiry to school systems in towns and cities near where you will be located. This, however, is rather a hit-or-miss operation. Here is where a teacher employment agency can be of particular value. If you contact an agency and describe to them the type of position you desire they will handle the problem for you. This service, you must remember, costs money, but may be well worth the investment.

---

[6]Ted Bass and Arnold Wolpert, *Teaching In California,* Howard Chandler, Publisher, 660 Market Street, San Francisco 4, California.

You might also find in your job hunting dilemma that a placement journal entitled *Crusade* is helpful. It is published monthly (except October) by the Advancement and Placement Institute, Box 99, Brooklyn 22, New York. This same publisher also produces the World-Wide Graduate Award Directory and the Annual World-Wide Summer Placement Directory. No fee is charged to subscribers locating jobs through *Crusade.*

In some instances the U. S. Office of Employment can be helpful to an applicant for a teaching position in another state. The U. S. Office of Employment operates as a part of the Department of Labor, Washington 25, D. C. In addition to the national office, the federal government financially supports the operation of state employment services in each state. For the most immediate employment help you therefore can contact the nearest state employment office in your particular state. These employment offices list job openings for teachers in their particular areas.

Last but not least is your own college placement office. It is probably the first place to check for information, advice and vacancies in the state you desire. Many placement offices, especially those in small colleges, do not handle teacher placement out of state. For this reason all the foregoing information was provided.

Should I Teach In a Private School?

This is a question which ultimately only you can answer in the light of your own teaching goals. A private school founded upon a sound educational premise can offer certain teachers a rich teaching experience. A private school whose existence is based largely upon some type of undemocratic segregation or social snobbery is automatically operating within an unwholesome educational framework.

Many private schools offer valuable and unique curricular programs which are more rigorous than average public school programs. Still other private schools are geared toward a particular religious or occupational point of view. If one of these educational paths is particularly congruent with your educational philosophy then you should consider the private school in your employment prospects.

In fairness to all concerned, some private schools expect a greatly expanded role for the teacher. This may include such things as residing at the school, proctoring dormitories in the evening, teaching a wider variety of academic subjects, and a longer work day in general. A teacher in a private school usually is not eligible for the state retirement program; however in a recent survey over 85 per cent of the private schools responding have some other type of retirement program.

Teaching in a private school may be tailored to *your* personal and professional talents and expectations. For further information related to private schools write to:

> National Council of Independent Schools
> 84 State Street
> Boston, Massachusetts

Letter of Inquiry.

One alternative to locating a teaching position when you are unsure of whether or not a vacancy exists is to write a letter of inquiry to the hiring officials of the school. If you are unfamiliar with the hiring procedure in the school then address your letter of inquiry to the superintendent of schools. The purpose of the letter is to determine if the school has any vacancy or anticipates any vacancy on their teaching staff, and the nature of the vacancy. The letter frequently states the candidate's interest in seeking a teaching position and the type being sought.

In your letter of inquiry it is proper to request an employment application form be sent to you if a vacancy exists. Since the letter of inquiry may be your initial contact with a school it is important to make it an exemplary bit of prose. A sample letter of inquiry is as follows:

> 16 Oakwood Avenue
> Nowheresville, Texas
> May 3, 1964

Mr. Everette Sherwood
Superintendent of Schools
120 Main Street
Notown, Texas

Dear Sir:

I am a senior majoring in elementary education at Ivy Wall University. I am seeking a teaching position in the primary grades beginning in September of this years.

Information has reached me regarding the fine opportunities that your school system offers to its staff members. Do you expect to have any vacancies at the beginning of the next school session, commencing in September? I am very interested in teaching in your school system.

Kindly send me an employment application form if you are interested in my candidacy and anticipate a vacancy in the primary grades.

Sincerely,
Charlotte Burke

Application Materials

There is nothing mysterious or hazardous about job application materials. Irrespective of the occupation, the purpose of application materials is to introduce you to the prospective employer.

The Application Form.

Once a school is interested in you as a teacher candidate, it will send you a job application form to complete. This form usually precedes the personal interview, and is designed to ferret out your general qualifications for the job. There are some standard commercial formats which many schools use. Other schools have an individualized application form which they have created to suit their own needs. Two sample application forms are as follows:

FOR USE BY CENTRAL OFFICE ONLY

Receipt Acknowledged ....

References Requested ....

Card Made ....

A P P L I C A T I O N

Department of Personnel
MONTGOMERY COUNTY PUBLIC SCHOOLS
850 North Washington Street
Rockville, Maryland

FOR USE BY CENTRAL OFFICE ONLY

Degree ....

Years Experience ....

Step on Schedule ....

Salary ....

Date ....

1. Name .... Soc. Sec. Number ....
   (Last)   (First)   (Middle or Maiden)
2. Permanent Address: 3. Present Address (until):

   Street ....   Street ....

   City ....   City ....

   State .... Phone .... State .... Phone ....

4. Sex: Male ..... Female ..... Date of Birth .... Place of Birth ....
                                                              Place of
5. Citizen of U.S.A.: Yes .... No .... If naturalized, give date .... naturalization ....

6. Height .... Weight ....   7. Marital Status: Single ..... Married .....
                                                 If married--name of spouse ....
8. Ages of Children .... Widowed ..... Divorced ..... Separated ....

9. Physical Defects, if any ....

10. Your Present Salary .... 11. Date Available ....

12. Type of Transportation: Own Transportation .... Public Transportation ....

13. Position You Prefer: (give details such as grade, subject, or field)

    First Preference ....   Second Preference ....

14. Do you hold a Maryland teaching certificate: Yes .... No .... Number ....

    Type .... Date Issued .... Expiration Date ....

15. Do you hold teaching certificates from other states?

    Issuing Authority .... Type .... Date Issued ....

    Subject(s) or grade(s) ....

16. If you took the National Teachers' Examination, please indicate your score: ....

    Breakdown: Nonverbal Reasoning .... Weighted Common Exam Total .... Science & Math ....

    Professional Information .... English Expression .... Social Studies, etc. ....

17. Have you previously filed an application with Montgomery County? Yes ..... No ..... Date ....

18. List professional and/or fraternal organizations of which you are a member: ....

    ....

    ....

19. List all full-time experience in chronological order.

EMPLOYER	CITY	COUNTY	STATE	POSITION GRADE OR SUBJECT TAUGHT	DATES INCLUSIVE	NUMBER OF YEARS

20. Education

HIGH SCHOOL	LOCATION	DATES

COLLEGE OR UNIVERSITY	LOCATION	DATES INCLUSIVE	DEGREE OR CREDITS	DATE RECEIVED	DATE EXPECTED

21. Practice Teaching Experience

SCHOOL	LOCATION	GRADE OR SUBJECT TAUGHT	DATES INCLUSIVE

22. In your own handwriting please express your philosophy of education in relation to your particular field.

23. Please list below all credits earned. This section **must** be completed. Minimum requirements for Junior and Senior High School (Secondary) and Elementary School positions:

    Completion of a standard four-year college course with credits in academic subjects and methods courses

	SECONDARY Not less than 24 semester hours in one of the following fields of study:		ELEMENTARY Not less than 80 semester hours in academic content courses including:	
	Required	Earned	Required	Earned
ENGLISH	24	_____	12	_____
SOCIAL STUDIES	36		15	
U. S. History	6	_____	6	_____
History	12	_____	3	_____
Economics	6	_____		_____
Geography			3	_____
Sociology, Geography, and Political Science	12	_____		_____
Other College Social Studies		_____	3	_____
HISTORY (including 6 s.h. of U. S. History)	24	_____		_____
GEOGRAPHY	24	_____		_____

MATHEMATICS	24	6
High School Mathematics	_____	
College Algebra	_____	_____
Trigonometry	_____	_____
Solid Geometry	_____	_____
Analytics	_____	_____
Other College Math	_____	_____
SCIENCE	36*	12**
Chemistry	_____	_____
Biology	_____	_____
Physics	_____	_____
Other College Science	_____	_____

*(At least 18 s.h. in Chemistry, Biology, or Physics and at least 6 s.h. in each of the other two fields of science)

**(4 s.h. in Physical Science, 4 s.h. in Biological Science, and 4 s.h. in Other Science)

CHEMISTRY	24	_____
BIOLOGY	24	_____
PHYSICS	24	_____
FRENCH	24	_____
SPANISH	24	_____
OTHER LANGUAGE	24	_____
ART	30	2 _____
MUSIC	30	2 _____
PHYSICAL EDUCATION	30	2 _____
SPECIAL SUBJECT (underscore subject)	30-40	_____
(Home Arts, Industrial Arts, Business Education, other: _____)		
PROFESSIONAL EDUCATION COURSES	18 _____	26 _____

Certificates shall be issued to post-1956 graduates from teacher-preparing institutions approved by the National Council for the Accreditation of Teacher Education; or to applicants who hold valid certificates from one of the states in the Northeast Reciprocity Compact Area or submit a statement of eligibility therefor; or to applicants who hold a bachelor's degree from an accredited institution and meet the above requirements.

24. Have you ever served in the U. S. Armed Forces: Yes ..... No ..... (If "no" go immediately to item 25; if "yes" complete the following items)

Dates Served: From .... to .... Branch of Service: ....

Original Entry: Inducted ..... Enlisted ..... Other ..... Did you enlist, reenlist, or otherwise

voluntarily extend your service after original entry in the armed service? Yes ..... No .....

25. All part-time experience and travel: (Give dates)

....

....

26. List extracurricular activities you have participated in as:

a. A Student ....

b. A Teacher ....

Underscore the following areas in which you are skilled:

a. Sports: Baseball; Basketball; Football; Track; Other (List) ....

b. Music: Singing; Piano or Other Musical Instrument (List) ....

27. REMARKS: (Please submit any additional information which may seem appropriate) ....

....

28. REFERENCE: Please give names of four persons in a supervisory capacity (critic teacher, supervisor of student teaching program, or college professor) who know of your success or probable success as a teacher. Experienced teachers please give names of the four most recent superintendents and/or principals.

PLEASE PRINT

	NAME	OFFICIAL POSITION	ADDRESS	DATES OF EMPLOYMENT
a				
b				
c				
d				

29. Have you ever been arrested, summoned into court as a defendant, convicted, fined, imprisioned or placed on probation; or has any case been instituted against you? Yes ( ) No ( ) Have you been ordered to deposit collateral for an alleged breach or violation of any law, ordinance or police regulation within the past five years? Yes ( ) No ( ) Do not include traffic violations for which a fine of $25 or less was imposed. All other charges must be included even if they were dismissed. If your answer is "Yes" to either of the above questions, please provide complete details on a separate sheet stating approximate date, charge, place and action taken. This may be submitted at the time of interview.

30. Teacher employees are required to be fingerprinted by the Montgomery County Board of Education.

31. Teacher employees of the Montgomery County Board of Education are required to join the Teachers' Retirement System of the State of Maryland; and are required to submit evidence of one of the following: Chest X-Ray, Intradermal Tuberculin Test or Physical Examination by a Physician prior to reporting for duty and annually thereafter.

32. Falsification of any information submitted on this application shall be cause for dismissal from service.

The information as submitted on this application is accurate to the best of my knowledge. I concur in the above statements and requirements.

....
(Signature)

APPLICATION NOT CONSIDERED
COMPLETE WITHOUT PHOTOGRAPH

ATTACH

SMALL PHOTOGRAPH

HERE

(APPLICANT -- DO NOT FILL IN. FOR USE BY CENTRAL OFFICE)
Interviewed by ....
Date of Interview ....
Comments: 1   2   3   4   5

Interviewed by ....
Date of Interview ....
Comments: 1   2   3   4   5

Number...

NEW BEDFORD PUBLIC SCHOOLS
New Bedford, Massachusetts

APPLICATION BLANK

Name in full .... Date ....

Present Address .... Telephone Number ....

Permanent Address .... Telephone Number ....

Date of Birth .... Height .... Weight ....

General Health .... Estimate of occupational time lost during last five years on account

of illness .... Physical Defects ....

Marital Status: Single................ Married................ Widow(er)................ Separated................ No. of children................

Are you a citizen of the United States of America? ....

Present Position ....

Grade and Subject   School   Place

Present Salary................ What salary will you accept?................ When can you accept a position?................

Are you willing to come to New Bedford for an interview at your own expense?...

Have you taken the National Teacher Examinations?................If so, please submit results with this application.

Position for which you are applying: (Check the grades; write the subjects)

Elementary (Kdg. - 6)................ 1st choice .... 2nd choice .... 3rd choice ....

Junior High School................Subjects: 1.. 2..

3.. 4.. ....

Senior High School .... Subjects: 1................................ 2................................ 3................................

Other ....

— Do not write in the space below —

Notes and Comments of Admininstrative Staff

....

....

....

....

....

Assignment: Salary: $

EDUCATIONAL AND PROFESSIONAL PREPARATION

Kind of School	Name and Location of School	Dates Attended	Summer Sess. in Weeks	Degree or Diploma	Major Subjects	Minor Subjects
High School						
College or University						
Other Schools						

NOTE: A transcript of college record must be filed with this application, before it can be considered complete.

Do you hold the Massachusetts Teacher's Certificate? Yes................ No................

Certificate Number: .... Date: .... Area: ....

If the answer is "No" what are your plans to obtain this certificate?

....

Have you ever been arrested or convicted of a crime?................If "yes" give full particulars.

EXPERIENCE AND EMPLOYMENT RECORD

Within the four catagories that follow, list all experience, employment and military, chronologically, including intervals of unemployment, if any. Leave no gaps in your records since graduation from high school or college. If additional space is required, attach a sheet of paper.

A. Teaching Experience

Name and P. O. Address of School	From Mo. Yr.	To Mo. Yr.	Hours Per Day	Months Per Year	Subjects or Grades	*Kind of Teaching	Name and Address of Official who can Best Certify To Service

* (S Substitute; R Regular; E Evening; SS Sumer School; PT Practice Teaching)

B. Administrative or Supervisory Experience in Educational Fields

Name and P. O. Address of School	From Mo. Yr.	To Mo. Yr.	Title and Duties of Position Held	Name and Address of Official Who can Best Certify To Service

C. Other Employment Experience (Commercial, Industrial, Trade)

Employer—Name and Address of Person or Firm	From Mo. Yr.	To Mo. Yr.	Hours Per Week	Months Per Year	Title and Duties of Position Held; (Indicate Number of Persons Under Your Supervision)

D. Military Service Record

Branch of Service	From Mo. Yr.	To Mo. Yr.	Title or Rank	Date Discharged	Name and Address of Official Who Can Best Certify To Service

Other Professional Experiences (Educational travel, lecturing, study, publications, scholastic honors, etc.)

Dates	Nature of Experience	Time

Membership in Professional Organizations

1..   3..

2..   4..

If you are applying for a position in Kindergarten or Grades 1 - 4, please answer the following questions:

1. With what systems of primary reading are you familiar?

2. What systems have you taught?

3. Do you sing? .... What musical instrument do you play?

REFERENCE (Give the names of those who have closely observed your work as a teacher or employee or as student. Do not enclose letters of reference, or duplicate information contained in placement papers.)

—FOR OFFICE USE ONLY—

Name	Official Position	Present Address	Sent	Rec'd

College Placement Bureau where references may be obtained:...

Activities - Athletics, School Organizations, Hobbies, etc. ....

....

Describe briefly the nature and extent of your participation in those activities which you feel **qualified to direct**:

....

....

....

Write briefly on one of the following topics, giving additional information of interest or value regarding your candidacy; for instance, participation in community or professional activities, membership in professional organizations, interest in New Bedford, your philosophy of education, your professional aspirations. Use additional piece of paper if necessary.

....
                                                                                   Signature of Applicant

The application form is the initial screening device used by the employer. Simple common sense rules should govern the manner in which you handle the application form.

1. Read all questions carefully.
2. Follow directions meticulously.
3. Write (or print as the form may request) legibly.
4. Be neat, as neatness is always appreciated.
5. Give strictly honest answers.
6. Be brief yet answer the questions fully.
7. Employ correct spelling and grammar.

College placement offices and teacher employment agencies utilize written forms which you may have to complete. These forms are necessary in order that the employment agent can catalog your qualifications and pinpoint your employment needs. The seven simple rules listed under application forms also apply to them.

Any one of the initial written forms which you are asked to fill out by employment officials or agencies can make an impression upon the reader. You want to make a favorable impression. As superficial as these materials might seem to some of you, employers often consider the manner in which you handle employment forms as indicative of your general work habits. The authors strongly encourage job candidates to make all of their written contacts with a prospective employer the best examples possible. Forms and letters that are messy or contain spelling and grammatical errors are poor advertisements for candidacy as a new teacher.

Smile At the Birdie! Many teacher employment application forms request a photograph of the applicant. Photographs often are included as part of a professional résumé. In *some* states, due to fair employment practice laws, it is unlawful for an employer to *require* a photogarph of the job applicant. As in all matters concerning employment application, common sense should guide your actions. Considerations relative to the job application photograph are no exception. The photograph you submit with any job application form or résumé should be one which presents your physical attributes as attractively as possible. To achieve this you may need to have several pictures taken by a professional photographer. After selecting the most favorable one, have several copies made. The photo should picture you in professional attire with a natural, pleasant expression on your face. The photo should not be misleading or misrepresentative. Try to avoid submitting the passport-type photo which often has the character of an F.B.I. "wanted" poster. Also avoid submitting the type of candid shots which belong in the family album but not on an employment form. Young ladies should definitely refrain from using the publicity oriented type photos. Remember, male applicants, that you are not entering a Mr. America contest and the young ladies are not running for Miss Universe. You are seeking admittance to a profession. While it is conceivable that your physical dimensions might influence some hiring officials, submitting such a photo is professionally in bad taste.

Season liberally your choice of photo with the grains of common sense.

The Personal Résumé

A résumé is a written factual summary of your vocational academic training and experiences as well as personal vital statistics. A résumé should *not* contain subjective material or personal value judgments.

Personal résumés are not as frequently used in the education field as in business and industry. The employment application form which most schools use supplants the need for the résumé. Personal résumés are used more frequently in the teaching profession in relation to filling higher administrative and supervisory positions.

A personal résumé can be returned to the school in addition to the application form if it contains information not asked for on the application. Sometimes a résumé is included with a letter of inquiry which precedes the application form.

The seven basic rules listed under "application forms" also apply to the construction of a résumé. A résumé should be written in ink or typewritten and be about one page in length. A personal résumé is your "story." It should help "sell you" to an employer. The following is a sample personal résumé which you might want to use as a guide in writing your own:

PERSONAL RÉSUMÉ[7]

NAME: John Dean Walpole

PRESENT ADDRESS: 48 Valequez Drive

TELEPHONE: MX 8-6498

BIRTHDAY: May 16, 1930

BIRTH PLACE: Rome, Georgia

SEX: Male

HEIGHT: 5' 8 1/2"

WEIGHT: 162 lbs.

PHYSICAL DEFECTS: Wear glasses (for astigmatism)

MARITAL STATUS: Married

NO. OF CHILDREN: Three

NAMES AND AGES: John Jr., 6; Scarlet. 8; Alice. 4.

SOCIAL SECURITY NO.: 282-8466

MILITARY SERVICE RECORD: 3 years, '49-'52 — honorable discharge.

MOTHER: Rita Noreen

FATHER: Frederick George

PHOTO

TYPE OF POSITION SOUGHT:
El. school teacher — 5th or 6th grade preferred

HOBBIES OR SPECIAL INTERESTS:
Photography
Reading
Tropical fish

Pre-College Education	NAME	LOCATION	DIPLOMA
Elementary	Horace Mann	Rome, Ga.	– – –
Senior High	Oggelthorpe	Rome, Ga.	Academic diploma

College Education	NAME	LOCATION	DATES	DIPLOMA
Duke University	Durham, North Carolina	'53-'57	B.S.—El. Ed.
Columbia University	New York, New York	Summer '57	6 grad. —cred. hrs.

Work Experiences	EMPLOYER	LOCATION	TYPE OF WORK	DATES
William S. Rogers	Cedertown, Ga.	5th grade	'58-'60
Camp O-Well-No	Crabtree, Vt.	arts & crafts instructor	Summers '58 & '59
Jefferson El. School	Canton, Ga.	6th grade	'60-'62

---

[7]The information given on this resume is fictitious.

Personal References — The Stamp of Approval.

College placement offices, employment agencies and employers will frequently request that you provide them with personal references. This is usually handled in one of two ways. You are either asked to submit names of people to whom reference forms may be sent or you are given the forms to deliver personally to your reference people. It is common courtesy to provide an addressed stamped envelop with the reference form so no postage fee need be paid by your reference person. Personal references carry much weight in the eyes of some employers and little in the eyes of others.

Choose those people who really know you, your work, or both, well. Personal references thus can be in relation to your character, your ability to perform some occupation, or both.

Refrain from asking a person who knows you only casually to write a personal reference for you. A person not well acquainted with you can honestly give you only a lukewarm recommendation. Sometimes this type of vague, general recommendation is worse than none.

Very often a school principal is too busy too observe student teachers assigned to his school. It therefore would be unwise for the student teachers to ask the principal to write a personal reference (recommendation) for them if he had not observed their work.

Choose your references carefully. Select the most prominent and influential people you know and who know you in a favorable light. One solid reference from a clergyman is generally advantageous.

Get your reference requests and/or forms to your reference people well in advance of the time they are needed. It is unpleasant to be rushed into writing a personal reference.

Interviewing

There are three common types of basic interviews which are employed by school hiring officials. The authors call these the tried-and-true trio. As a job candidate you usually have no advanced knowledge as to which type you will experience. It is therefore wise to be familiar with all three.

The "One to One" Interviews.

As the name implies, this involves the job candidate and one interviewer who has the power to hire you directly or makes a recommendation to another school official who has said power. Your whole "case" as a candidate for the job depends upon the impression you make upon this *one* individual. The strengths and weaknesses of this type of interview are obvious.

The Team Interview.

This particular interviewing pattern is used a great deal by business and industry and has crept substantially into the field of education. A "team" of two or more hiring officials from the same school system interview you together. The team might, for example, be composed of the principal, the elementary supervisor and the superintendent of schools. During the interview they all may "fire" questions at you. By employing this type of interview, all three school officials meet you and listen jointly to your responses. The evaluation of your job interview now rests with *three* individuals instead of one. This can be to your advantage as it is then possible to win a favorable two to one vote of the team and obtain the teaching job. This type of interview naturally saves time for you. Instead of having a separate interview with each of the team members (three interviews) you interact with all of them at once. There are, of course, negative aspects to this type of interviewing. Greater anxiety is often created in the job candidate when confronted (or outnumbered) by three formidable interviewers. What other disadvantages can you envision as being inherent in the team interview?

Pyramid Interviewing

Large school systems are more apt to employ this pattern of interviewing than small ones. In the literal sense this is not a type of interview but a pattern of scheduling "one to one" type interviews. To save the time and energy of very busy, high-echelon school officials, job candidates are subjected to a series of interviews beginning with lower level administrative personnel. If the candidate obtains a satisfactory rating in the first interview he is then scheduled for an interview with a staff member at a higher level of responsibility. If the candidate passes this interview, he is again passed upward until he either fails an interview and is rejected or reaches an administrator who has the power to hire him and does so. As you can see, the lower administrative interviewers act as a screening device. This allows the higher administrative executives to spend their time interviewing only the highly desirable candidates since others have been weeded out along the way. While this process may appear to be rigorous and time-consuming for the job candidate, it is a most efficient procedure when large numbers of job candidates are required. If a school system needs to fill 200 or 300 vacancies in a four-month period (May to August), many hundreds of applicants must be screened. It would be most wasteful for a top-echelon school executive such as the superintendent of schools to interview all of the applicants. Furthermore, it would take *all* of his working hours. A typical pyramid interview structure is shown in illustration (right). The purpose of all job interview patterns is the same — the employment of a suitable job candidate.

Perhaps the general description of the three interview patterns just given will eliminate for you some of the uncertainties.

Your personal job interview carries great importance. Many superintendents, principals, and hiring officials base their final decision regarding your employment upon the impressions that you make during your interview. They have access to college records, also in-

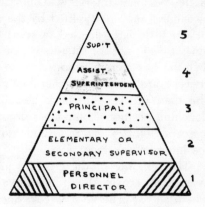

PYRAMID INTERVIEW PLAN

cluding your personal references. Armed with the information that they obtain in a candidate's written records they proceed to meet each candidate "in the flesh." It is more often than not the interview in which they seek to conclude "the case" for you as a teacher candidate for their school system.

Currently great emphasis is placed upon the human relations aspect of the teaching job and rightly so. This of course leads the employer to look carefully at any evidences the candidate may reveal in to his attitudes toward: (1) cooperative work; (2) contacts with the public; (3) respect for his fellow man; (4) verbal evidence of enthusiasm for the profession (or lack of it); (5) a zest and curiosity regarding life; (6) animation of personality; (7) physical vitality.

"Those applications without personal interview evaluations will not be consulted for potential employment until all applications *with* personal interview evaluations are exhausted."[8]

Your employment interview might be the most important minutes in your life, yet many applicants come to job interviews without any

----

[8]Dade County Board of Public Instruction, Form Ap-12, Miami, Florida, Oct., 1959.

thoughtful preparation. They often have not formulated the questions they want to ask or points of information they need clarified. Remember that the interview is a two-way street as it presents an opportunity for you, the applicant, to raise questions you may have as well as to answer the questions put to you by the principal, superintendent, or other hiring official. There are at least two extremes in attitude related to the personal interview. One extreme, that of detachment or over-casualness, may be typified by the applicant who appears for the interview a little late, dressed in sport clothes. She is dressed for a day at Jones Beach, not an interview. She has an air about her which implies that she has merely dropped in to be accommodating. You (the interviewer) are interrupting her lively social calendar, so please be brief. She then proceeds to park herself (in the nearest chair assuming a slouching position), blinks her drooping eye lids covered with too much mascara, lights a cigarette and blows a draft of secondhand smoke in the interviewer's face.

The opposite of the creature just described is the applicant who is overly concerned about making a favorable impression to the point where she is a nervous wreck. She walks into the interview as though she were walking her last mile. Her facial expression is that of one who expects to be burned at the stake. When she is confronted with a direct question the best answer she can muster is a stammered mono-syllabic one.

Preparing Yourself for the Interview.

Get ready — get set! Some of the fears and anxieties regarding a personal interview can be alleviated by familiarizing yourself with the mechanics of an interview and by making a few simple preparations before the interview to get yourself ready. The following are some suggestions which we hope will be useful to you:

1. Write down the time, place and person's name with whom you are to have the interview. It is best not to rely on your memory for such important matters. You should assume nothing about any of these matters. Simply because you know that a friend's interview is to be held at a certain location does not mean that yours is. Be very certain to check these facts long before the day of the interview.

2. Be certain of the pronunciation of your interviewer's name (if this is possible in advance) and know what position, office, title, or rank he holds in the school district.

3. Take a pencil or pen and some kind of paper with you as you may want to take some notes during the interview. A small notebook or

some other diminutive supply of paper that is not going to be conspicuous and cumbersome to manage will do. Have more than one writing implement in the event one should fail. Pens are subject to having their ink supply run out or ink cartridge run dry, so have an emergency one handy. Of course you would want to ask permission of the interviewer to take notes during your interview before doing so.

4. Clothes. A good rule of thumb in relation to suitable clothes for an interview would be to "dress to suit a tailor and not a king." In other words avoid regal splendor. It is true, of course, that conservative dress means many different things in various parts of the country. Your dress ought to be congruent with what most members of the teaching profession wear in your particular locale. Remember that you are not going to a dance or stepping before the footlights of the "Met" for your world première. Comfort is naturally one consideration here, yet it should not be the primary one. If your interview occurs at such a time as to prevent a change of wardrobe — (i.e., you are called out of a college class or laboratory to be interviewed) then explain in a simple unobtrusive way that time did not permit you to dress differently for your interview. We suggest you look at the illustration which offers some additional check points regarding your appearance.

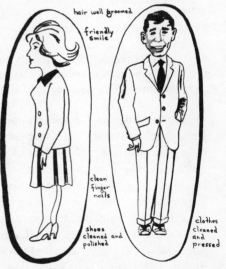

CHECK YOUR APPEARANCE IN THE PROFESSIONAL MIRROR. HOW DO YOU REFLECT?

5. Since many of the interview rooms are small it is particularly important for the applicant to use discretion regarding the use of toiletries such as deodorants, colognes, perfumes, and (with men), after-shave lotions. Heavy scents should be avoided and whichever ones you select they should be used sparingly. The fact that you may be somewhat nervous should prompt the use of antiperspirants. Here again, be conservative and use your "common sense."

6. We suggest that you become familiar with the kinds of questions that are frequently asked by interviewers. You will find a partial list on page 241. While you do not want to exactly rehearse your answers you might try having a friend ask you some of the questions so

as to become familiar with the types, thereby alleviating some of your uncertainty.

If possible corral a friend and ask him to read to you the various sample questions listed on page 241 while you employ a tape recorder so as to enable you to listen to your answers played back. Try to judge the impact that your voice and speech mannerisms have upon other people by surveying the reactions of some impartial folks whom you can persuade to help you in this experiment. In doing this you might want to keep the following questions in mind:

1. Do you sound sincere and forthright in your replies?
2. Does a general note of enthusiasm characterize your replies?
3. What about your fluency with language? Do you "grope" a great deal for suitable words?
4. Have you any obvious speech mannerisms which might be particularly annoying such as repeating "ands" or too much emphasis on "I"?
5. Is your general voice quality sonorous?
6. What about the volume and pitch of your voice?
7. How are your enunciation, diction, and most important, grammar?

These and other considerations can help you to do an analysis of your "verbal impact" at least as it affects the persons you choose to help you evaluate it. Needless to say, the more sensitive the individuals (whom you ask to be judges) are to language the more astute will be their judgments. If for no other reason than your own self-improvement, such an analysis of your verbal communication should be extremely valuable to you as a prospective teacher. The ability to communicate effectively is a hallmark of a good teacher. It would be unnecessary to tape a mock interview previous to every interview; in fact one taping may make you fully aware of your speech problems and general impact.

We should note here that in taping your mock interview you may want to employ several individuals as interviewers if you expect to be faced with a team interview. Having several parties involved may help you to get the "feel" of this type of interviewing technique. Team interviewing is further discussed on page 236 of this text if you desire additional information regarding its mechanics and general implementation.

Questions that the interviewer frequently asks during an interview for a teaching position follow.

Pertaining to High School and College Experiences

1. In what school activities have you participated? Why? Which did did you find most enjoyable?
2. Which courses did you like best? Least? Why?
3. How do you feel about your general preparation for teaching?
4. What extracurricular offices have you held?
5. If you could begin college over again, which courses would you take?
6. Why did you decide to go to this particular college?
7. How did you rank academically in your high school graduating class? Where do you think you rank in your college class?
8. Were your high school and college extracurricular activities worth the additional time and effort you put into them? Why?
9. Did you ever change your major field of study while you were in high school or in college? Why?
10. At what point in your education did you choose your major field?
11. Do you feel as though your scholastic achievement reflects your best ability? If not, why not?
12. Why did you decide to go to college?
13. Have you ever had a great deal of difficulty in getting along with your yellow students or faculty?
14. Which college year was the most enjoyable for you? Why? Which was the most difficult? Why?
15. Do you plan to do graduate work? Where?
16. Have you enjoyed your four years of college? In what ways?

Pertaining to Salary

1. What are your personal ideas and needs in relation to salary?
2. How much do you believe a good teacher is worth?
3. How much money do you hope to be earning when you are 30 years old? At 40 years of age?
4. From what source do you now obtain your spending money?
5. Do you have any debts?
6. Have you ever been completely self-supporting? When?
7. What would be the least amount of money you would accept as a beginning salary?

Pertaining to Personal and Family Life

1. Are you in good health? What do you do to maintain it?
2. How do you usually spend a Sunday?
3. Have you any handicaps or injuries?
4. Is it difficult for you to tolerate any particular race or nationality?
5. What kinds of books and/or magazines do you read?
6. What types of people "get on your nerves"?
7. What special abilities do you believe you have?

8. Do you enjoy travelling?
9. Do you smoke? How much?
10. Do you drink alcoholic beverages? To what extent?
11. What do you do in your spare time? What hobbies do you have?
12. What kind of relationship do you have with your family? How do you feel towards them? Are both of your parents living?
13. Are you interested in sports? To what extent?
14. Do you have any current marriage plans? Are you going steady? Is it serious?
15. What personal characteristics do you believe are vital to the success of a teacher?
16. What is your father's occupation?
17. What was your childhood like? Describe it briefly.
18. In general, are you usually eager to please?
19. Do you enjoy working with other people or would you really rather work by yourself?
20. For what kind of person do you prefer to work?
21. Can you accept supervision and criticism without becoming upset?
22. Are you living with your parents? Which parent has the more influence upon you? Why?
23. Are you a church member?
24. What do you believe are your personal weaknesses?
25. What are your goals in education?
26. Do you believe you have an analytical mind? Creative mind?

Pertaining to Military Service

1. How long did you serve? Where? In what capacity?
2. What rank did you hold when you were discharged?
3. What was your record during military service?
4. How were your academic grades before military service as compared with those after military service?

Pertaining to General Information

1. What famous person do you admire most?
2. What would you say you have learned from other kinds of jobs (in addition to anything related to teaching) you have held?
3. Will previous employers give you complimentary recommendations?
4. What size community do you prefer to live in most?
5. How many close friends do you have?
6. How would you define cooperation?

Pertaining to Teaching

1. What are the reasons you chose our school system to teach in?
2. Do you prefer to teach at a particular grade level? What is it and why?

3. Why did you choose teaching as your profession?
4. What particular qualities and qualifications do you believe you possess that will make you a successful teacher?
5. What do you know about our school district or system?
6. Is geographic location a major factor in choosing our school to teach in?
7. What do you believe determines a teacher's promotion or professional advancement in education?
8. What do you know about the opportunities for advancement in the teaching profession?
9. Are you interested in a temporary or a permanent teaching position in our school?
10. How long is the average elementary school teacher's day, in your opinion? How many working hours?
11. Do you enjoy routine type work?
12. Do you prefer to teach in a small or large school (number of pupils enrolled).
13. If you could choose any job in a school system, which one would you select? Why?
14. What is your idea of a sound classroom reading program?
15. In your opinion, what are the advantages and disadvantages in teaching?
16. What do you think about progressive education?
17. What do you feel should be the role of the teacher in the community?
18. How would you provide for individual differences in your social studies program?
19. Briefly state your general philosophy of education.
20. What are the greatest satisfactions you have gained through working with children?
21. Describe a classroom in which there is a wholesome disciplinary climate.

In many states it is illegal for an interviewer to ask you any questions pertaining to race, religion or national origin.

What to Expect From Your Interviewer.

As a general rule interviewers are anxious to help the applicants succeed at the interview. This is especially true of interviews for teaching positions. You will find that most interviewers strive to give the applicant a good measure of objectivity, sincere interest and patience. Teaching job interviews are, as a general rule, set in a predetermined favorable climate due to many factors, among which of course is the teacher shortage. In any event teaching interviews are quite different from most commercial and industrial job interviews in general character. This is to your benefit.

Despite the healthy job market for teachers many good candidates fail to get the particular position that they want through their own ignorance. An interview is an opportunity to sell yourself. Unfortunately all too many candidates lack this ability or are thoughtless in the manner in which they approach a job interview.

Being rejected as a job candidate is probably the most serious negative outcome of any job interview. You therefore may be interested in the elements which have elicited negative reactions from interviewers and frequently lead to the applicant's being rejected. While the following data is based upon interviews with applicants for business and industrial positions the items are nevertheless pertinent to interviews in general.

Negative factors evaluated during the employment interview which frequently lead to rejection of the applicant: (As reported by 153 companies surveyed by Frank S. Endicott, Director of Placement, Northwestern University)

1. Poor personal appearance
2. Overbearing — overaggressive — conceited
3. Inability to express himself clearly — poor voice, diction, grammar.
4. Lack of planning for career — no purpose and goals
5. Lack of interest and enthusiasm — passive — indifferent
6. Lack of confidence and poise — nervousness — ill-at-ease
7. Failure to participate in a variety of activities
8. Overemphasis on money — interest only in the best dollar offer
9. Poor scholastic record — just got by
10. Makes excuses — evasiveness — hedges on unfavorable factors in his or her record.
11. Lack of tact
12. Lack of maturity
13. Lazy
14. Indication of low moral standards
15. Cynical
16. Intolerant — strong prejudices
17. Narrow interests
18. Spends much time in the movies
19. Poor handling of personal finances
20. No interest in community activities
21. Condemnation of past employers
22. Lack of courtesy — ill-mannered
23. Lack of social understanding
24. Lack of vitality
25. Fails to look interviewer in the eye
26. Limp, fishy handshake

27. Indecision
28. Loafs during vacations
29. Unhappy married life
30. Friction with parents
31. Sloppy application blank
32. Merely shopping around
33. Wants the job for only a short time
34. Little sense of humor
35. Lack of knowledge in field of specialization
36. Parents make decisions for her (or him)
37. Emphasis on who he knows
38. Inability to take criticism
39. Lack of appreciation of the value of experience
40. Radical ideas
41. Late to interview without good reason
42. Asks no questions about the position
43. High pressure type
44. Indefinite response to questions
45. Failure to express appreciation for the interviewer's time.

The fact that interviewers all are individuals naturally lends uniqueness to all interviews. Some hiring officials have certain pet elements which they stress as being important in any teacher candidate. Most of these which they hunt for in candidates are very valid, some are not. Be that as it may, the authors have given you in the foregoing list some of the elements which have proven to be a detriment to job candidates. The authors would like to add to this list the results of a survey which they have conducted pertaining directly to teaching job interviews. It has already been mentioned that interviewers often have certain "pet" positive elements (traits, attitudes, etc.) that they vigorously hunt for when interviewing candidates. Many also have very strong feelings toward specific negative elements which they find in candidates which we will call "pet peeves." The authors do not attempt here to evaluate whether or not any of these "pet peeves" should be rated as negative or to what degree, but only report the results of a questionnaire. If you are not familiar with the use of the questionnaire as a research tool, it is imperative you realize that there are many limitations and weaknesses involved. It is not a first-rate, scientific device and the authors caution the reader against making any sweeping generalizations from the data presented. The authors do feel, however, that the findings are worth consideration and certainly can be helpful to the candidate to a limited extent. For those of you who wish to investigate the merits of questionnaires as a research tool, we suggest the following:

1. ———, "Ask Questions That Get Results," Nation's Bsns., Vol. 47, pp. 34-35, July, 1959.
2. Kingsley, H. L., and Ralph Garry, *The Nature and Conditions of Learning* Prentice-Hall, Inc., 1957, Englewood Cliffs, N. J., Chapter II, pp. 32-33.
3. McNemar, Q., "Opinion-Attitude Methodology," *Psychology Bulletin*, 1946, pp. 37, 289-374.
4. Payne, S. L., *The Art of Asking Questions*, Princeton; Princeton University Press, 1951.
5. Thorndike, R. L., and E. Hagen, *Measurement and Evaluation in Psychology and Education*, New York: Wiley, 1955.
6. Wellington, J., and C. B. Wellington, "What Is A Question?" *Clearing House*, Vol. 36, pp. 471-2, April, 1962.

The questionnaire[9] was sent to two hundred superintendents and principals in eight states asking them to state any "pet peeves" they have about interviewing teacher candidates. One hundred and fifty usable responses were received. The states that were sampled include New York, Massachusetts, Connecticut, Maryland, Florida, Oklahoma, Illinois, and California. One superintendent stated that he had interviewed well over 10,000 teaching candidates in his career to date, so this sampling represents the experience of a great many seasoned administrators over a large geographical area. The results follow:

My Pet Peeve When Interviewing Teacher Candidates Is:	*Per Cents*
1. General overaggressiveness	13
2. Overconfidence in their own abilities	10
3. Poor English usage	10
4. "Failure to look me in the eye"	6
5. Poor and/or sloppy grooming	6
6. Professional indifference	6
7. A retiring attitude	5
8. Lack of poise	4
9. Overconcern with salary	4
10. Bad manners	2
11. Too much interruption by the candidate when I'm talking	2
12. Punctuality (being late for the interview)	2
13. Lack of enthusiasm (in general)	2
14. Overconcern about "extra" school duties	2
15. Asking trivial questions just to impress me	2
16. Lacking the ability to ask questions well	2
17. An attitude of "just shopping around"	2
18. Lack of a friendly smile	1

[9]Alvin M. Westcott, State University of New York, College at Oswego, Oswego, New York, December-February, 1959.

19.	Continued use of indirect answers	1
20.	Bringing another person to the interview	1
21.	Demanding inconvenient interview times	1
22.	Demanding that they be given a specific grade level	1
23.	Evidence of a lack of professional ethics	1
24.	Patronizing attitude, too agreeable	1
25.	The candidate who changes the subject constantly	1
26.	The candidate who talks too loudly	1
27.	Individual items not cited frequently enough to be statistically significant	11

As mentioned previously, proper dress and a general knowledge of the mechanics of an interview will also aid your poise and confidence. This is extremely important as many interviewers regard poise and confidence as the most notable qualities to be looked for in applicants.

Having armed yourself with the general procedures of an interview (as well as the types of questions asked and the pitfalls to be avoided) you can approach any interview relatively free from anxiety.

As previously indicated, an interview is a two-way street. It permits the employing official to get to know you better and presents you with an opportunity to ask questions and gain specific information about the job. Regrettably all too many job candidates do not avail themselves of this privilege and come away from an interview with inadequate information to suit their needs or just plain confused. We heartily recommend that you make a list of the various items which you desire to know about the school before you are faced by the hiring official. You will find that most school officials welcome your questions and very often rate your astuteness by the kinds of questions you ask. The candidate who has no questions about a position is viewed very skeptically.

In terms of aiding you to compile your questions, permit us to cite the following data:

Topics Discussed During Job Interviews With Beginning Teachers[10]

Are you curious about the topics which arise as school officials interview beginning teachers who are seeking their first teaching position? One college placement bureau studied the problems of initial interviews and secured these results:

Most frequently discussed items (in order from most to least discussed items)

1. Specific classes, grades candidate is to teach — 1
2. School enrollment — 1

---

[10]Taken from Siggelkow, Richard A., "Meaningful Interviews with Beginning Teachers." Reprinted, with permission, from The Nation's Schools, June, 1954. Copyright 1954 The Modern Hospital Publishing Co., Inc., Chicago. All rights reserved.

3. Extraclass, cocurricular assignments — 1
4. Size of classes candidate is to teach — 1
5. Population of the community — 1
6. Condition of the physical plant — 1
7. Location of the community — 1
8. Room facilities (school) — 1
9. Number of teachers — 1
10. Typical living accommodations for teachers — 3
11. Transportation facilities — 1
12. General educational and cultural level of population — 1
13. Enrollment trends — 1
14. Practice teaching experience — 2
15. Size of the community in which the candidate was raised — 2
16. Financial ability of community to support schools — 1
17. Number of new teachers in school — 1
18. Dominant nationality groups — 1
19. Philosophy of the school — 1
20. Other schools in the community — 1
21. Cost of room and board — 1
22. Recreational opportunities — 1
23. Churches in the community — 1
24. Dominant vocational groups — 1
25. Engagement or marriage plans — 2

1—Introduced into discussion by both candidate and hiring official; more frequently hiring official.
2—Asked by hiring official
3—Introduced into discussion by both candidate and hiring official; more frequently by candidate.

Least discussed items in interviews recorded (in order from most to least discussed items)
(In less than 20 per cent of 106 initial interviews)

1. Type of work experiences of the candidate
2. Teaching philosophy
3. Your interest in children
4. College grade point average
5. Professional ambitions
6. Preparation and qualifications which you believe will help you in teaching
7. Why you want to teach
8. Honors, college distinctions
9. How much you enjoy working with people
10. Percentage of expenses earned while in college
11. Personal traits which you believe will help you as a teacher
12. Travel experience

Some of the little frustrations which sometimes occur and for which you should be alerted:

1. Having to wait a lengthy time before the interviewer arrives
2. Repetition of questions
3. Interviewer's eccentricities, prejudices, opinions, etc.
4. Prejudices already made in favor of another candidate
5. Interviewer failing to recognize your point of view
6. An arrogant attitude on the part of the employer
7. The interviewing official's unfamiliarity with your personal data
8. Lack of courtesy on the part of the interviewer
9. Many disturbing interruptions during the interview such as telephone calls, etc.

Preparing Mentally

There is nothing more beneficial to your mental and physical fitness for an interview than a good night's rest preceding the interview. Regardless of how many butterflies you may have in your stomach the day of the interview, they will be somewhat tranquilized by a totally rested physique.

Many employing officials contact candidates to arrange personal interviews after having looked over their college records. This does not mean employment is any more certain simply because you have been personally invited to come for an interview. It means only that you are being given the chance to be compared firsthand with other applicants for the position. It is safe to say, however, that the more searching the interview, the better chances are for being hired. One fatal mistake is to assume that because you have been beckoned for an interview the position is yours.

Many school officials are not well seasoned in the mechanics of interviewing and often the interview is as much a trial for them as it is for you. Consequently you may find there are awkward moments and/or discourtesies that arise. They are more than likely unintentional and should be ignored by the applicant. Use these to show your poise and self-control.

You undoubtedly have noted from this list that some of the most vital elements for the candidate to ascertain about a job are frequently neglected. Endeavor to avoid these mistakes by making your own list more inclusive.

This section devoted to preparing for a personal interview is an attempt to help the job candidate become familiar with some of the basic mechanics of an interview and to help eliminate some of the anxieties which might develop from fear of the unknown. For organizational purposes you may want to use the following guide as a reference for interview preparation.

A Preparation Check List for the Job Candidate

Decide in your own mind what you want in a teaching position.

Prepare a written list of questions to which you seek answers (in relation to the job).

Check the components of proper dress

Get plenty of sleep the night before

Establish a positive, friendly attitude in your own mind toward the interview itself

Think out previous to the interview your strongest qualifications — accentuate them whenever you can at the interview. Adopt, if possible, the idea of "selling yourself."

Review mentally the social amenities pertaining to a personal interview.

Review the types of questions often asked during an interview.

Role play with others a mock personal interview.

Special Requirements Often Requested by Employers.

Space limitations will not permit a detailed description of each requirement that follows. Your college placement office or employment agency can supply you with any details you desire. Not every school system requires *all* of these; however the ones marked by an asterisk are very common:

*A. A physical examination and other health data and requirements
*B. Transcript or other record of college work
*C. Written personal character references
*D. Student teaching performance records
 E. Special written examinations administered by the school system itself (the New York City examination, for example)
 F. Signing of a loyalty oath
*G. Citizenship and residence requirements
 H. Fingerprinting
 I. An academic course pertaining to the history of the particular state

The Teaching Contract

When a new teacher is hired for a school system she is given a teaching contract which usually encompasses one school year (ten months). A few schools still employ a twelve month contract. Under a twelve month contract a school system could *require* a teacher to work without extra remuneration during the summer months if it so desired. This is *not* a common occurrence. If the school authorities decide to hire her for a second year, another ten month contract is offered to her. And so the process goes until the teacher has served the probationary period in the school system which ranges anywhere from three to five years. At the end of this time a continuing contract may or may not be offered to the teacher. This continuing contract is what is commonly referred to as receiving tenure. For further details related to tenure see page 196 of Chapter 8.

The teacher's employment contract with the school authorities is considered a legal document, yet in most instances it is treated more as a gentleman's agreement. As a generalization, all schools employing more than eight teachers issue some form of teacher contracts. The legality of the teacher's contract has withstood many severe tests in courts of law. A few sample cases can be found in reference No. 4 at the close of this chapter. Historically the teacher employment contracts have been more binding upon the school than upon the teacher who signs the contract. Legally both parties are equally bound by the stipulations of the contract; however schools for the most part have been reluctant to resort to strict enforcement. Supposing a teacher candidate signs a contract with a school system early in March then in July is offered a much more attractive job in another school system. She then asks the first school system if she can be released from her contract in order to take what she believes to be a better job. Most schools under these circumstances would release her from her contract since no school wants someone on their staff against her will. Technically if this girl took the second job without being released from her first contract she could be sued by the first school for breach of contract.

While schools have been reluctant to use legal procedures to force teachers to adhere to contractual agreements, teachers have been quick to sue schools for any deviation from a contract. The authors emphasize that contracts *should* be equally binding on all parties involved.

In the spring and summer of each year many school administrators have to fill vacancies in their teaching staff two or three times as a result of teacher candidates' breaking signed contracts. Yould should not sign a teaching employment contract unless you have sincere intentions of fulfilling it. Suits against teachers for breach of contract have resulted in the teacher's forfeiting her state teaching certificate — (license). Irrespective of the penalties involved, it is unethical and a blot upon the status of the teaching profession when a professional commitment is ignored. The NEA code of ethics states:

Fourth Principle: The members of the teaching profession have inescapable obligations with respect to employment. These obligations are nearly always shared employer-employee responsibilities based upon mutual respect and good faith.

In fulfilling the obligations of this fourth principle the teacher will —

6. Adhere to the conditions of a contract until service thereunder has been performed, the contract has been terminated by mutual consent, or the contract has otherwise been legally terminated.

7. Give and expect due notice before a change of position is to be made.

Opinion 15: *Contracts, Subsequent Negotiations* — If a teacher has entered into a contract with one school district, it is improper for him to initiate or continue negotiations for a contract with another school district without the consent of the district to which he is obligated. By the same token, it is improper for a superintendent knowingly to negotiate with a teacher already under contract without the approval of the school district to which the teacher is obligated.[11]

You Got It — What Now? Once a contract is offered to you there are several immediate steps to take. First you should read the contract thoroughly and be certain you understand what it says. If you are uncertain about some clause in it seek legal advice. Most teachers' contracts are worded simply and are free of legal traps. On page 253 are two samples of teacher employment contracts.

After reading the contract thoroughly decide whether or not you are going to sign it. Return the signed contract within the time limit you are allotted. The usual time allotment is a week to ten days.

If you are negotiating with another school at the time and cannot decide immediately whether you will sign the contract, notify the school authorities. Ask for extended time to make up your mind. If the school wants you badly enough they will grant you extra time to consider the matter. If they have many other fine candidates they may not be patient as this might result in their losing other prospects for the position.

Sign only one contract for employment. It is highly unethical to do otherwise. As soon as you have signed your employment contract communicate this fact to all of the schools to which you may have made employment application. This will permit them to cross you off their list and make another choice. It is also very important to notify the college placement bureau on any other placement agency with which you may have been working that you have accepted a teaching position. It saves them time, money and embarrassment. It is very disconcerting

---

[11]NEA Code of Ethics, adopted by the Representative Assembly in 1952.

TEACHER'S CONTRACT

STATE OF MARYLAND,

COUNTY OF ....

IT IS HEREBY AGREED by and between the COUNTY BOARD OF EDUCATION of ....
.... County and
that the said teacher shall be and is hereby employed to teach in the public schools of the said County as
...., subject to
assignment by the County Superintendent or transfer to some other teaching position within the County, provided
that if the transfer be made during the school year or after the opening of the school *for any year*, the salary shall
not be reduced for the *remainder of the year*. The salary of said teacher shall be fixed by the County Board of
Education, which salary shall be not less than the minimum salary provided by law.

AND IT IS FURTHER AGREED that the teacher named herein shall become a member of the Maryland
Teachers' Retirement System as of date on which h......... teaching service begins.

AND IT IS FURTHER AGREED that the said teacher will not vacate the position to which assigned during
any school year, except in case of emergency, of which the County Board of Education shall judge.

AND IT IS FURTHER AGREED that either of the parties to this contract may terminate it at the end of the
first or second school year by giving thirty days' notice in writing to the other during the month of June or July.

AND IT IS FURTHER AGREED that if the teacher named herein wishes to vacate his or her position after
the second year, thirty days' notice in writing shall be given the County Board of Education during the month of
June or July, except in case of emergency, of which the County Board of Education shall judge.

If any of the conditions of this contract shall be violated by the teacher named herein, salary already accrued
will be forfeited, in the discretion of the County Board of Education.

This contract shall continue from year to year, subject to the aforegoing conditions, provided that if the teacher, on recommendation of the County Superintendent, is suspended by the County Board of Education in accordance
with the provisions of Sections 64 and 102 of Article 77 of the Annotated Code of Maryland, 1957 Edition, said
teacher shall have the right of appeal to the State Superintendent of Schools, if the decision of said board is not
unanimous.

This contract is made in accordance with the provisions of the school law, and is subject to Sections 64, 99, and
102 of Article 77 of the Annotated Code of Maryland, and any amendments thereto, and will be filed among the records of the County Board of Education.

The said teacher on his or her part hereby accepts said appointment, to take effect on the ....
.... day of .... 19...............

Date of signing this contract .... 19...............
WITNESS OUR HANDS:

(SEAL)

....
President, County Board of Education

....
Secretary, County Board of Education

....
Teacher

OATH OF OFFICE

I, ..., having been appointed a teacher in the public schools of
.... County, State of Maryland, do swear (or affirm) that I will obey
the school law of the State of Maryland and all rules and regulations governing my position as teacher, passed in
pursuance thereof by the proper authority; that I will, to the best of my skill and judgment, diligently and faithfully, without partiality or prejudice, discharge the duties of a teacher in the public schools of said county, including attendance on teachers' institutes and associations when legally called thereto and will honestly and correctly
make all reports as required by law or the school authorities of said county.

....
Teacher

STATE OF MARYLAND .... County, to wit:

Sworn (or affirmed) before the subscriber ....
by ...., teacher, who in my presence has thereto
affixed h............ signature this .... day of ...., 19...........

NOTARIAL SEAL

....
Signature

THOS. G. PULLEN, JR.
STATE SUPERINTENDENT OF SCHOOLS

MARYLAND STATE DEPARTMENT OF EDUCATION
Baltimore 1

The sections of the law referred to in the body of the prescribed form for teacher's contract, as printed on the other side of this sheet, are given below. The form of contract was adopted by the State Board of Education, June 6, 1918, under the authority of Section 21 (Annotated Code of Maryland, 1957 edition) of the school law.

THOS. G. PULLEN, JR.
State Superintendent of Schools

Annotated Code of Maryland, 1957 edition, Article 77, Sec. 99

99. No person shall be employed as county superintendent, assistant superintendent, supervisor, principal or teacher unless such person shall hold a certificate issued by the superintendent of public education and for the grade required for the position, but any county of the State may require as a condition of employment a higher standard for a certificate of a similar kind and grade than is required by the State. Provided that all teachers' certificates and diplomas in force on April 18, 1916, shall continue in force for the full time for which they were issued or are valid, and shall remain valid for the grade and position for which issued. Provided, that no renewal or extension of such certificates shall be granted under this section by the State superintendent of schools, nor shall the renewal or extension of any certificate by a county superintendent expiring between the time this section goes into effect and September the thirtieth, 1916, be for more than one year. Provided also that no certificate issued by a county superintendent of schools between April 18, 1916, and September the thirtieth, 1916, shall be valid for more than one year. Provided further that no certificate heretofore issued shall be valid after April 18, 1916, for appointment to the position of county superintendent, assistant superintendent, supervisor, high school principal or elementary school principal in elementary schools having three or more teachers, including the principal, except in case of persons holding the foregoing positions on April 18, 1916, and then valid only for the particular position they are then holding and in the particular county.

Annotated Code of Maryland, 1957 edition, Article 77, Sec. 110

110. (Membership.) The membership of this retirement system shall be composed as follows: (1) All persons who shall become teachers after the date as of which the retirement system is established, **(June 1, 1927) (For exceptions see remainder of this section.)**

Annotated Code of Maryland, 1957 edition, Article 77, Sec. 102

102. Any county board of education may, on the recommendation of the county superintendent, suspend any teacher, principal, supervisor, or assistant superintendent for immorality, dishonesty, intemperance, insubordination, incompetency, or wilful neglect of duty, and may recommend to the state superintendent of schools the revocation of the certificate of such person, stating in writing the grounds for such recommendations, and giving an opportunity, upon not less than ten days' notice, to be heard in defense, in person or by counsel, and the state superintendent of schools may order such investigations as he may deem necessary. If he approves the recommendation, the teacher's certificate shall be revoked and the teacher shall be dropped from the service.

Annotated Code of Maryland, 1957 edition, Article 77, Sec. 64

64. The county board of education shall appoint, on the written recommendation of the county superintendent, all principals and assistant teachers, and fix their salaries, subject to the provisions of Chapter 8 of this Article. The county board may suspend or dismiss without appeal any teacher so appointed, on the written recommendation of the county superintendent, for immorality, misconduct in office, insubordination, incompetency, or wilful neglect of duty, provided that the charges be stated in writing, and that the teacher be given an opportunity to be heard by the board upon not less than ten days' notice; provided further that in all cases when the board is not unanimous in its decision to suspend or dismiss, the right of appeal shall lie to the state superintendent of schools.

By-law 14

All contracts with teachers, both principals and assistants, employed after June 1, 1918, shall be in writing and on one of two contract blanks furnished by the State Board of Education. For teachers who hold non-emergency certificates the blank entitled "Teacher's Contract," the form for which follows, shall be used; for teachers who hold emergency certificates, the blank entitled "Emergency Teacher's Contract," the form for which also follows, shall be used. The contract shall be signed by the teacher, and the president and the secretary of the county board of education, and when so signed shall be filed by the secretary in the office of the board; provided teachers employed prior to June 1, 1918, and continuing in the service, shall have the contract herein prescribed when they so desire. The following shall be the forms of contract and, under the foregoing conditions, no others shall be recognized:

(Only the non-emergency "Teacher's Contract" is printed on the reverse side of this page.)

(Over)

(FIRST PART)

PUBLIC SCHOOLS

CITY OF NEW BEDFORD, MASS.

To _____

You are hereby notified that you have been elected a Teacher in the Public Schools of the City of New Bedford, for the school year commencing September _____ 196___, at a salary at the rate of $ _____ per year.

It is now expected that you will be located in the _____ School, but the right is reserved to make such changes as the exigencies of the school service may require.

Should you accept the position, please sign your name below, and return the "First Part" of this contract to the Superintendent of Schools within one week from date. Any position not accepted on that day will be considered vacant.

_____

Secretary of the School Committee.

I hereby accept the above election, and agree to perform faithfully the duties required of me to the best of my ability; I further agree to give to the Secretary of the School Committee eight weeks' notice of my intention to resign said duties, resignation not to take effect during the months of June or September, except for personal illness, and to cheerfully conform to all requirements of said Committee.

_____

(Signature of Teacher)

(SECOND PART)

PUBLIC SCHOOLS

CITY OF NEW BEDFORD, MASS.

To _____

You are hereby notified that you have been elected a Teacher in the Public Schools of the City of New Bedford, for the school year commencing September _____ 196___, at a salary at the rate of $ _____ per year.

It is now expected that you will be located in the _____ School, but the right is reserved to make such changes as the exigencies of the school service may require.

Should you accept the position, please sign your name below, and return the "First Part" of this contract to the Superintendent of Schools within one week from date. Any position not accepted on that day will be considered vacant.

_____

Secretary of the School Committee.

I hereby accept the above election, and agree to perform faithfully the duties required of me to the best of my ability; I further agree to give to the Secretary of the School Committee eight weeks' notice of my intention to resign said duties, resignation not to take effect during the months of June or September, except for personal illness, and to cheerfully conform to all requirements of said Committee.

_____

(Signature of Teacher)

to a placement bureau to recommend you for a teaching position only to learn that you have already accepted another job without notifying them.

If teaching is to become truly a profession then its members must behave in a professional manner. This of course applies to job procurement as well as all other phases of a teacher's role.

TOPICS AND QUESTIONS FOR STUDY AND DISCUSSION

1. How might the character of a letter of inquiry which a teacher candidate writes to a school affect his chances of obtaining a teaching position in that school?
2. To insure procurement of a suitable teaching position some teacher candidates have been known to sign three or four contracts with different schools. Then they reject all but the most attractive one at the last minute. Why is this practice extremely unethical?
3. What is your ultimate employment goal at this stage of your professional career? What are your reasons for selecting this particular goal? Is it a realistic one in terms of your personal and professional qualifications? What factors do you think might cause you to change your ultimate employment goal as time moves on?
4. Make out a budget of estimated personal expenditures (what it will cost you to live) for your first year of teaching. What salary will you need to cover your budget? Is this salary attainable from your present bargaining position? Why or why not?
5. Set up a mock job interview between yourself and another person who is taking the role of employing officer for a school system. Record the interview for later evaluation. Employ some of the frequently used interview questions listed in this chapter.

SELECTED REFERENCES

1. Bingham, Walter, and Bruce Moore, *How To Interview*, New York: Harper and Bros., 1959.
2. Eye, Glen G. and Willard Lane, *The New Teacher Comes To School*, New York: Harper and Bros., 1956.
3. Hageny, William J., *Handbook on New York State Education Law*, New York State Boards Association, Albany, New York, 1958.
4. Mason, Ward S., *The Beginning Teachers Status and Career Orientations*, U. S. Dept. Health, Education and Welfare, Washington 25, D. C., 1961.
5. National Education Association, Research Division, "The Teacher's Day in Court," *Review of 1958*, Washington, D. C., May, 1959.
6. Redefer, Frederick and Dorothy Reeves, *Planning A Teaching Career*, New York; Harper and Bros., 1960.
7. Von Haden, H. I., "Is a Teaching Contract a Oneway Street," *N.E.A. Journal*, February, 1962.
8. Abraham, Willard, *A Handbook For The New Teacher*, New York: Holt, Rinehart and Winston, Inc., 1960.

Part III

Educational
Frontiers

Chapter 10

Topics, Problems, Frontiers and Issues In Education

"A man's reach should exceed his grasp, or what is heaven for?"

Robert Browning

The authors have designed this chapter to be used in one of two specific ways. It can be used by the individual student of education for independent study or by an education class, seminar or workshop for group study.

Seminar Around the Flag, Boys! Many teacher preparation programs include some type of professional seminar following student teaching or running concurrently with it. Such seminars provide education students with an opportunity to study and discuss immediate educational problems derived from the student teaching experience. The authors strongly subscribe to the principles of learning implied in the location of such a seminar in close proximity to student teaching.

Separate Sheep From Goats! Perhaps the title of this chapter caused some confusion in your mind as to the nature of a problem as contrasted with an issue or of an issue as contrasted with a topic. If this is so then you will want to investigate and discuss the semantic and contextual differences among these terms as an initial task before proceeding any farther.

Upon completing this task in a seminar setting, your group may want to consider with your seminar leader such matters as:

1. The elements of group dynamics that are or can be inherent in a seminar setting.
2. The aims (objectives) of the seminar as viewed by its members including the seminar leader (instructor).
3. The seminar structure or format which will accomplish best the expressed objectives of the seminar (discussion, reporting, lectures, individual reading, etc.).
4. Some of the topics, problems, issues or frontiers that are of immediate interest to the members of the seminar and could be studied in the seminar.
5. The techniques and devices to be employed in evaluating individual achievement in the seminar as well as general success of the total seminar.

As a resource in selecting topics for your seminar or individual study the following list is provided:

1. The Exceptional Child
2. Grouping Children Within the School
3. The Intelligence Quotient
4. Classroom Discipline
5. Foundations of Curriculum
6. Core Curriculum
7. Evaluating and Reporting Pupil Progress
8. Effective Teacher Planning
9. Utilizing the Teacher's Manual
10. The Role of Workbooks in the Classroom
11. The Ideal Classroom and/or School
12. Promotion Policies
13. Establishing a Professional Library (personal one)
14. Teachers' Unions as Compared to Other Professional Organizations
15. The First Few Days In Your Own Classroom (as a new teacher)
16. Creativity and/or Creative Teaching
17. Implementing Democratic Procedures Into the Classroom and the Total School
18. The Role of the Teacher in Our Society
19. Grading Systems
20. Homework Policies
21. The Teacher's Role In Public Relations
22. Educational Research and the Classroom Teacher
23. The Merit System of Rating Teachers
24. Faculty Meetings — Their Function and Values
25. Teacher Certification
26. Parent-Teacher Associations — Their Advantages and Disadvantages
27. In-service Teacher Education
28. Education Law
29. Tenure For Teachers
30. Elementary or Secondary School Supervision
31. Public School Administration As It Relates To The Classroom Teacher
32. An Education for The Children of Migrant Workers
33. Religion — Its Place in the Public Schools

34. Professional Ethics and the Teacher
35. Educational Philosophy In Practice In the Classroom

It Can Be Merely A "Gab Session." Extreme caution must be taken by seminar groups to insure against the seminar's becoming a matter of students' (members of the seminar) sharing only personal opinion, biases or misinformation. Due to this danger, seminar discussions should be well fortified by outside reading and study by those participating. Resource people can also be called upon to add "meat" to the discussions.

The eventual success of any seminar is predicated upon active, intelligent participation by all of its members. The professional seminar can have unique value for students as it is one type of college experience which is totally problem centered.

You'll Have to Beat the Bushes. A large volume of material is available in professional literature relative to the various topics suggested by the authors for seminar consideration. This fact is not true for educational frontiers. For this reason the authors are providing a skeletal description and a bibliography for each frontier.

Educational Frontiers

A frontier implies that there is something that is unconquered, unexplored, or undeveloped. It may be material or purely intellectual in nature. To some it may connote the existence of a far distant horizon which is chiefly unknown in character. To meet such a challenge imaginative and even visionary people are needed.

The frontiers of education rest fundamentally upon unborn ideas. In many respects these frontiers are created by the swiftly moving technology of the space age. In other respects the frontiers have been created by exploding population and the skyrocketing costs of education. Basically, however, the frontiers have been created by men who dare to dream. Yet "dreaming" alone is not sufficient. In order for dreams to come to tangible fruition they must be coupled with action. A vision, an idea, a dream, a goal is a dormant entity until it manifests itself in some concrete form. The embryo of the concrete, tangible end-product, however, is an idea or dream. In some respects then, pursuing a frontier is like chasing a rainbow or reaching for a cloud. Its dimensions are unknown and the frontier can be pushed ahead only by new ideas and patient experimentation.

A nationally famous inventor once remarked that he already had performed 9,000 experiments without finding the solution to a problem. A colleague of his who heard the remark asked if this apparent failure discouraged him. "No," said the inventor, "quite the contrary. I know 9,000 possible solutions which will not work. This places me closer to the correct one."

Wanted — Fearless Frontiersmen.

As a classroom teacher you can have a part in exploring the exciting

frontiers of education. To accomplish this you must not wait for someone else to take the lead or to show you exactly what needs experimentation and what ideas need airing. If you can contribute at least one new idea to some phase of teaching you will be making a significant contribution to education and to children. If you will view your classroom as a learning laboratory for yourself as well as for children, then you have established fertile ground upon which the seeds of creativity and innovation can grow heartily. An excellent rule of thumb is to vow to try out at least one new idea in your classroom each year you teach.

As a classroom teacher you can also encourage your school faculty to engage in some "total school" experimentation. Not only is it exciting to be a part of a controlled research study but it can help to advance the educational frontiers which are defined in this chapter. Experimentation in the total school or individual classroom — "action research" as it is sometimes labelled — can shed some light in the dark recesses of educational frontiers. You should encourage those (including yourself) who have experimented with an idea to write up their work and submit it to a professional journal for publication. Share the method and results of your work with others in the profession.

As stated in the introduction, this chapter is designed to introduce the student of education to *some* of the frontiers of education. Volumes could be written relative to any one of these frontiers but the authors can provide only the first foothold for your further investigation and study. This chapter can also serve as a framework of topics around which a post student teaching workshop or seminar can be structured.

Since the areas presented in this chapter are frontiers rather than well-worn paths, you will find a shortage of written material available.

Much of the present literature related to these frontiers is located in current periodical literature, as you will observe in the bibliographies. A few full length books are available in some of the areas, but in general you will have to ferret out information from periodicals.

Chapter 10 is organized in such a manner that each frontier mentioned contains three separate subdivisions. For each frontier you will find:

1. A brief description of what constitutes the frontier
2. Some questions or problems related to the frontier which may serve to arouse your interest or curiosity
3. A selected bibliography of references which may aid you to investigate the far-reaches of these educational frontiers.

Automation In Education

Automation involves the application of electronic and mechanical devices to tasks ordinarily assigned to human labor. Automation usually reduces the long-term cost of accomplishing a particular job while doing it more rapidly and efficiently. Some current applications of automation to education include the use of teaching machines, educational TV, automated microfilm libraries, library cataloging and indexing, translation of publications into foreign languages, language laboratories, and automatic record keeping, e.g., school attendance cards and students' course scheduling. These are only a few.

We are merely at the threshold of the age of automation. Automation has already created a change in labor requirements. What will be its impact upon education of the future? Should teachers be concerned about the possibility of being replaced by machines?

"Good Morning Boys and Girls. I'm Miss Auto Matic, Your New Teacher"

Perhaps some of the following questions will guide your personal study and investigation of this frontier:

1. What are the types of jobs which automation can assume in the over-all school program?
2. What are the instructional strengths and weaknesses of teaching machines as presently designed?

3. What principles of learning undergird the use of teaching machines?
4. How did the early work of Sidney L. Pressey affect the development of modern day teaching machines?
5. What facets of the role of a teacher do you feel can be satisfactorily automated? Defend your choices.
6. How might the influx of automation in a school change the character of the personnel needed to operate the school?
7. What quality of learning has resulted from automated teaching?
8. Does automation pose any threat to full employment for teachers?
9. What provisions can be made to preserve individuality and the importance of recognizing individual differences while incorporating automation into our school programs?
10. What parts of the school curriculum thus far have been "programmed" for use in teaching machines?
11. In what ways might automation change the type of preparation necessary to become an effective teacher in the era of the automated school?
12. Approximately how much additional expense is incurred by installing various types of automation in a school? Is automation presently priced out of reach of most school systems?
13. In those schools where it has been employed, what is pupil and teacher reaction to specific types of automation?

Selected References

(General)

1. Finn, J. D., "Technology and the Instructional Process," *Phi Delta Kappan,* Vol. 41, June, 1960.
2. Galanter, Eugene, "The Mechanization of Learning," N.E.A. Journal, Vol. 50, pp. 16-19, November, 1961.
3. Ginther, J., "Man, Values and the Machine," *Elementary School Journal,* Vol. 60, pp. 179-89, January, 1960.
4. Huffman, Harry, "Machine Age Enters The Classroom," *Virginia Journal of Education,* Vol. LIII, pp. 22-25, May, 1960.
5. Kowitz, G. T., "Administering The Automated Schools," *American School Board Journal,* pp. 13-16, February, 1961.
6. Krugman, Herbert E., "Education and The New Learning Devices," *N.E.A. Journal,* Vol. 51, April, 1962.
7. Kvaraceus, William, "Future Classroom — An Educational Automat?" *Educational Leadership* Vol. 18, February, 1961.
8. Lang, C. H., "Automation and Education," *New York State Education,* Vol. 45, pp. 622-25, June, 1958.
9. Maxwell, W. L., "Impact of Automation on Education," *Education Digest,* pp. 23-6, September, 1959.
10. Olds, R., "Automated Education," *Ohio Schools,* Vol. 38, pp. 8-9, April, 1960.
11. Rock, W. C., "Automation Challenges Education," *Amer. School Board Journal,* pp. 18-20, April, 1961.

12. Rollins, S. P., "Automated Grouping," *Phi Delta Kappan,* Vol. 42, pp. 212-14, February, 1961.
13. Schweickhard, D. M., "Electronics In Public Schools," *Minnesota Journal of Education,* Vol. 41, pp. 20-21, January, 1961.
14. Stolurow, L. M., "Problems In Evaluating Automated Instruction," *Teachers College Record,* Vol. 63, pp. 66-67, October, 1961.
15. Winebrenner, D. K., "Launderettes and Learn-O-Mats," *School Arts,* Vol. 52, p. 52, May, 1961.
16. Weisenberg, C. M., "Automation In The Classroom," *Clearing House,* 36:287, January, 1962.

Selected References
(Teaching Machines)

1. Baroff, David, "The Three R's and Pushbuttons," *New York Times Magazine,* September 25, 1960.
2. Blyth, J. W., "Teaching Machines and Human Beings," *Educational Record,* Vol. 41, pp. 116-25, April, 1960.
3. Coulson, J. E., and Harry Silberman, "Effects of Three Variables In A Teaching Machine," *Journal of Educational Psychology,* Vol. 51, pp. 135-43, June, 1960.
4. Cram, David, "Explaining 'Teaching Machines' and Programming," Fearon Publishers, San Francisco, 1961.
5. Deterline, Alexander William, *An Introduction to Programmed Instruction,* Englewood Cliffs, New Jersey: Prentice-Hall, 1962.
6. Finn, James D., and Donald G. Perrin, *Teaching Machines and Programmed Learning, 1962 A Survey of the Industry Technological Development Project of the National Education Association,* Washington, D. C., 1962.
7. Gorman, A. H., "Challenge of The Machine," *Clearing House,* Vol. 36, p. 357, February, 1962.
8. Grinder, C., "Place and Value of Teaching Machines," *The Nation's Schools,* Vol. 67, p. 10, May, 1961.
9. Henderson, Robert, "Listen Son," *The New Yorker,* December, 5, 1959.
10. Hough, J. B., "Research Vindication for Teaching Machines," *Phi Delta Kappan,* Vol. 43, pp. 240-42, March, 1962.
11. "How Machines Do A Teaching Job," *Business Week,* pp. 111-114, September 17, 1960.
12. Luce, G., "Can Machines Replace Teachers?" *Saturday Evening Post,* September 24, 1960.
13. Lumsdaine and Glaser, *Teacher Machines and Programmed Learning,* N.E.A. Department of A.V. Instruction, Washington, D. C., 1960.
14. McNeil, J., "Teaching Machines Can Help Improve Status of Teachers," *Chicago School Journal,* Vol. 43, pp. 178-80, January, 1962.
15. Morrill, Charles S., "Teaching Machines: A Review," *Psychological Bulletin,* Vol. 58, 1961.
16. Porter, D., "Teaching Machines," *Harvard Graduate School* Educ. Bull., pp. 1-5, 1958.
17. ———. "Push Button Brains," *Newsweek,* p. 95, October 26, 1959.

18. Robinson, D. W., "But This A Machine Can Not Do," *California Teach: Assoc. Journal*, pp. 16-17, September, 1960.
19. Skinner, B. F., "Something Good Happens To A Child," *Phi Delta Kappan*, October, 1960.
20. Skinner, B. F., "Teaching Machines," *Science*, pp. 969-977, 1958.
21. Skinner, B. F., "Teaching Machines and Behavior," *Scientific American*, Vol. 205, pp. 90-102, November, 1961.
22. Skinner, B. F., "Why We Need Teaching Machines," *Harvard Educational Review*, Vol. 31, p. 380, fall, 1961.
23. Stockman, Verne, "Teaching Machines You Can Make," *The Instructor*, Vol. 70, June, 1961.
24. ———. "Teaching Machines," *Time*, pp. 91-2, November 7, 1960.
25. ———. "Use of Teaching Machines Will Grow, But They Won't Replace Textbooks," *The Nation's Schools*, Vol. 68, December, 1961.
26. ———. "Will Teaching Machines Revolutionize Education?" *Michigan Education Journal*, Vol. 38, pp. 300-301, December, 1960.
27. Wittich, Walter A., "Teaching Machines: Practical and Probable," *The Nation's Schools*, Vol. 66, August, 1960.
28. Zachokke, Theo. O., "Mr. Brain Helps In The Classroom," *California Teachers Association Journal*, Vol. 56, p. 13, September, 1960.

Resourceful School Plant Planning

The frontier of school plant planning involves not only an issue of quality but one of quantity. Our present classroom shortage runs in the neighborhood of 250,000. School is being held in bus garages, church basements, fire houses and public libraries. Added to these conditions is the fact that we need to provide school facilities for over 1 1/4 million additional pupils each year.

All this needs to be accomplished without financially smothering the already heavily-burdened taxpayer. Adequate schools which are functional and durable yet nominal in cost need to be planned. The National Council On Schoolhouse Construction has made some interesting studies along these lines.

One obstacle to the frontier of school plant planning in some communities is the traditional stereotype of a school building which the general public harbors. "A school building must look like a school building." By this they mean a school building must not vary too much in appearance and physical construction from the schoolhouse they attended. "It was good enough for me, so it's good enough for my children." A similar traditional stereotype is held by many communities for church buildings and municipal buildings. It is difficult to shake off the narrowness and rigidity of thought which in some instances is part of our heritage.

Another imposing hurdle is that of public misinformation. Very often communication breaks down between those who are planning the school and the community at large. False rumors begin circulating about supposed "frills" being incorporated into the building or the exorbitant raise in taxes which will result if the new school is approved. Some school proposals therefore are voted down by the general public before they are off the drawing board. This problem is strictly a matter of communicating accurately and effectively with the public. If the public is given *all* of the correct information they will make a sound decision. This is the foundation of our democratic system. These obstacles and limitations notwithstanding, school plant planners are forging ahead with some creative and visionary ideas for new buildings and facilities.

Prefabrication is being employed in school building construction yet we have only scratched the surface of its possibilities. Schools are appearing with folding partitions and multi-purpose rooms. There are in existence schools which are circular in design, "see-thru" schools, movable schools, schools containing modular units, underground schools, schools without windows, and completely air conditioned ones. Architects and school planners are searching for designs which provide a maximum of flexibility at minimum price. Of course a school building should have esthetic value as a piece of architecture. This, too, is of concern. Some types of construction materials needed today by school planners have not yet been invented. Planners always have to work within the scope of available materials.

To date the frontier of school plant planning has only been touched upon. A vast gulf of presently unbelievable yet workable ideas lies before us. We desperately need to set sail upon it.

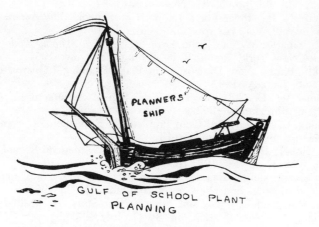

IT'S TIME TO SET SAIL

Questions and Activities to Spur Investigation and Discussion

1. What factors should determine the design of a school plant? What hierarchy, if any, should exist among these factors?
2. What are the advantages and disadvantages of a single story school building as compared to a multi-level school building?
3. Name some of the innovations in school building construction which have evolved in the last ten years.
4. What role should each of the following groups play in determining and approving school plant design: Architects; teachers; school administrators; children; board of education; local citizenry; state education department; federal government?
5. What constitutes a "frill" in school construction? What criteria should be employed as the measure?
6. Can a school be economical in cost and still be expensive looking in appearance? If so, how can it be accomplished?
7. What features can be incorporated in school plant construction so as to make the building flexible (in terms of accommodating a diversity of school activities and programs)?
8. Compose a list of what you consider the most pressing problems faced by school plant planners.
9. Formulate an argument either for or against the installation of air conditioning in all new schools.
10. What approach and what avenues should be used in presenting proposed plans for a new school to the general public (a community)?
11. Make a sketch of what you envision to be the physical design of an ideal classroom. (Include furniture, cabinets, and all such fittings.)

SELECTED REFERENCES

1. Brubaker, C. W., "The Big-City School of Tomorrow," *Nation's Schools,* Vol. 66, p. 74, December, 1960.
2. Buehring, L. E., "Schools Where The Walls Fold Away," *Nation's Schools,* Vol. 68, pp. 53-61, November, 1961.
3. Burbank, N. B., "Ideas For a Junior High School," *The American School Board Journal,* Vol. 142, pp. 20-23, March, 1961.
4. Bursch, Charles W., and John Lyon Reid, *High Schools Today and Tomorrow,* New York: Reinhold Publishing Company, 1957.
5. Castaldi, Basil, "New Dimension in Plant Planning," *Overview,* Vol. 3, pp. 44-46, January, 1962.
6. Cocking, W. D., "Recent Trends in School Architecture," *Overview,* Vol. 3, p. 85, March, 1962.
7. DeYoung, C. A., "Physical Plant Problems in Education," *Current History,* Vol. 41, pp. 97-101, August, 1961.
8. Dietz, Robert H., "The See-Through School," *American School and University,* Vol. 1, pp. 135-138, 1958.
9. ——. *Environmental Engineering for the School,* U. S. Department of Health, Education and Welfare, Washington, D. C., 1961.
10. Featherstone, Richard L., and others, "One-Story vs. Multi-Story Construction," *Overview,* Vol. 2, pp. 40-41, July, 1961.

11. Foxhall, William B., "Air-Conditioning For Schools," *Architectural Record*, Vol. 130, pp. 183-194, July, 1961.

12. Hechinger, Fred M., "The Old Schoolhouse Is Going Modern," *Parents*, Vol. 36, pp. 38-39, February, 1961.

13. Heffernan, Helen, *Curriculum and the Elementary School Plant*, Association for Supervision and Curriculum Development, N.E.A., Washington, D. C., 1958.

14. Goldhammer, K., "Concepts of Educational Research for School Plant Planners and Designers," *American School and University*, Vol. 1, pp. 11-14, 1960.

15. Kelsey, F. L., "Building Today for Tomorrow's School Programs," *The Nations Schools*, Vol. 69, pp. 73-80, May, 1962.

16. Kump, Ernest J., "The Facts About Modular Construction," *School Management*, Vol. 4, p. 54, January, 1960.

17. McDonald, Eva G., and Burt E., "Opinions Differ on Windowless Classrooms," *N.E.A. Journal*, Vol. 50, pp. 12-14, October, 1961.

18. McQuade, Walter, *Schoolhouses*, New York: Simon and Schuster Publishing Company, 1958.

19. "Movable School," *Overview*, Vol. 3, pp. 37-38, February, 1962.

20. Olsen, Leroy C., "School Architecture and the Learning Process," *American School Board Journal*, Vol. 143, pp. 28-31, October, 1961.

21. Orput, Raymond A., "Emerging Instructional Patterns and School Design," *American School Board Journal*, pp. 24-28, January, 1961.

22. Pearson, William A., "Everybody's School," *N.E.A. Journal*, Vol. 51, p. 20, March, 1962.

23. Shaw, A. B., "Educational Construction In 1960," *American School and University*, Vol. 1, pp. 5-14, 1961.

24. Taylor, James L., "Learning Laboratories for Elementary School Children," *School Life*, Vol. 41, pp. 17-19, January-February, 1959.

25. Wells, Charles Jr., "Anatomy of the School Building Process," *The American School Board Journal*, Vol. 142, pp. 24-35, March, 1961.

26. Wright, Henry, "About Air Conditioned Schools," *School Management*, Vol. 4, p. 62, April, 1960.

More Efficient Use of Our Teacher Resources

If an industrial personnel director or efficiency expert were to survey staff utilization in most schools he would be appalled. Certainly industrial personnel practices and problems are not totally the same as those of a public school. The fact still remains, however, that school staff utilization historically has been a "hit-or-miss" proposition. It is inconceivable that any business or industry would be guilty of such misuse of a professionally trained staff as has typified school staff utilization in the past. Teachers and administrators who are trained to perform a valuable professional service find themselves obligated to do many kinds of custodial, secretarial and menial tasks. These represent a tremendous waste of a professional teacher's time and energy plus a loss to children and of tax dollars.

The teaching staff represents the primary educational resource of any school. The manner in which this resource is deployed is all important. Too many fine teachers are spending their valuable time and energy patrolling school cafeterias, collecting milk money, supervising playgrounds, and performing routine bookkeeping and secretarial chores.

A teacher who has spent half of her noon hour patrolling a playground will not be as physically ready to teach in the afternoon as one who has had a full hour's rest. Teachers need to be freed to teach. They also need to be utilized in such a fashion so as to capitalize upon their individual talents and academic specialties. School authorities and the general public are beginning to become aware of these facts; consequently many new ideas aimed at improving staff utilization are coming into practice. Teacher aids and extra secretarial help are being organized into "teams" so as to capitalize upon academic strengths and to present many points of view to the students. Teacher work load is being carefully examined in many school systems. Teaching by closed circuit TV is being employed to increase the exposure and sphere of influence of the exceptionally fine teacher.

We have gained at least a foothold along this frontier. Perhaps we have even blazed a few trails — yet the forest remains largely dense and uncharted.

Questions for Study

1. What kinds of professional abilities, talents, resources might a teacher possess?
2. Select some special professional ability such as music, dramatics or foreign language. Discuss how this ability can best be capitalized upon by proper staff utilization.
3. How can team teaching make provision for the individual academic strengths and weaknesses of teachers?
4. Outline a possible day's work schedule for three teachers (specify grade level) who are employing team teaching.
5. What special educational facilities do you feel are necessary (if any) to stage a good setting for team teaching?
6. What has educational research shown about team teaching as regards general reaction of the teachers using it; quality of learning which resulted from it as compared to a conventional classroom and its effects upon children?
7. Make a list of the tasks (which you recall from student teaching) the classroom teacher engaged in which you consider to be a waste of the teacher's time and energy.
   How might these tasks be accomplished using other school personnel?

8. Investigate through current periodical literature the use of "teacher aides" in the public schools.
9. Through what means can a school administration best come to know the individual talents, abilities and resources of its teaching staff?

SELECTED REFERENCES

(General)

1. "Aides and Secretaries — One Way to Solve Your Classroom Teacher Shortage," *School Management*, Vol. 2, pp. 36-37 and 74-75, May, 1958.
2. Bowen, John J., "Methods For Better Utilization of Teachers' Professional Skills," *Elementary School Journal*, Vol. 56, pp. 403-408, May, 1956.
3. Claxton, B. C., "How Are We Classified: Teacher or Device?" *Bal. Sheet*, Vol. 43, pp. 362-363, April, 1962.
4. Cronin, Joseph M., "What's All This About 'Teacher Aides'?" *California Journal of Secondary Education*, Vol. 34, pp. 390-97, November, 1959.
5. Grayson, J., "Teacher Aide: Mother," *El. Sch. Journal*, Vol. 62, pp. 134-38, December, 1961.
6. Norton, M. S., "Extra Duties For Teachers," *Nat. Assn. Sec. Sch. Prin. Bul.*, Vol. 45, pp 105-110, December, 1961
7. Singer, I. J., "Survey of Staff Utilization Practices In Six States," Vol. 46, pp. 1-13, January, 1962.
8. "Time To Teach," *Mich. Ed. Journal*, Vol. 39, pp. 416-417, February, 1962.
9. Trump, Lloyd J., "Better Staff Utilization," *N.E.A. Journal*, January, 1958.

SELECTED REFERENCES

(Team Teaching)

1. Anderson, Robert H., "Team Teaching," *N.E.A. Journal*, pp. 52-54, March, 1960.
2. Anderson, Robert H., "Team Teaching In Action," *The Nation's Schools*, pp. 62-65, May, 1960.
3. Anderson, Robert H., "Team Teaching In The Elementary School," *Education Digest*, pp. 26-28, November, 1959.
4. Anderson, Robert H., and Donald P. Mitchell, "Team Teaching, New Learning Concepts Demand Changes in School Plant Design," *Nation's Schools*, pp. 75-83, June, 1960.
5. Becker, H. A., et al., "Team Teaching," *Instructor*, Vol. 71, pp. 43-45, June, 1962.
6. Brownell, J. A., and H. A. Taylor, "Theoretical Perspectives for Teaching Teams," *Phi Delta Kappan*, pp. 150-157, January, 1962.
7. Clinchy, Evans, ed., *Schools For Team Teaching*, Educational Facilities Laboratories, New York City, 1961.
8. Crandell, E., "Birmingham Tries Team Teaching Experiment," *Michigan Education Journal*, January, 1961.
9. Cunningham, L. L., "Keys to Team Teaching," *Overview*, Vol. 1, pp. 54-55, October, 1960.
10. Dean, Stuart E., "Team Teaching A Review," *School Life*, pp. 5-7, September, 1961.

11. Drummond, H. D., "Team Teaching: An Assessment," *Education Digest*, pp. 5-8, February, 1962.
12. Elliot, R. W., "Team Teaching: Effective In-Service Training," *American School Board Journal*, p. 19, February, 1962.
13. Fischler, A. S., "Use of Team Teaching in the Elementary School," *School Science and Mathematics*, Vol. 62, pp. 281-288, April, 1962.
14. Goodlad, John, "Experiment In Team Teaching," *Elementary School Journal*, pp. 11-13, October, 1958.
15. Hahn, Robert O., et al., "Team Teaching: A Second Look," *Journal of Teacher Education*, pp. 508-510, December, 1961.
16. Hoopes, Ned, "Team-Teachers Play A Winning Game," *P.T.A. Magazine*, pp. 29-31, March, 1961.
17. Hoppock, Anne, "Team Teaching: Form Without Substance?" *N.E.A. Journal*, pp. 47-48, April, 1961.
18. Horn, E. G., "Experiments In Team Teaching," *Illinois Education*, pp. 111-115, November, 1961.
19. Lambert, P., "Team Teaching For The Elementary School," *Educational Leadership*, Vol. 18, pp. 85-88, November, 1960.
20. Lobb, M., "What Are Some Promising Practices in Team Teaching?" *Nat. Assoc., Sec. School Principals' Bulletin*, 44: pp. 2-7, April, 1960.
21. Marsh, R., "Team Teaching: New Concept," *Clearing House*, pp. 496-499, April, 1961.
22. Morse, Arthur D., *Schools of Tomorrow — Today*, Garden City, New York: Doubleday and Co., Chapter I, 1960.
23. Petruzello, P. R., "Report On Team Teaching," *Clearing House*, pp. 333-336, February, 1962.
24. Rzepka, L., "Team Teaching In The Elementary School: What Is It?" *Ohio Schools*, pp. 14-15, January, 1962.
25. Simon, A. et al., "Experiment In Team Teaching," *Ohio Schools*, pp. 34-35, March, 1961.
26. Smith, G. et al., "Team Teaching A Challenge To Change," *Arizona Teacher*, Vol. 50, pp. 20-24, November, 1961.
27. Ward, J. O., "Another Plan For Co-ordinate Teaching," *American Sch. Bd. Jr.*, 140:10, February, 1960.

Well Controlled Programs of Educational Research and Dissemination Of Information

An age-old debate rests on the question — is teaching a science or an art? Many classify it as both. If it is a science, then its practictioners ought to perform in a scientific manner. Research established principles should undergird what is taught and how it is taught, yet much of current methodology and curriculum has flimsy, if any, research foundation. Student teaching is a good example of this fact. We are carrying on a traditional practice with little research to justify it. There are of course techniques of teaching which will never be proven either more or less effective than others since there are many human variables involved. This fact may justify the classification of teaching, in part at least, as an art.

Educational research must meet certain criteria to be helpful. It must be well structured and controlled in order to be a valuable contribution. Much of the early educational research lacked these qualities. There are at least two other phases of this frontier which need attention if it is to be conquered.

Research Into Practice. Research in quality and quantity is a useless tool hanging lonely on the rack unless it affects practice. Somehow we need to stimulate the flow of research findings to the classroom teacher. Other professions are devoutly concerned about constantly informing their members of new research developments. Many teachers and school administrators just do not have time to ferret out research findings from the many different publications in which they appear. Perhaps a central research information center could be established which, if automated, could compile and catalog educational research done both nationally and internationally.

Let's Spread It Around. Rapid dissemination of accurate information is vital to high quality teaching. Teachers should have the most current knowledge at their fingertips. Unfortunately, its disssemination is amazingly inefficient in our otherwise highly technological society. We have many effective mass communication media at our disposal but employ them on a very limited basis in spreading knowledge. Description and results of current basic research and scholarly studies in law, medicine, mathematics, teaching, etc. are painfully slow in becoming available to the professions, much less the general public. There are many reasons for this fact.

Helter-skelter Shelter. Because research foundations and graduate schools are widely dispersed across our country, frequently they are unaware of what research is being done or has been done by others. Doctoral studies, for example, often get tucked away on library shelves without receiving proper circulation. Scholars in allied fields are sometimes unaware of their existence. One solution to this dilemma might be some sort of national (or perhaps international) warehouse of knowledge. Literally all of the knowledge of the world which appears in written form could be stored in orderly fashion by employing modern methods of automation and microprinting.

Imagine what a timesaver such a knowledge center could be. If a student were contemplating doing some research he would not have to spend hours "hunting" for what was already known about his particular research area. Rather, a question could be fed into the auto-mated knowledge warehouse and out of the machinery would come a bibliography containing *all* of the information relative to his topic.

By using the knowledge warehouse a physician could find out almost instantly the current research findings concerning a particular ailment.

The federal government, the United Nations, or almost any public or private agency could operate this knowledge warehouse providing it had the capital investment necessary. The long range values of such an informational resource would be inestimable. We have the tech-nology to establish the knowledge warehouse *now* if we can find the human motivation to do it. An amazing automated library has already been demonstrated at the Seattle World's Fair.

One Thousand Books Printed On the Head of A Pin! Books are major vehicles for disseminating knowledge. Books as we presently know them still have some serious limitations in terms of their accessi-bility to the general public. If a private individual or small library would like to own a great number of books the cost of buying thousands of volumes would be prohibitive. The space required to store vast numbers of books also may prohibit ownership. A new frontier in printing may serve to wipe away the factors preventing the owner-ship of a large personal library. This new technique, called micro-printing, can put the estimated twenty million volumes of the *world's* libraries at the disposal of the general public for a cost of approxi-mately three to five thousand dollars. Many professional people and students pay about this sum for books and magazines over say, a twenty year span of time.

Just how small can books be printed? Richard Feynman of the California Institute of Technology, speaking before the American Physical Society, theorized that we could print on a thin metal film with a delicately controlled "pencil" of electrons. By reaching the level of electronmicroscopic reduction an ordinary page of printed matter could be reduced to a size one micron by two microns (in area). This would mean that the head of a pin (one square millimeter) could hold about 1,000 books of 500 pages each. Projected further, one sheet of paper eight by eleven inches could hold over twenty million books (the approximate number of different books contained in all of the libraries of the world). There may never be any practical need to compress printed matter to this degree, but at least it is possible to do so.

At the present time we are already reducing printed material 40 to 60 times by utilizing photography and 35-millimeter film. A newer process reduces print 500 to 1,000 times so that an entire book can be printed on a regular-sized library catalogue card.

A third system employing the micro-dot shrinks printed matter photographically. It then can be read through a high-powered microscope. This technique frequently has been used in espionage work.

The wholesale use of micro-books may not be far off. By using a high-powered projector we could read books from a movie screen in the privacy of our own homes. Most important we could own enormous numbers of micro-books at a fraction of the cost of full-sized volumes. An entire library could be stored on one small shelf of a den. Micro-books represent an educational frontier.

Funds for Educational Research Scarce. One reason for the scarcity of educational research has been a lack of funds. Research grants in other academic areas such as science (chemistry, electrical engineering, physics) and mathematics have enjoyed fine support, due to their business and industrial applications. Private individuals seeking new products have been their benefactors. Research in education, on the other hand, has been starved for financial backing with the exception of funds provided by nonprofit foundations and philanthropic sources. This situation needs to be corrected if we are to pursue excellence at all levels of the teaching-learning process.

Brain-teasers for Further Study

1. Study individually or with others the structuring and procedures relative to educational research. What constitutes well structured research? What are some of the pitfalls?
2. Become familiar with some of the publications which report educational research, i.e., Journal of Educational Research; N.E.A. Research Reports; Encyclopedia of Educational Research.
3. Select some area of the curriculum such as handwriting instruction or the teaching of spelling and survey the available research pertaining to it. Does the research point to any specific classroom methodology?
4. Define each of these terms associated with educational research: Variables; sample; mean; median; mode; standard deviation from the mean; control group.
5. Select a report of one research study and try to locate any variables which were not provided for in the research.
6. Teachers have very little time to read professional journals. Make a list of possible ways they can be kept informed about important, pertinent educational research in spite of limited time.
7. What areas of student teaching do you feel need to be researched? Make some suggestions as to how it could be accomplished.

SELECTED REFERENCES

1. Anderson, K. E., "Avenues For The Improvement of Research," *Science Ed.*, Vol. 45, pp. 418-424, December, 1961.
2. Brower, G., "Hunches and Hypotheses," *Michigan Ed. Journal*, pp. 312-313, December, 1961.
3. Bruce, W. C., "Research in School Administration," *Am. Sch. Bd. Journal*, Vol. 144, p. 39, March, 1962.
4. Clark, D. L., "What's Next For Research In Education?" *Theory Into Practice*, Vol. 1, pp. 61-63, April, 1962.
5. Hall, R. M., "Education On The Move," *Theory Into Practice*, Vol. 1, pp. 105-112, April, 1962.
6. Hunnicutt and Iverson, *Research In The Three R's*, New York: Harper and Bros., 1958.
7. Krathwohl, D. R., "Scope of The Research Problem," *Theory Into Practice*, Vol. 1, pp. 98-104, April, 1962.
8. Massialas, B. G., and F.R. Smith, "Quality Research; A Goal For Every Teacher," *Phi Delta Kappan*, Vol. 43, pp. 253-256, March, 1962.
9. McGoldrick, J. H., "Research Starting With The Textbook," *Clearing House*, Vol. 36, pp. 31-32, September, 1961.
10. Moore, S. A., "How Not To Report Research," *Overview*, Vol. 2, pp. 24-25, December, 1961.
11. Moriarity, T. E., "Every Teacher A Researcher," *Sci. Ed.*, Vol. 46, pp. 164-66, March, 1962.
12. Passow, A. H., "Curriculum Research: Status, Needs, and Prospects," *Ed. Res. Bul.*, Vol. pp. 197-205, November, 1960.
13. Provus, M., "Research and Uncertainty In The Modern Classroom," *Sch. Sci. and Math.* Vol. 62, pp. 276-280, April, 1962.
14. Rossetti, A. D., "Research and Administration," *Clearing House*, Vol. 36, pp. 346-349, fall, 1962.
15. Simpson, R. J., "Constant Quest: Quality Education," *Mich. Ed. Journal*, Vol. 38, pp. 418-419, February, 1962.
16. Taylor, C. W., et al., "Bridging The Gap Between Research and Teaching," *N.E.A. Journal*, Vol. 51, pp. 23-25, January, 1962.

Exploring the Limits and Horizons of Educational TV

Several of the frontiers discussed in this chapter overlap each other. Educational television could be considered a part of automation in education or a part of the utilization of teacher resources. The authors felt, however, that educational TV presented so many unique problems and facets in and of itself that it should be treated as a separate frontier.

What's Your Best Camera Angle?

This question may become a common part of modern day teaching terminology. A student passing a teacher in the school corridor may be more apt to say, "I saw your great science lesson on TV yesterday, Miss Roberts," than merely a simple, "Good morning, Miss Roberts."

Educational television promises to make many exciting innovations in our total school program. It can lift the limitations of classroom equipment, time and resources. It can expand the sphere of influence of the topnotch teacher to limitless proportions. Many institutions and organizations are experimenting with this sleeping communications giant. Among these are the Ford Foundation and the Fund For the Advancement of Education. How much of the role of the teacher can and should be assigned to educational TV? There are a myriad of questions related to its use in education which remain unanswered. One very big question mark related to educational TV is: Who is going to finance it? At the present time some private institutions, together with philanthropic funds, are carrying the major burden of limited experimental usage. But what about the mountainous costs of expanded usage? Should the federal government be enlisted? The cost problem remains an ominous one.

Despite the financial hurdles we must put this electronic marvel to work in an era of mushrooming school enrollments and increasing academic demands upon the school. It could revolutionize school staff utilization and teacher work load; however, we must not let it become a mechanical monster which injects impersonality and regimentation into our educational programs. Through the wonders of electronics we have been given a remarkable teaching tool. How can we employ it to enhance the quality of education at all levels?

TANTALIZING TORMENTERS ABOUT TV

1. Would all classroom teachers be suitable as television teachers? What special qualifications would be necessary to be successful as a TV teacher?
2. What are the limitations of educational TV as indicated by current research findings?
3. What is meant by closed circuit and open circuit educational TV?
4. Trace the brief history of educational TV from the early experiments of the 1930's to present day usage.
5. Plan a field trip to an educational TV studio.

6. What varied communication functions can educational TV provide for teachers, pupils, school administrators and the community?
7. List some possible sources for financing educational TV.
8. Investigate some of the present educational TV experiments such as the Midwest Airborne Project, the Chelsa Project of New York City, and the Washington County, Maryland, Experiment.
9. How can educational TV change the school staff utilization picture?
10. What modifications of teaching techniques and lesson planning might be necessary for teaching on television?
11. List some types of educational experiences which can be provided through educational TV which would be out of the range of a regular classroom setting.
12. What additional staff and school physical facilities are necessary to maintain closed circuit educational TV within a school building?
13. Does the advent of TV on the educational scene dictate any changes in our teacher preparation programs?

SELECTED REFERENCES

1. Bassett, F., "Education's Newest Resource," *California Teachers' Association Journal,* Vol. 57, pp. 11-12, January, 1961.
2. Besvinick, S. L., "TV Teaching: Some Assumptions and Conclusions," *School and Society* Vol. 88, pp. 30-31, January, 1960.
3. Bridges, C. C., "Attention Scale for Evaluation of Educational Television Programs," *Journal of Educational Research,* Vol. 54, pp. 149-52, December, 1960.
4. Broadrick and others, "TV Teachers' Report," *Speech Teacher,* Vol. 11, pp. 153-157, March, 1962.
5. Burns, J. L., "Promise of Classroom TV," *National Parent Teacher,* Vol. 55, pp. 8-11, November, 1960.
6. Fagan, E. R., "Educational TV: What's The Story?" *Clearing House,* Vol. 35, pp. 259-264, January, 1961.
7. Foshay, A. W., "Instructional Television," *Virginia Journal of Education,* Vol. 54, pp. 18-22, February, 1961.
8. Gable, M. A., "Educational TV: Catastrophe or Opportunity?" *Education Digest,* Vol. 26, pp. 14-16, October, 1960.
9. Guba, E. G., "Measuring the Effectiveness of Instructional Television," *Educational Research Bulletin,* Vol. 40, pp. 153-61, September, 1961.
10. Himmelweit, Hilde T., *Television and The Child,* New York: Oxford University Press, 1958.
11. Ivey, J. E., and B. D. Godbold, "MPATI: Breakthrough in Educational Television," *Phi Delta Kappan,* Vol. 42, pp. 192-6, February, 1961.
12. Jewett, R. E., "Effects of Television Teaching On the Classroom Teacher," *Educational Research Bulletin,* Vol. 40, pp. 141-5, September, 1961.
13. Levy, D., "Don't Make the Mistakes We Did," *Education Screen and A.V. Guide,* Vol. 40, pp. 201-2, April, 1962.
14. Maranz, I. L., "Afraid of Educational TV?" *New York State Education,* Vol. 49, pp. 32-33, March, 1962.
15. Minnow, Newton, "Our Common Goal: A Nationwide Educational Television System," *The Education Digest,* May, 1962.

16. Morse, Arthur D., *Schools of Tomorrow-Today*, New York: Doubleday and Company, Chapter 8, 1960.
17. Perry, A., "Teaching By TV In Today's Schools," *Educational Forum*, Vol. 24, pp. 389-395, May, 1960.
18. Remley, F. M., "TV Playback On Tape or Film," *Overview*, Vol. 2, pp. 48-49, December, 1961.
19. Schramm, Wilber, *Television in the Lives of Our Children*, Stanford California: University Press, 1961.
20. Shayon, R. L., "And After TV?" *Saturday Review*, June 2, 1962.
21. Siepmann, Charles Arthur, *TV and Our School Crisis*, New York: Dodd, Mead and Company, 1958.
22. Skeleton, M., "SOS For Educational Television," *P.T.A. Magazine*, November, 1961.
23. Smith, Mary, ed., *Using Television In The Classroom*, (Midwest Program on Airborn Television Instruction), New York: McGraw-Hill, 1961.
24. Tanner, D., "Needed Research in Instructional TV," *School Review*, Vol. 69, pp. 4-5, January, 1960.
25. ———. "Ten Years of Educational TV," *Education Digest*, Vol. 27, pp. 28-30, September, 1961.
26. Tarbet, Donald, *Television and Our Schools*, New York: Ronald Press, 1961.
27. Zorbough, H., "Television in American Schools," *Journal of Ed. Socio.*, Vol. 32, p. 413, May, 1959.

Greater Individualization of Instruction

There is nothing so unequal as equal treatment of unequals.

Fundamentally education is a person-to-person process. Its successful practitioners claim to modify human behavior. Logically, then, its final measure of quality must be its impact upon human beings — individual human beings. It thus would appear sequentially that a greater individualization of instruction would result in a higher quality of learning, assuming other variables are held constant. Does this mean that the most favorable teaching ratio becomes one teacher to one student? This one-to-one ratio is a so-called advantage of teaching machines. Is it a misnomer? What are the advantages and disadvantages of individualized instruction? Some critics of education feel that we should move toward more large group instruction through such devices as educational TV. If we individualize instruction in our public schools to a greater extent, can we keep within reasonable costs? Assuming we can, does this movement warrant the expenditure of extra tax dollars?

Keep in mind while probing this problem that, like so many terms in education, individualization of instruction has many interpretations.

To some it means a very low pupil-to-teacher ratio. To others it may mean supplying educational materials on many grade levels within one classroom. It can also mean permitting students to proceed through graduated learning tasks at their own learning speed, eliminating grade level lock steps. The nongraded school is an example of this idea. The term individualization of instruction can mean all of these things and more; therefore define clearly the frame of reference for this frontier as you do your exploratory reading. If we supersensitize our school program to the similarities and differences of individual students we may have found the keystone factor in the educative process. If this is desirable, is it obtainable? Perhaps its proponents are the Don Quixotes of education?

To Tease Your Gray Matter

1. What is meant by individualized reading instruction?
2. How does educational research indicate how school class size affects the general achievement of children?

3. How might an educational guidance and counseling program in an elementary school serve to further individualize the total school program?
4. What general provisions can be made in lesson plans to facilitate more individual or small group instruction?
5. What "extra" or special educational materials would need to be available to truly individualize classroom instruction?
6. Faced with skyrocketing school enrollments how can we preserve a reasonable degree of individual recognition and instruction for the students? What techniques, devices, organizational patterns, and aids can assist in doing this?
7. Assuming that students are given academic work suited to their abilities, do all need about the same amount of individual instruction? Defend your answer.
8. Are there types of classroom lessons or activities which do not lend themselves to individualized instruction? If so, what are some of them?
9. What factors should determine to what extent individualized instruction is utilized in the classroom?

You may want to add other questions to this list as your interests and background dictate.

SELECTED REFERENCES

1. Barron, J. Roy, "Individualized Learning," *Education Screen*, Vol. 17, pp. 20-21, January, 1960.
2. Bowden, M. G., et al., "Quality Through Individualized Instruction," *Childhood Education*, Vol. 36, pp. 361-370, April, 1960.
3. Bush, Robert N., "Individualizing Learning In An Age of Conformity," *Journal of Secondary Education*, Vol. 36, p. 385, November, 1961.
4. Chase, Linwood, "Individual Differences in Classroom Learning," *Social Studies in the Elementary School*, Fifty Sixth Yearbook of N.S.S.E., University of Chicago Press, 1957.
5. Cutts, Norma, and Nicholas Moseley, *Providing for Individual Differences in The Elementary School*, Englewood Cliffs, New Jersey: Prentice-Hall, 1960.
6. Flourner, Francis, "Meeting Individual Differences in Arithmetic," *The Arithmetic Teacher*, Vol. VII, February, 1960.
7. Frazier, Alexander, "More Opportunity For Learning Or Less," *Education Leadership*, Vol. 18, pp. 266-270, February, 1961.
8. Goodlad, John, and Robert Anderson, *The Nongraded Elementary School*, New York: Harcourt, Brace and Company, 1959.
9. ———. "Individualized Learning." *Overview*, Vol. 2, p. 45, March, 1961.
10. Kessie, Eleanor, "Good-by To The Reading Group," *Grade Teacher*, Vol. 78, pp. 30-31, November, 1960.
11. Lazar, May, "Individualized Reading: A Dynamic Approach," *The Reading Teacher*, pp. 75-83, December, 1957.
12. Morrison, Nellie C., "Instead of Reading Groups — What?" *Childhood Education*, Vol. 36, pp. 371-3, April, 1960.
13. Morse, Arthur, *Schools of Tomorrow — Today*, Chapter II, New York: Doubleday and Company, 1960.
14. Noall, Mabel S., "Individualized Instruction," *Journal of Education*, Vol. 143, pp. 33-43, April, 1961.

15. Stauffer, Russell, "Individualized Reading Instruction — A Backward Look", *Elementary English,* pp. 335-341, May, 1959.
16. Veatch, Jeannette, *Individualizing Your Reading Program,* New York: G. P. Putnam's Sons, 1959.
17. White, Verna, *Studying The Individual Pupil,* New York: Harper & Bros., 1958.

More Effective and Functional Grouping In the Classroom and Total School

Elementary School Organization, published by the Department of Elementary School Principals of the N.E.A., predicts that the school of the future will have no grades. There are many signposts which indicate that we are moving in that direction. To many the appearance of the nongraded school seems to be a very natural outgrowth from the past years of "fumbling around" with various grouping schemes. For more than fifty years schools have committed themselves to the notion that chronological age was the most functional criterion for grouping children within the school. Modern day research tells us that this method of grouping children for instructional purposes is at best cumbersome. It ignores completely the individual uniqueness of children. Since those concerned with education came to the realization that improved grouping patterns were needed, there have been many interesting experiments and innovations.

The student of education is reminded that this frontier being discussed does not include "the group process" which is a part of teaching methodology. Rather, this frontier involves grouping patterns or organizational schemes for grouping children which are a part of total school and classroom organization and management. Grouping, then, is never an end in itself but is a process or organizational consideration by which we accomplish other goals.

The nongraded school poses new criteria for grouping children and offers many exciting challenges to the teacher. In Torrance, California,[1] there has been some experimentation with multi-grade groupings. Some sections of Ohio[2] have experimented with yearly achievement grouping. All these are coupled with the innumerable experiments to establish various types of so called homogeneous groups. The point to be made is that the school is given a group of children. Logically it seems as though possible grouping schematics would be practically limitless

---

[1] J. H. Hill, "A Three Year Study in Multi-Graded Teaching," *The Nation's Schools,* Vol. 60, July, 1958, pp. 51-53.
[2] Bryan Crutcher and Marian Smith, "The Grouping Dilemma," *Ohio Schools,* Vol. 37, November, 1959, p. 18.

if all variables were considered. Thus far we have experimented with relatively few grouping patterns considering the range of possibilities. In addition to experimenting with new possibilities there is a need to establish, through sound research, the strengths and weaknesses of many existing patterns. Many in education feel that to hunt for a grouping schema which is far superior to what has already been suggested is like a hunt for the "pot of gold." The feeling is also expressed that educators should concentrate upon improving the overall quality of teaching as it is a most important variable. There still remain those who, with a far distant look in their eyes, envision grouping schemata which truly reflect recognition of the uniqueness of children. Enfolded in today's wildest dreams lie tomorrow's realities.

SELECTED REFERENCES

1. Bahner, John, "Grouping Within A School," *Childhood Education*, Vol. 36, pp. 354-356, April, 1960.
2. Blumberg, Arthur, and Edmund Amidon, "Students Reactions To Group Teaching Methods," *The Journal of Teacher Education*, Vol. 12, pp. 458-462, December, 1961.
3. Byers, Loretta, "Ability Grouping — Help or Hindrance to Social and Emotional Growth?" *School Review*, Vol. 69, pp. 449-455, winter, 1961.
4. Cartwright, Dorwin, and Alvin Zander, *Group Dynamics: Research and Theory*, Elmsford, New York: Row, Peterson and Company, 1960.
5. Clausen, Robert, "Grouping for Continuous Learning: Why Probe Grouping Practices?" *Childhood Education*, Vol. 36, pp. 352-3, April, 1960.
6. Crutcher, E. Bryan, and Marian Smith, "The Grouping Dilemma," *Ohio Schools*, Vol. 37, pp. 18-19, November, 1959.
7. Davis, O. L., "Grouping For Instruction: Some Perspectives," *The Education Forum*, Vol. 24, pp. 209-216, January, 1960.
8. Della-Dora, Delma, "What Research Says About Grouping," *Michigan Education Journal*, Vol. 37, pp. 513-542, April, 1960.
9. Feely, Martin J., "Ability Grouping," *Journal of Health, Physical Education and Recreation*, Vol. 32, p. 18, November, 1961.
10. Gerberich, J. Raymond, and Jay Blaha, "Using Test Results to Make Decisions About Pupil Placement, Grouping and Promotion," *National Elementary Principal*, Vol. 41, pp. 18-22, November, 1961.
11. Harris, Janet D., "Group Dynamics for Young Children? Of Course," *The National Elementary Principal*, Vol. 40, pp. 10-13, April, 1961.
12. Jensen, Gale E., ed., *The Dynamics of Instructional Groups*, 59th Yearbook, N.S.S.E., University of Chicago Press.
13. Lifton, Walter M., *Working With Groups*, New York: John Wiley & Sons, 1961.
14. Mann, Maxine, "What Does Ability Grouping Do To The Self-Concept?" *Childhood Education*, Vol. 36, pp. 357-360, April, 1960.
15. Morrison, Nellie C., "Instead of Ability Grouping, What?" *Childhood Education*, Vol. 36, pp. 371-373, April, 1960.

16. Passow, Harry, "The Maze of the Research on Ability Grouping," *The Educational Forum*, Vol. 26, pp. 281-288, March, 1962.
17. Riley, F. C., "Grouping Gives Each Child A Chance," *The Nation's Schools*, Vol. 58, pp. 51-56, August, 1956.
18. Roberts, Bernice, "So We Grouped, Now What?" *Michigan Education Journal*, Vol. 37, pp. 400-401, February, 1960.
19. Rollins, Sidney, "Automated Grouping," *Phi Delta Kappan*, Vol. 42, pp. 212-214, February, 1961.
20. Schottman, Thomas, "Still Groping in Grouping?" *National Elementary Principal*, Vol. 41, pp. 53-54, September, 1961.
21. Shane, Harold, "Grouping in the Elementary School," *Phi Delta Kappan*, Vol. 41, pp. 313-319, April, 1960.
22. Shane, Harold, "We Can Find Better Ways of Grouping Children," *Childhood Education*, Vol. 36, pp. 350-1, April, 1960.
23. Strevell, Wallace, and Pauline Oliver, "Grouping Can Be Flexible Within The Classroom," *The Nation's Schools*, Vol. 59, pp. 89-92, February, 1957.
24. Torrance, Paul, "Can Grouping Control Social Stress in Creative Activities?" *Elementary School Journal*, Vol. 62, pp. 139-145, December, 1961.
25. Wolfson, Bernice, "The Education Scene — Multi-Grade Classes," *Elementary English*, Vol. 38, pp. 590 ff, December, 1961
26. Wood, Robert F., "Random Grouping," *Grade Teacher*, Vol. 79, pp. 10 and 83, December, 1961.
27. Woodall, Vaughn C., "More Effective Grouping," *Illinois Education*, Vol. 50, p. 294, March, 1962.

Creative and Functional Curriculum Development and Implementation

Curriculum often is defined as all those experiences for which the school assumes responsibility. Dramatic curriculum changes are being implemented in the public schools of this nation. The laymen almost needs an interpreter to decipher what is going on. As a teacher you will be hard pressed to keep abreast of it. New rapid fire developments in all phases of curriculum and methodology make it imperative that teachers return to college campuses periodically for further study and professional orientation. This frontier is being explored with increased vigor especially since the sputnik amazed the world.

Curriculum, of course, deals with the question of what should be taught in our schools while methodology concerns itself with how it shall be taught. In studying this frontier dealing with curriculum the student of education should realize that "the what" cannot be completely divorced from "the how." They affect each other.

For some people one of the frustrating characteristics of curriculum development is that it has no closure. Since the world in which we live is dynamic and constantly changing, it dictates that school curriculum must also be in a constant state of flux. It need not be changed in its entirety, of course, but some phases are always in need of revision.

Exploding fields of new knowledge and technology mandate this. As a result, much experimentation and investigation relative to curriculum is occurring. Many of these experimental projects are known by their initials, which creates an alphabetical maze. For example, there is UIESSP — University of Illinois Elementary School Science Project; SMSG — School Mathematics Study Group; HSGP — High School Geography Project; BSCS — Biological Sciences Curriculum Study; SWEMP — Syracuse Webster Elementary Mathematics Project. These are but a few.

"ALPHABETICAL MAZE"

Curriculum development fundamentally involves the question: what can we teach children today to prepare them best to meet the problems of today's as well as tomorrow's world? It is a vital and profound challenge. If the past tells us anything relative to curriculum planning, it is that in general we have underestimated the intellectual capacities of children. The space age must be ushered in with a space age curriculum. What shall it be?

JUST A FEW QUERIES

1. How big a role should each of the following have in determining the school curriculum: teachers, pupils, school administrators, boards of education, parents, general public?
2. What educational goal or goals should lend direction to school curriculum?
3. Name some kinds of pressure groups who would like to influence public school curriculum. Assign possible motives to each group named.
4. Determine through reading their published works what suggestions or direction for curriculum each of the following critics of education is pointing up:
   a. Conant
   b. Bestor
   c. Rickover
   d. Hollingshead
   e. Flesch
5. Excluding the so-called "tool subjects" such as reading, writing and arithmetic calculation, is there a group of topics or subjects which should always be the core of curriculum content? Does the "great books" curriculum answer this question? Is there a girth of basic subject matter which should be taught to all youths regardless of whether the year is 1963, 1993, or 2063?

6. What are some basic steps that a school staff should take in re-examining or planning a new curriculum for the school?
7. How does a curriculum get implemented into practice? What might be some of the hazards of implementing a new curriculum in a school?
8. Through curriculum planning, should the school be an organ of social change? Is it a legitimate function of a public school?
9. Select a school nearby and secure copies of its curriculum guides. Discuss and evaluate them.
10. What role, if any, should the state and federal government play in determining school curriculum?

SELECTED REFERENCES

1. Alexander, W. M., "Assessing Curriculum Proposals," *Teachers College Record*, Vol. 63, pp. 286-93, January, 1962.
2. A.S.C.D., "Balance In The Curriculum," *Association For Supervision and Curriculum Development*, 18th Yearbook, Washington, D. C., NEA, 1961.
3. Beck, Robert, and Walter Cook, *Curriculum in the Modern Elementary School*, Englewood Cliffs, New Jersey: Prentice-Hall Inc., 1960.
4. Blade, G., and J. Steffensen, "Testing Tool For Curriculum Development," *Overview*, Vol. 2, pp. 59-60, November, 1961.
5. Chase, F. S., "Some Effects of Current Curriculum Projects On Educational Policy and Practice," *School Review*, Vol. 70, pp. 132-47, spring, 1962.
6. Gwynn, J. Minor, *Curriculum Principles and Social Trends*, New York: Macmillan Co., 1960.
7. Hass, C. G., "Who Shall Plan the Curriculum?" *Educational Leadership*, Vol. 19, pp. 2-4, October, 1961.
8. Heath, R. W., "Pitfalls in the Evaluation of New Curricula," *Sci. Ed.*, Vol. 46, p. 216, April, 1962.
9. Jennings, W., "Status of the Core Program," *Nat. Assn. Sec. Sch. Principals Bul.*, Vol. 46, pp. 55-57, March, 1962.
10. Kennedy, R. H., "Teacher Readiness For Curriculum Improvement," *Nat. Assn. Sec. Sch. Prin. Bul.*, Vol. 45, pp. 70-74, September, 1961
11. Leese, Frasure and Johnson, *The Teacher in Curriculum Making*, New York: Harper & Bros., 1961.
12. Littrell, J. H., "Lay Participation: A Guide For Educators in Working With Citizen Groups," *Clearing House*, Vol. 36, pp. 137-39, November, 1961.
13. Parker, Edwards & Stegeman, *Curriculum In America*, New York: Thomas Y. Crowell Company, 1962.
14. Parsons, E. D., "Curriculum Experimentation: Road To Revival?" *Av. Instr.*, Vol. 7, pp. 80-81, February, 1962.
15. Ragan, William, and Celia Stendler, *Modern Elementary Curriculum* (Revised), Chapter I, New York: Holt-Dryden, 1960.
16. Robinson, G. "Legislation Influences Curriculum Development," *Educational Leadership*, Vol. 19, pp. 26-30, October, 1961.
17. Rucker, Ray W., *Curriculum Development in the Elementary School*, New York: Harper & Bros., 1960.
18. Salisbury, M. B., "Bridged: Subject Mastery With Creativity," *Nation's Schools*, Vol. 69, pp. 79-80, March, 1962.

19. Sand, O., "Six Basic Issues In Determining What To Teach," *Chicago Sch. Journal*, Vol. 43, pp. 170-177, January, 1962.
20. Van Til, W., "A.S.C.D.'s Role in Curriculum Experimentation," *Educational Leadership*, Vol. 19, pp. 314-315, February, 1962.
21. Vorce, M. B., and W. C. Miller, "Brainstorming The Curriculum," *Mich. Ed. Journal*, Vol. 39, pp. 22-23, September, 1961.
22. Wilhelms, F. T., "Curriculum and Individual Differences," *Nat. Soc. Study Ed. Yearbook*, Part I, pp. 62-74, 1961.

Professional Maturity and Recognition of Teaching As A Profession

As pointed out in Chapter 6, teachers have been slow to become aware of the significance of professional status. Teaching has lagged behind the other professions in this respect.

A reason for this lag has been the lack of unity and solidarity common to a mature, unified and strong professional organization. Some regard the lag as being due in large measure to the turnover rate of teachers. Certainly our national value system has something to do with recognizing teaching as a profession. Historically, teachers have been regarded by many as among those who can't do very much else!

The condition of the teacher and/or scholar is still unfavorable, in spite of great gains in recent years, as contrasted with some of our other professions. Naturally, respect and recognition must be earned, and teachers at large have not been too aggressive in promoting and interpreting the values and merits of their profession.

The Merry-Go-Round. In our culture, success unfortunately often is equated with the acquisition of financial wealth. To many, the worth or degree of recognition of a particular service is typified by the monetary value it commands. Using this yardstick alone, teaching ranks below other professions. It seems that high financial reward brings recognition and recognition brings higher financial reward. Around and around it goes.

To some it may sound mercenary, but poor salaries are an important factor in maintaining poor recognition of teachers. A teacher

"Around and Around It Goes"

as a second class citizen financially is often relegated to being a second class citizen in other respects as a result of finances. Before we achieve any major breakthrough in the financial rewards for teaching there therefore must be a shift in our social values relative to teachers and teaching. The public image of the teacher needs to be considerably modified. The poor monetary rewards of teaching are only one barometer of how the general public feels about its teachers. There are others. Teaching does not enjoy the high public esteem allotted to medicine, law and similar professions, though a recent Gallup Poll indicates it has made some significant gains. Teachers in the past often have been reluctant to police their membership to root out incompetence and have permitted unqualified persons to be licensed. In short, they have failed to stand together in support of high standards.

Public esteem is hinged to many elements of a profession. Teaching has a definite frontier to conquer to achieve full recognition for the vital public service it performs.

What are the current prospects for a breakthrough? The authors regard the work of the organized teaching profession in promoting the professional standards movement as most significant for teaching as well as for the general welfare of society. This expression comes largely through the National Education Association and particularly its National Commission on Teacher Education and Professional Standards, or TEPS, as it is more familiarly known.

Since 1946, the National TEPS Commission has led the fight for higher standards. Gradually, the 54 state and territorial associations have joined the movement through their own state TEPS or professional education committees. There are even a number of local TEPS committees.

What are the major aspects of the professional standards movement which appear to offer the promise of professional maturity? In brief, it is the achievement of the right of the profession itself to establish and enforce standards of preparation and competent, ethical practice of its members. Involved are:

1. The identification, selection and retention of the most able people for the profession.
2. Accreditation of all teacher education programs by a nationally recognized and fully qualified accrediting agency.

The National Council for Accreditation of Teacher Education, or NCATE for short, has been active since 1952. A description of its general structure is given in Chapter 6.

Recognition of NCATE as the profession's accrediting agency is growing. By June, 1962, teacher preparation institutions had been accredited by NCATE in 48 states. In addition, 24 states had accepted

NCATE accreditions as the bases for reciprocity. This means that in the states adopting reciprocity the certifying agency in each of them accepts certificates to teach from the other states in the compact.

NCATE, though very young, is potentially powerful as an agency for professional improvement. Will it make necessary changes in procedures and revisions of standards in the immediate years ahead to meet the challenges facing the profession? If so, and if the accrediting personnel are carefully chosen so as to secure the best available people in each case, NCATE may prove to be a frontier in the steady move toward professional maturity.

The New Horizons Report recommends NCATE as the national accrediting agency.

3. Higher certification requirements: a five year program for the qualified teacher, elimination of emergency and other substandard permits, and simplification of certification procedures. The "approved-program" approach is gaining in favor.
4. Professional standards boards composed of teachers to establish machinery to protect and discipline members.
5. Defining teacher competence[3] and professional ethics or ethical practices.

A FEW THOUGHT PRODDERS

1. What do you believe is implied by the phrase "appropriate recognition of teaching as a profession"?
2. Trace and compare the rise in average teachers' salaries with that of other professions and with the cost of living index. Use the years 1940-1960.
3. Conduct a poll in your community which asks the question: How much is a good teacher worth? (What should be the minimum and maximum salary?)
4. In past years many high school guidance counselors have been reluctant to steer topnotch students toward the teaching profession. Why do you suppose this is true?
5. What positive steps can teachers take to improve general public recognition of the teaching profession?
6. What kinds of services does teaching provide for mankind that would justify its being held in high esteem?
7. Explain the following sentence: If all teaching ceased for one generation man would have to reinvent the wheel and rediscover fire.
8. Discuss the relationship between teacher recruitment, practices and professional standards.

---

[3]See Commission on Teacher Education, *Teacher Competence: Its Nature and Scope,* (Burlingame: California Teachers Association, 1957), or Appendix in L. G. Thomas, et al., *Perspective on Teaching,* Englewood Cliffs, N. J.: Prentice-Hall, Inc., 1961, pp. 418-425.

9. Investigate the purposes and functions of TEPS.
10. What are some common avenues or devices through which standards are raised in any profession, be it teaching or whatever?
11. Since teachers' salaries remain generally poor to fair in relation to other professions, why should the profession attempt to raise its standards?
12. Who would profit from implementing higher standards in the teaching profession?
13. What elements are actually involved in the "standards" of a profession?
14. Who is initially responsible for establishing and maintaining professional standards for teaching?
15. Trace the evaluation of teacher certification in your state. How is it related to professional standards?
16. At the present time (in your state) what constitutes incompetency in teaching according to state law?
17. How can a regular classroom teacher actively participate in raising the professional standards of teaching?

Selected References

1. Abbott, J. C., "Attracting Better Teachers," *Education*, Vol. 82, pp. 242-244, December, 1961.
2. Ahrens, Maurice, "Tomorrow's Elementary Teacher," *NEA Journal*, January, 1958.
3. ———. "Aim For Excellence Chosen Theme of Fifth Teaching Career Month," *Art Education*, Vol. 15, p. 17, January, 1962.
4. Anderson, G. L., "Professional Education: Present Status and Continuing Problems," *Nat. Soc. Study Ed. Yrbk.*, 1961, Part 2, pp. 3-26.
5. Angell, George, "Courage In A Profession," *New York State Education*, Vol. 48, December, 1960.
6. Barnes, D. L., and C. D. Shipman, "Changing Patterns in State Requirements for Teacher Certification," *Clearing House*, Vol. 36, pp. 158-60, November, 1961.
7. Chandler, B. J., "What It Takes To Professionalize Teaching," *The School Executive*, Vol. 77, pp. 48-49, December, 1957.
8. Cottrell, Donald, Ed., *Teacher Education For a Free People*, American Association of Colleges For Teacher Education (AACTE), Oneonta, New York.
9. Cronin, J. M., "Reformation of Teacher Education," *Clearing House*, Vol. 36, pp. 464-466, April, 1962.
10. Darland, D. D., "Role of the Profession in Teacher Certification," *Journal of Teacher Education*, Vol. 11. pp. 201-5, June, 1960.
11. Drake, W. E., "Challenge of Professionalization," *School and Community*, Vol. 45, pp. 14-16, September, 1958.
12. Ehlers, Henry, and Gordon Lee. *Crucial Issues in Education*, New York: Henry Holt and Company, 1959.
13. Epley, I., "Single Code of Ethics," *NEA Journal*, Vol. 50, pp. 70-71, March, 1951.
14. Green, J., "Enemies From Within," *Clearing House*, Vol. 36, January, 1962, pp. 291-2.
15. Griffin, W. M., "Schools of The Future, Now," *Nat. Assn. Sec. Sch. Prin. Bul.*, Vol. 46, pp. 51-57, May, 1962.

16. Hansen, Carl F., "On Becoming a Profession," *Journal of Teacher Education*, Vol. 10, pp. 132-33, June, 1959.

17. Harris, Raymond, *American Education: Facts, Fancies and Folklore*, New York: Random House, 1961.

18. Heming, Hilton P., "One Set of Goals, One Profession," *New York State Education*, Vol. 48, pp. 16-17, December, 1960.

19. Huggett, Albert, and T. M. Stinnett, *Professional Problems of Teachers*, New York: Macmillan Company, 1956.

20. Lawler, William V., D.D.S., "Respected Status Must Be Won," *California Teacher Association Journal*, Vol. 56, p. 9, March, 1960.

21. Lieberman, Myron, *Education As A Profession*, Englewood Cliffs, N. J.: Prentice-Hall, 1956.

22. ———. *The Future of Education*, Chicago: The University of Chicago Press, 1960.

23. Marting, B., "Professionalism: Are We Digging Its Grave?" *Bal. Sheet*, Vol. 43, pp. 16-17, September, 1961.

24. Massey, Harold W., and Edwin Vineyard, *The Profession of Teaching*, New York: The Odyssey Press, Inc., 1961.

25. McPhie, W. E., and L. B. Kinney, "Professional Autonomy in Education," *Journal of Teacher Education*, Vol. 10, pp. 285-290, September, 1959.

26. ———. "New Horizons In Teacher Education and Professional Standards," *NEA Journal*, Washington, D. C., pp. 55-68, January, 1961.

27. Pence, Audra M., "Let's Start Being Professionals," *Illinois Education*, Vol. 49, pp. 8-9, September, 1960.

28. ———. "Professional Autonomy," *Journal of the National Education Association*, Vol. 51, pp. 69-76, March, 1962.

29. ———. "Professional Teacher," *New Republic*, Vol. 145, pp. 3-4, December, 1961.

30. Same, O. J., "Are You Living By The Code?" *Ariz. Teacher*, p. 9, March, 1962.

31. Stiles, Lindley J., *The Teachers Role in American Society*, New York: Harper and Bros., 1957.

32. ———. "Teacher Education: The Decade Ahead," Nat. Commission on Teacher Education and Professional Standards (Report of the De Kalb Conference), Washington, D. C., 1956.

33. ———. "Teachers Rank Low in Prestige," *Science Digest*, Vol. 41, p. 27, May, 1957.

34. Thomas, Lawrence, and others, *Perspective on Teaching*, Englewood Cliffs, N. J.: Prentice-Hall, Inc., 1961.

35. Thompson, Scott, "Are We The Punchboard Profession?" *The Clearing House*, Vol. 35, p. 342, February, 1961.

36. ———. "Toward Improved School Organization; Toward Improved Horizontal Organization," *Nat. Elementary Principal*, Vol. 41, pp. 93-106, December, 1961.

37. Trump, J. L., "Future Setting For Teacher Education," *Journal Teacher Education*, Vol. 13, pp. 19-23, March, 1962.

38. Tyler, Catlin, E., "Is Teaching a Profession, Craft or Job?" *Virginia Journal of Education*, Vol. 53, pp. 11-15, October, 1959.

39. Vander Werf, Lester, "A Single Profession for All Teachers," *School and Society*, Vol. 88, September 24, 1960.

40. Vander Werf, Lester S., "Improving The Status of Teachers," *American School Board Journal,* Vol. 143, pp. 14-16, September, 1961.
41. Yeager, Herman V., "Profession, Anyone," *Journal of Teacher Education,* Vol. 11, pp. 460-463, December, 1960.

Visionary Public School Finance

There are historically and currently three sources of support of our public schools, namely local, state and federal governmental units. All are, of course, based on taxes of various kinds. The local district and area tax is primarily a property tax. The states levy various forms of taxes. Currently 34 states have an individual income tax. The sales tax also is popular with the states, since all of them have various forms of excise or sales taxes with rates ranging from less than 1 per cent to 4 per cent on general sales. Other kinds of excises exist such as state taxes on tobacco and liquor sales and other forms of use and consumption. Thirty-five of the states currently have the general sales tax referred to. Other kinds of state-imposed taxes are corporation income taxes, licenses, severance taxes (on the removal of oil, gas and other natural resources), gift taxes, poll taxes, motor fuel and property taxes.

In 1960, according to an NEA Research Division report,[4] state tax collections totaled a record-breaking $18 billion! At the same time local units collected approximately $15 to $16 billion.

The federal government relies heavily on individual and corporation income taxes. Various excises, customs taxes and estate and payroll taxes account for much of the remainder of federal collections. Total federal collections in 1961 approached $95 billion. Historically and currently the first source mentioned (the local unit) leads the others in amount and percentage of support of public education. Formerly most of the cost of public education was borne by local units. In recent years, with the increase in state support, the percentages have changed gradually. Currently, public education over the nation is supported by the three units of government as follows: local — about 55 per cent; state — approximately 41 per cent; federal — about 4 per cent. As among the several states, there is much variation in the amount and percentage of state and local support. There is even some variation in the matter of federal support among the states.

You may deduce from the foregoing that the governmental unit collecting the most income (federal) supports public schools the least,

[4]NEA Research Bulletin 39, No. 1, Feb., 1961, Washington: The NEA, 1961, p. 19.

with the unit receiving the least in total collections (local) supporting public education in the largest degree.

You should note that the property tax, which is the mainstay of local units and therefore a main support of public schools, has limitations. Though it has been a stable source of support of local government, it has relatively little relationship to ability to pay. A definite weakness lies in the assessment system with regard to the property tax. Inequalities exist in the assessment of properties in most areas. In addition, this tax form is slow to respond to such matters as general economic growth and dramatic changes in local industrial development and increases in pupil population. Tax economists are likely to look with little favor on the property tax and its attendant assessment procedures and inequalities.

Finally, there are great variations in wealth in the several areas in individual states as well as among the states. Let us note a few more figures as to cost. In 1959, public schools (elementary, secondary, college and university) cost approximately $16 to $17 billion. Studies[5] of future needs in terms of increasing enrollments, increasing school plant needs, increases in teachers' salaries, and other factors point to a cost of $31 billion by 1969-70. The projected range for 1969-70 costs is from $31 billion to $38 billion. In any event, it is very likely that 1959 public education costs will, of necessity, double by 1969-70 unless the public is willing to tolerate an inadequate educational program.

The foregoing is a brief presentation of the general setting in the nation with respect to the bases of support of education and some of the costs involved. The big question now is how will the mounting costs of public education be met? Where and what is the frontier in financial support of education?

There are some things that we know relative to these questions. There is abundant evidence to support them. Among them are:

1. The quality and cost of education are definitely related.
2. Education is an investment that returns dividends in terms of ever higher standards of living, general economic growth, and a literate and intelligent citizenry far out of proportion to cost. Such dividends are both current and long-range.

---

[5]See — (1) White House Conference, 1955 — Report of Committee on Education. (2) Rockefeller Brothers Fund, 1958 — "Challenge to America: Its Economic and Social Aspects." (3) NEA — Committee for Economic Development "Paying for Better Schools," 1959. (4) NEA — Committee on Education Finance Reports: (a) New Directions in Financing Education, 1960; (b) Financing Education for our Changing Population, 1960; (c) Financing the Changing School Program, 1962.

3. Quality education is bound to cost more than is afforded presently. As indicated, costs will increase as enrollments, plants, salaries and related items increase.
4. The nation can pay the cost of education in whatever degree it chooses to provide for its citizenry.

As long as the public now spends more for liquor and tobacco, recreation, gambling, and beauty aids and related services, than it does for education, it can surely afford necessary increased costs of education! The U. S. Department of Commerce is authority for the fact that current public expenditure is considerably more for each of the foregoing than for educational purposes.

As to the sources of funds, there are several possible choices, or perhaps combinations of choices. The federal government is a prime source. It pre-empts approximately 70 per cent of the tax dollar. It invests heavily in military defense or national security functions and related items. In recent years, such costs have ranged from between 60 and 70 per cent of the federal budget. It proposes some $30 billion for a "man-on-the-moon" venture.

Is there a frontier here for adequate financing of public education?

The NEA Committee on Educational Finance[6] estimates that a relatively modest increase of 15 per cent in federal revenues for education over 1958 figures would finance a $10 billion increase in public school expenditures.

Local support of public education has a long tradition. It is a basic to our system. There are many who feel that local initiative must be retained and encouraged. Public education is also a function of the state. Through state support children and youth in the entire state can be enabled to receive a more nearly equal educational opportunity.

There is little question of the fact that certain local and state taxes can and should be improved. Reforms in the property tax and the attendant assessment procedure, for example, are mandatory. Even with such reformation, however, the local and state sources are hardly adequate to support education in terms as described.

A possible and reasonable proposal which would definitely involve federal support might be to divide the cost of public education among the three units in this manner:

---

[6]NEA Committee on Educational Finance, "What Everyone Should Know About Financing Our Schools," Washington, D. C.: The NEA, 1960, p. 56.

Federal — 25%
Local — 25%
State — 50%

Another possibility might be:

Local — 30%
State — 45%
Federal — 25%

In each case, local support would be reduced percentagewise, and state and federal support would be increased. There would still be opportunity for local initiative.

In any case, it appears that increased federal support is imperative. There is the possibility of securing large sums of money by diverting revenue from off-shore oil reserves to education. This was actually proposed in the U. S. Senate some years ago. Such a plan would involve no tax increase or new taxes since it would tap an entirely new source! Admittedly, this would require changes in the federal law, or a court decision. Who can be sure that such will not come to pass if the people desire it?

The proponents of federal aid to education point to the fact that large sums of money could be made available for education purposes without its being closely connected to the taxpayer. Since local taxes are presently segregated from other taxes, John Q. Public knows exactly what he is spending for education. In contrast, he pays vastly greater amounts to the federal government through income tax and other taxes and usually does not know how the money is spent. Psychologically, it may be a poor idea to keep the costs of education so close to home. The result has been that the federal government can spend millions for some dubious project unchallenged by the taxpayer while this same taxpayer will scream loudly if his local school tax goes up a dollar. There are a host of pros and cons to federal aid to education, so from here on in the problem is left to you, the student of education.

We must find new and imaginative means of meeting the high costs of high quality education. Moreover, we must do it in a manner which is most equitable and tolerable for all of our citizens and taxpayers. Herein lies the challenge of this frontier.

Is there a frontier in terms of the values held by our citizenry? As pointed out in the foregoing, our present valuation of certain material things as evidenced by our expenditures for them cries loudly for modification. It would seem that herein education faces a tremendous challenge.

Can the public be brought to understand that educational expenditures for quality education are a long-term investment in democracy? If so, then the money should be forthcoming. It is available. We only have to possess the willingness to use it.

PROBLEMS OF PURSE AND POCKETBOOK

1. Is a general sales tax in a community to support public education equitable to all income groups in the community?
2. Compare the amount of state aid per pupil supplied by your state and other selected ones.
3. How and through what means can the public schools interpret the increasing costs of education to the general public?
4. Should federal or state aid be given to private or parochial schools? Why?
5. What types of aid to education is the federal government currently providing?
6. How can a school budget be an instrument (1) of school evaluation? (2) for long term school planning?
7. What percentage of educational costs is met through taxation at the district, county and state level?
8. What does the term equalization encompass as applied to school taxes?
9. Regarding state and federal aid to education: Explain in what manner financial support might be related to control of education.
10. Secure and discuss a copy of a school budget in terms of the percentage of the budget allotted for:
    a. Maintenance of the plant
    b. Fixed charges
    c. Community services
    d. Pupil transportation
    e. Instructional services

SELECTED REFERENCES

1. Alford, A., "School Finance As a Part of Public Finance," *School Life,* April, 1961.
2. Barr, Monfort, W., "*American Public School Finance,* New York: American Book Company, 1960.
3. Benson, Charles S., *The Economics of Public Education,* New York: Houghton Mifflin Company, 1960.
4. Burke, Arvid J., *Financing Public Schools in the United States,* New York: Harper and Brothers Publishers, 1957.
5. Harrison, F., "Investment of Idle School Funds," *School Life,* January, 1962.
6. Hutchins, C., and D. Steinhiller, "Financial Trends in Public Education," *School Life,* January, 1962.
7. Johns, Roe, and Edgar Morphet, *Financing the Public Schools,* Englewood Cliffs, New Jersey: Prentice-Hall, Inc., 1960.

8. Mort, Reusser, and Polley, *Public School Finance,* New York: McGraw-Hill Book Company, 1960.
9. ———. "New Directions in Financing Public Schools," *N.E.A. Research Bulletin* 38:107-110, December, 1960.
10. Ovsiew, Leon, and William Castetter, *Budgeting for Better Schools,* Englewood Cliffs, New Jersey: Prentice-Hall, Inc., 1960.
11. Pierce, David A., *Saving Dollars In Building Schools,* New York: Reinhold Publishing Company, 1959.
12. Stautz, Carl H., *Planning Your School Building Dollar,* Philadelphia: Chilton Company, 1960.

High Quality, Consistent, Democratic Inspirational School Administration, Supervision and Leadership

It is generally agreed upon by both educators and laymen that the teaching profession has a great deal of growing and maturing to accomplish in its pursuits of general excellence and professional autonomy. To reach our professional goals we will need sound leadership from among our ranks. This leadership must be not only at the national and state level but at the grass-roots level.

The school principal and supervisor of instruction are the most immediate agents of local educational leadership. Their contribution, however, is contingent on the way in which they conceive their role. For too long a time in the evolutionary development of school administration and supervision, their function has been rigidly and narrowly defined primarily as one of inspection and policing. Such a role for the school administrator or supervisor is degrading not only to him but to the "professionals" (teachers) who fall under his jurisdiction. The authors feel that in the past too many important decisions at all levels of education have been decided arbitrarily. Leadership which inspires teachers to constantly strive toward self-improvement is based upon democratic principles. Professional goals *imposed* by educational leaders will never be wholeheartedly sought by its membership. Strong leadership in the wrong direction can be fatal to the profession.

In the past, certification for school administrative and supervisory positions has been very lax. The result has been the placement of individuals in educational leadership positions who are not highly qualified for these jobs in terms of college training. The idea of appointing an aging football coach as principal of an elementary school in the district, as a kind of reward for years of service, must go! Positions of educational leadership are too vital to be handed out like lollipops or used as political plums.

The word consistent is included in the heading for this frontier. It was included because the goals of the teaching profession have been so ineptly defined that often different factors of its leadership were pulling in opposition to each other. Perhaps there should be a hierarchy of professional goals set up to prevent the educator from "jumping on his horse and riding off in all directions." If we are to advance toward the goals of true professionalism, teachers must be able to identify with strong, intelligent leadership figures at all levels of educational organization. Professional improvement eventually will be based upon the kinds of decisions made by the great mass of individual classroom teachers and their ability to make these decisions known through the avenues of professional leadership.

In our society, the general acceptance of democratic administration and supervision in our schools is most desirable. This statement applies at all levels — elementary, secondary, college and university — for, at all levels, human relationships are involved. Good human relationships engender good working conditions in any kind of institution. In the school, this should mean a fertile climate for good education. Democracy in action implies that the free mind can be trusted; that cooperation is more productive of good than is domination or any kind of authoritarianism, and that reason is conducive to intelligent judgment and action. Historically, school administration in America has been cast in an authoritarian mold. The line-and-staff concept of leadership or administration is still probably more common than is a cooperative approach. Essentially, this concept involves a flow of authority from the superintendent, or principal, or director or president or chairman on top to the staff at the bottom. It resembles typical big business enterprise organization in which the top man is "boss" and his word is "law."

Democratic administration or leadership involves less of the "line of authority" and more of sharing on the part of all involved members

"TAKE ME TO YOUR LEADER"

in making decisions and policy and sharing responsibility. Cooperation is a keynote. Leadership is gained more by merit than by situation or position. It should be noted, of course, that a line and staff structure need not be autocratic. It can be so structured by the total group faculty or staff that democratic action can prevail. This demands a mutuality of respect one for another, a cooperative approach to policy and decision making, and sharing of responsibility. Obviously, this kind of structure requires highly professional teachers as well as administrators. Probably a majority of the school systems of the nation operate to some degree or on occasions along authoritarian lines. The trend for some years however has been toward more democratic action in school administration and organization. It is to be hoped that this trend continues unabated. It will mean better staff morale and better education for the children and youth of the nation. This may be the frontier in school organization and adminis-tration.

Some Rib Ticklers

1. Discuss what is meant by the term "leadership."
2. Are there specific human qualities inherent in all leader-type figures?
3. Construct a job analysis for a school principal, a grade supervisor and/or superintendent of schools. (Perhaps interviews and questionnaires could be employed here.)
4. Find out what the certification requirements are in your state to become a school administrator or supervisor. Are they commensurate with the responsibilities of the job?
5. Review the leadership role played by teachers' unions and/or teachers' organizations such as NEA. Toward what types of goals are they aiming?
6. Discuss the extent of relationship which can exist between the quality of educational leadership within the profession and the achievement of pro-fessional goals.
7. What variables in our society may act upon and perhaps modify our struggle toward professional autonomy regardless of the quality of profes-sional leadership present?

Selected References

1. Bartholomew, W. G., "Challenges of Supervision," *Pa. Sch. Journal,* Vol. 110, pp. 214-216, January, 1962.
2. Bass, Bernard M., *Leadership, Psychology and Organizational Behavior,* New York: Harper & Bros., 1960.
3. Brahou, V., "Must Teachers Remain In The Shadows?" *Education Forum,* Vol. 25, pp. 473-480, May, 1961.
4. Burnett, L., "Creativity Challenges the Supervisor," *Education Forum,* Vol. 26, pp. 221-228, January, 1962.
5. Campbell, Roald, and Russell Gregg, *Administrative Behavior in Educa-tion,* New York: Harper & Bros., 1957.
6. DeYoung, Chris, and Richard Wynn, *American Education,* New York: McGraw-Hill Book Company, (Part V), 1961.
7. Douglass, Bent. and Boardman, *Democratic Supervision in Secondary Schools,* New York: Houghton Mifflin, 1961.
8. Foshay, A. W., "Freeing Teachers To Teach," *Childhood Education,* Vol. 38, pp. 367-369, April, 1962.

9. Franseth, Jane, *School Supervision As Leadership*, Elmsford, New York: Row, Peterson & Co., 1960.
10. Glennon, V. J., "Updating the Theory of Supervision," *Syracuse University Frontiers El. Ed.* VII, pp. 45-55.
11. Greer, E. S., "Human Relations in Supervision," *Education Digest*, Vol. 27, pp. 21-23, April, 1962.
12. Grieder, Pierce, and Rosenstengel, *Public School Administration*, Ronald Press, New York, 1961, Chap. II.
13. Gross, Neal, *Who Runs Our Schools?* New York: John Wiley & Sons, Inc., 1958.
14. Jensen, G., "Dangers of Too Much Administration," *Ed. Digest*, Vol. 27, p. 13, January, 1962.
15. Kim, E. C., "Five Realities Important to Faculty Human Relations in School Administration," *Nat. Assn. Sec. Sch. Prin. Bul.*, Vol. 46, pp. 120-124, April, 1962.
16. Lucio, William, and John McNeil, *Supervision: A Synthesis of Thought and Action*, New York: McGraw-Hill Company, 1962.
17. Manla, G. N., "Administration in Transition," *Am. Sch. & University*, pp. 145-54, 1960.
18. McCarty, D. J., "Organizational Influences On Teacher Behavior," *Am. Sch. Bd. Journal*, Vol. 143, pp. 13-14, July, 1961.
19. Nelson, L. W., "Newer Trends and Experiments in American Education Which Have Implications For School Administrators," *N. Y. State Education*, Vol. 49, pp. 22-24, April, 1962.
20. See, O. and H. B. Tate, "Block-of-Time Program In Educational Administration," *Journal Teach. Ed.*, Vol. 12, pp. 511-512, December, 1961.
21. Selznick, Phillip, *Leadership In Administration*, Elmsford, New York: Row, Peterson and Co., 1957.
22. Severson, J., "Conflicts in Academic Discipline," *California Teachers Association Journal*, Vol. 57, pp. 24-25, November, 1961.
23. Shane, Harold, and Wilbur Yauch, *School Administration in Elementary and Junior High Schools*, New York: Holt-Dryden, 1954.
24. Spain, Charles. Harold Drummond, John Goodlad. *Educational Leadership and the Elementary School Principal*, Holt-Dryden, 1956.
25. Stone, W. J., "Schools of the Future, Now," *Nat. Assn. Sec. Sch. Prin. Bul.* Vol. 46, pp. 241-49, May, 1962
26. Vars, G. F., "Administrative Leadership: Key to Core Program Development," *Nat. Assn. Sec. Sch. Prin. Bul.* Vol. 41, pp. 91-103, February, 1962.
27. Wood, L. K., "How To Use Democratic Processes In School Administration," *Nation's Schools*, Vol. 68, pp. 43-44, July, 1961.

Index

A

Accreditation of teacher education, 130-133
  American Association of Colleges for Teacher Education, 132
  history of, 130, 132
  National Council for Accreditation of Teacher Education, 131-133
    composition of, 132
    development of, 131-133
    establishment of, 132
    goals of, 132
    regional, 130
Accrediting agencies, 130-133
Administration, democratic school, 298
American Association of Colleges for Teacher Education, 132
American Association of University Professors, 145
Association for Childhood Education International, 145
American Education Fellowship, 145
American Federation of Teachers, 138-140
  goals, 139
  membership, 138
  organized, 138
American Teachers Association, 145
Audio-visual materials, utilization of, 69
Auditory impact, 41
Automation, in education, 263-266

B

Bachelor's degree, 161, 166-168, 171, 187, 188
  States requiring for certification, 189
Basic salary schedule, 161

C

Central States Conference (on reciprocity in certification), 193
Certification, teacher, 120, 128, 185-196
  background of, 186-187
  current status of, 187-192
  definition of, 185-186
  lack of uniformity, 187-190
  legal basis of, 186
  problems and issues, 192-194
  purposes of, 186
  requirements, 188-192
  multiplicity of, 193
  reciprocity of certificates, 195-196
  temporary and substandard certificates, 192
  trends, 194-195
Classroom
  climate, 36
  management of, 46
Classroom grouping, more effective and functional, 282-284
Clothing, 34
Codes of ethics, 121, 126, 127, 146-149
College supervisor, role of, 24
Community
  grading sheet, 65

Index of Names